Urban politics in the suburban era

THE DORSEY SERIES IN POLITICAL SCIENCE

Consulting Editor SAMUEL C. PATTERSON *University of Iowa*

Urban politics in the suburban era

THOMAS P. MURPHY
University of Maryland

JOHN REHFUSS
Northern Illinois University

 1976

The Dorsey Press   *Homewood, Illinois 60430*
Irwin-Dorsey International   Arundel, Sussex   BN18 9AB
Irwin-Dorsey Limited   Georgetown, Ontario   L7G 4B3

First Printing, March 1976

ISBN 0-256-01848-0
Library of Congress Catalog Card No. 75–39365
Printed in the United States of America

To our wives
MARCELLA and CAROL

and our children
KEVIN, MICHAEL, THOMAS, DOLORES, and
DANIEL MURPHY
and
DEBBIE, BRENT, and TODD REHFUSS

Preface

THIS TEXTBOOK is designed to present to the student of urban politics a comprehensive analysis of the current institutions, dynamics, and tensions of urban government. It focuses upon suburban political, economic, and social phenomena, not only as a point of departure, but as a dominant emphasis throughout the entire analysis.

We believe that the literature of urban and metropolitan government has not focused sufficiently upon the phenomenon of suburban growth. Many analysts tend to write about urban politics within too narrow a framework, concentrating primarily upon large central cities such as Chicago or New York. Others write about metropolitan areas as if they somehow could be abstracted from the governmental units which comprise them. But these approaches ignore suburbs, which now include most of the total metropolitan population.

We have found that, by emphasizing the political structures and problems characteristic of the burgeoning suburban units of government, we can broaden the student's insight into the matrix of issues and challenges confronting the entire metropolitan system. Our research suggests how contemporary suburban efforts to adapt to growth, provide effective services, and establish viable governmental systems are, to a large extent, representative of the entire metropolitan political drama currently being enacted. The reader, therefore, will be exposed to considerations and issues that extend far beyond the range of exclusively suburban phenomena.

Our primary purpose, in fact, is to review the altered relationships between suburbs and central cities, between suburbs and their metropolitan areas, and between individual suburban units. Such a purpose has been motivated by our firm conviction that, however complex the implications for urban policy makers, the futures of the city and the suburbs are inextricably related. Consequently, there can be no viable suburban policy except as a subset of urban and metropolitan policy.

One important fact, which will be stressed and demonstrated repeatedly in the chapters that follow, is that most stereotypes regarding suburbs can be proven invalid or in need of significant qualification. The fact is that there is a phenomenal diversity among suburbs in terms of their purpose, their size, their socioeconomic systems, their politics, and their relationships to other governments in their metropolitan area. In general, suburbs have in common only the basic formal criteria that defines them—they are all satellite areas of major cities. Almost any other generalization respecting suburbs must be qualified in order to account for their great diversity.

Certain inherent limitations are imposed upon any work of this scope. The dynamic nature of the subject, its inevitable complexity, and the absence of data relating to many of the significant questions all limit its possible comprehensiveness. It is subject to revision by new data that indicates demographic changes or that documents new theories of urban economics, social movements, or political cohesion.

ACKNOWLEDGMENTS

Because of the extensive scope of this project, the authors have relied heavily upon their assistants in the data gathering process. That need was ably met by graduate assistants Judy Bair and David Felzenberg, whose help was indispensible. They also were aided by former graduate assistants Patricia Atkins, Robert Kline, Ellen Pierce, John Shanley, and Connie Williams. Patricia Florestano contributed, first as a graduate assistant, and later as a faculty colleague. Other colleagues who reviewed chapters include Charles Christian, Mark Freeman, James Giese, Robert Janes, Elizabeth Knipe, Chesley McGinnis, Mavis Reeves, Clarence Stone, Susan Torrence, and David Walker.

The bulk of the production phase fell upon the shoulders of Ginny Karas, who also had to keep Maryland's Institute for Urban Studies on the tracks while the rest of the team was preoccupied with footnotes, revisions, and reviewers. She was assisted by Mary Bell, Yolanda Benedict, Angela Jones, Rosemary Minni, Dolores Pruett, and Dolores Vita. Linda Engberg, Sue Vaughn, and Lisa Parts provided the secretarial support at Northern Illinois University.

The project involved a total mobilization of our families, the staff, and almost all our colleagues with expertise on the subject. We also wish to thank our patient editors and their reviewers, Edwin A. Gere, Jr., Ronald W. Johnson, Samuel C. Patterson, and Vincent L. Marando, who made many helpful suggestions.

February 1976 THOMAS P. MURPHY
JOHN REHFUSS

Contents

List of figures and tables

Table

Introduction

BOTH POLITICAL decisionmakers and social commentators have misunderstood the complexities of suburban political life and the nature of metropolitan systems, which are predominantly "suburban" rather than "urban." Popular assumptions concerning suburbia generally are rooted in two prevalent stereotypes. First, the Jeffersonian myth of a nation of independent yeomen in agricultural villages has fostered the view that suburbs are homogeneous communities which neither need nor want aid from the state and federal governments. The Beverly Hills or Scarsdale stereotype enforces the view that suburban units are well managed, affluent, and conservative. Since they are free from the pathologies of the central city, any aid would be wasted on them.

Although the mass media and the public at large have begun to question the validity of these stereotypes, the actions of policymakers suggest that they still exert a strong influence. Both stereotypes imply that national and state policymakers need not be concerned with suburban problems and that federal and state intervention would be considered an undesirable infringement upon suburban independence.

It is unfortunate that these stereotypes persist, because suburbs always have been symbiotically linked to the central city and to other suburbs. Geographically defined as the urbanized areas bordering the central city, the suburbs actually exceed the population of the central cities in many metropolitan areas. By 1970, on a national basis, more citizens in metropolitan areas lived in suburbia than within the central cities.

1

In the first 3 years after the 1970 census, the central cities had a net loss of 4 million residents, most of whom moved to the suburbs.

Assumptions regarding suburban homogeneity also are unfounded. There are substantial distinctions among suburbs in terms of financial status, political affiliations, life styles, income levels and racial composition. As individual units, suburbs are usually, though not always, somewhat homogeneous. In the aggregate, however, they are enormously pluralistic. Intra- as well as intersuburban diversity is likely to increase in the future as low-income residents and ethnic and racial minorites join the exodus from the central city.

Suburban political influence will expand as suburban populations increase. However, since the suburbs do not have clearly compatible interests, suburban political potential may never be fully realized. In any case, suburbs will continue to grow. Political, economic, and social assessments of urban life must consider both the total potential suburban influence and the unique needs of particular metropolitan areas.

THE SUBURBAN CRISIS

The problems confronting suburbs are serious enough to be designated a "suburban crisis." They are a subset of the "urban crisis"—the cumulative impact of social problems on urbanized areas. These problems include high population density, substantial in-migration, and intra-metropolitan movements. Suburbs also are feeling the pressures resulting from racial tensions, crime, family instability, decentralization of industry and shopping facilities, youth cultures, the women's movement, and rural migration. The energy crisis has added new pressures, as gasoline shortages pose considerable problems for suburbanites heavily dependent upon the automobile. Each metropolitan area has a different capacity to absorb these pressures and changes.

In the second half of the 20th century, the continuing migration from rural areas to the cities occurred simultaneously with an out-migration from the central cities to the suburbs. These movements and the resulting social changes have exerted tremendous pressures on cities and suburbs, exposing the inadequacies of the 19th century local government system that is still used to govern sprawling urbanized areas. Even the waning of rural migration in the 1970s has not affected the decentralization process which is creating the "suburban crisis."

Migration causes social stress in many ways. Newcomers bring not only new ideas, expectations, and values, but also new demands and new problems. However, local governments are slow to respond to pressures created by increased suburban populations. The migration of blacks to formerly white suburbs introduces still another set of complex adjustment problems. Finally, the increasing significance of suburban governments raises new questions regarding their relationship to each other as well as to the central city, the metropolitan area, and the state government.

The institutional problems involved in suburban adaptation during the 1970s and 1980s may prove to be greater than those the cities faced in the 1950s and the 1960s. However great the pressures became for central cities, they had at least one advantage over the suburbs—most central city governments had the legal capacity to respond effectively. The very existence of a major city meant that there was a governmental jurisdiction with the power to make and enforce decisions. The suburbs of most metropolitan areas, however, usually are governed by a large number of small units that lack the economic, political, or home rule powers essential to deal with local issues. Many suburban residents live in unincorporated areas and must depend upon the county government to provide their essential public services. Consequently, suburbs will not be able to respond fully to change until the actions of a variety of suburban city, town, and county governments are coordinated and until they make peace with the central city. The classic political question is no longer "Who runs City Hall?" but "Is anyone in charge here?" Too often the answer has been "No."

GOVERNMENTAL RESPONSES TO SUBURBAN CHANGE

Governmental responses to metropolitan issues have been inadequate. More effective coordination of central city and suburban government is essential since their interests so often are identical. These common interests are most apparent in the suburban cities and counties closest to the central city, which have attracted more of its residents and its problems. These suburbs share common concerns with the central city in the handling of crime, health, and transportation problems. Even the affluent suburbs that resemble the popular stereotype will be affected as they come into closer contact with new economic and social forces. The stage·is set for more cooperation at the metropolitan level, to deal with the urban problems of the suburbs and the central cities.

The state response

Despite substantial constitutional power and complete legal responsibility, few state governments have provided all the help that local governments require. States determine the jurisdiction and powers of their cities and counties, including the powers of those local governments to raise and spend money. Yet state action has fragmented local strength by fostering numerous special districts for water, fire protection, sewers, and many other urban services. These actions have splintered the governing capacity of cities and counties.

Further, states rarely have provided their local governments with enough legal and economic flexibility to use annexation as a means of meeting the challenges of urban growth. This lack of state leadership has placed additional pressure on local government to meet those challenges. The burden first fell on central cities, but now suburban cities, towns, and counties are experiencing similar problems.

Except in the areas of public education, highway systems, and public welfare—all of which are funded at least partially by federal grants—states generally have lacked the expertise and initiative to provide leadership in developing needed programs. Thus, few states have legislated experimental social service programs or have developed positive approaches to meeting the service needs of their citizens. They generally have failed to legislate land use controls or to promote improved metropolitan planning.

Federal influences

The federal government has been more responsive to urban problems, but it also has been ineffective in delivering workable solutions or stable programs. In recent decades, the federal emphasis has been on investment in central city programs such as urban renewal, model cities, the teacher corps, and neighborhood health programs. The War on Poverty concentrated on the central cities, bypassed even low income suburbs, and paid only passing attention to rural poverty. These programs have not solved the housing, education, or community development problems of central cities, partly because the resources never really followed the promises. The expectations of city residents were raised, never to be fully satisfied. Year-to-year federal appropriations, combined with drastic fluctuations in the amounts appropriated, limited the federal impact on urban problems.[1]

It became clear in the late 1960s that few central cities could solve their problems in isolation. Therefore, the federal focus was expanded to include the entire metropolitan area. The federal policymakers recog-

---

[1] See, for example, books by Edward C. Banfield, *The Unheavenly City* (Boston: Little, Brown and Company, 1970); Anthony Downs, *Urban Problems and Prospect* (Chicago: Markham, 1970); Martha Derthick, *New Towns in Town: Why a Federal Program Failed* (Washington, D.C.: Urban Institute, 1972); Jay Forrester, *Urban Dynamics* (Cambridge: M.I.T. Press, 1969); Willis D. Hawley and David Rogers, eds., *Improving the Quality of Urban Management* (Beverly Hills, Calif.: Sage, 1974); A. D. Little, *Community Renewal Programming* (New York: Praeger, 1966); Daniel P. Moynihan, *Maximum Feasible Misunderstanding* (New York: The Free Press, 1969) and ed., *Toward a National Urban Policy* (New York: Basic Books, 1970); James L. Sundquist and David W. Davis, *Making Federalism Work* (Washington, D.C.: Brookings Institution, 1969); Jeffrey Pressman and Aaron Wildavsky, *Implementation* (Berkeley: University of California Press, 1973); and Oakland Task Force, San Francisco Federal Executive Board, *An Analysis of Federal Decision-Making and Impact: The Federal Government in Oakland* (New York: Praeger, 1971).

nized that few necessary metropolitan decisions could be made without the active collaboration of both the central city and the suburbs. They began to see that the fate of the suburbs is inextricably linked with that of the central city and that effective metropolitan action requires suburban participation.

Nevertheless, even this broader approach has been limited to supporting the development of metropolitan planning and coordinating units designed to deal with areawide technical problems such as transportation, sewers, water supply, air and water pollution, solid waste disposal, and law enforcement planning. Programs focusing on comprehensive health planning, housing, and manpower training have been less effective because their social ramifications have triggered the resistance of health professionals, the construction industry, and local businessmen. Further, many local governments have failed to see how new planning approaches could help to improve their effectiveness.

Metropolitan coordination efforts

One practical effect of the federal programs was the creation of metropolitan planning commissions and councils of governments (COGs), designed to relate suburban and central city planning. Federal legislation in the 1960s provided financial inducements to metropolitan areas to establish these mechanisms. The COGs and commissions review federal grant proposals from local units, establish regional priorities, and coordinate related governmental activities. As voluntary organizations, however, they often are unable to take strong action. Therefore, serious questions have arisen concerning their power and their credibility. It is still not clear whether they can elicit the kinds of tradeoffs essential for effective metropolitan decision making.

Further, the federal revenue sharing programs complicate metropolitan planning and coordination. Unlike the "Great Society" programs of the 1960s, which concentrated primarily on central cities and were based on specific project grants, revenue sharing dispenses federal money as bloc grants to suburban cities and to urban counties. Consequently, all local governments receive some of the additional resources needed for responding to increased urbanization. Further, the influence of federal strings and conditions has been curtailed. Thus to some extent, revenue sharing will reinforce the decentralizing tendencies already operating in metropolitan areas.

SUMMARY

The focus of this book is upon the growth dynamics of the metropolitan area, the impact of growth on the suburbs, the methods of improving suburban city and county government, and the nature of suburban participation in metropolitan decision making. As suburbs grow in size and as they expand the scope of their services, the lessons derived from analyses of central city service delivery systems will become more relevant to suburban problems. Applying these lessons requires analysis of the demographic and social aspects of urban change, the economy and governance of the suburbs, and the nature of intergovernmental relations in the metropolitan area. Since state and federal urban policies have substantial impacts on the suburbs and affect their participation in metropolitan approaches to urban problems, they also must be reviewed.

Providing effective suburban government, and coordinating it with central city government, presents a new challenge for political and community leaders as well as for professional administrators. If suburban political and administrative leadership can meet the demands of this new role, it will significantly enhance the effectiveness of suburban government. It also will affect the capacity of the central cities to stabilize their situation and to improve the quality of urban life, both for their own residents and for those of the total metropolitan area.

Urban Politics in the Suburban Era will explore the scope of these challenges. The following chapters are divided into three broad categories—the social and political dynamics of suburbs; the problem of governing; and the need for urban coherence in the metropolitan area. The authors are united in the belief that much hard work and clear thinking needs to be done before consistent urban policies can be developed from the federal, state, metropolitan, and local points of view. They have written this book in the hope that it may contribute to this process.

1

The dynamics of suburban growth

ONE LESSON to be learned from the 1960s is that the "urban crisis," which came to a climax during that decade, was actually a whole set of complex and interrelated problems. Efforts to find solutions to these problems have been complicated by continuing population migrations into urban areas and by the variety of preconceived notions about what constitutes an ideal urban environment. The expansion and increasing diversity of the suburbs is altering some of these preconceived notions about metropolitan areas, as well as some myths about the suburbs.

Until recently, citizens, politicians, and even researchers associated the urban crisis almost exclusively with central city problems such as social tensions, manpower dislocations, rising welfare budgets, ineffective school systems, deteriorating public housing, inadequate health services, drug addiction, inadequate public transportation systems, and increasing crime and violence. The association of these issues with the central city fostered an unnecessarily pessimistic view of central cities. Simultaneously, it contributed to an unjustifiably optimistic view of the suburbs.

The view that metropolitan systems were composed of two independent populations—central city residents pressured by the urban crisis and affluent suburbanities enjoying a high quality life-style—was too simplistic. The central city and its suburbs together constitute a metropolitan area that is politically, socially, and economically interdependent. The boundary lines that separate central cities from suburbs and suburban cities from each other are often arbitrary and, in some metropolitan areas, may not even be functional. Yet, if redrawing boundaries would solve the variety of urban problems, officials in many metropolitan areas probably would have redrawn them. This has not been done because the situation is too complex to be solved by simply eliminating fragmented units of government. In fact, even acceptance of a metropolitan government would solve only a few of the problems currently faced by metropolitan areas.

Suburbs developed haphazardly but not accidentally. Suburban cities generally were incorporated to preserve the social values of their residents, to prevent the central city from annexing their territory, and to provide needed services. Their residents preferred separation from the large city because they felt their specific needs would be of relatively low priority compared to those of central city residents. Thus, suburbs, which were so small as to be economically dysfunctional in terms of the cost of delivering public services, could be politically and socially functional.

Most suburban officials still view continued separation and isolation from central city involvement as essential for keeping the urban crisis from their doorsteps. While this attitude has hindered the development of central city-suburban intergovernmental cooperation, many suburbanites consider this a small price to pay to insure firm control over the destiny of their neighborhoods. Nevertheless, there is no way to quarantine the urban crisis at the borders of the central city. The problems of the central cities—and increasingly those of the suburbs—cannot be controlled or reduced unless some metropolitan considerations are included in the prescriptions for change.

When George Romney, then Secretary of Housing and Urban Development, revised President Johnson's "Great Society" urban program in 1969 and 1970, he used a broader and improved conceptual focus. Romney popularized the term "The Real City," which he defined as the whole metropolitan area and not just the central city. The underlying assumption was that federal urban policy could not be effective if it related only to cities and excluded their suburbs. Increasing metropolitan population accompanied by speculative land development have spurred suburban growth. Consequently, the central city, which once constituted almost the entire metropolis, is fast becoming only the center of a multinucleated urbanized area.

This chapter will examine the nature of 20th century population migrations and the theories that have attempted to explain suburban growth. The resulting economic and political changes and their ramifications for the suburbs also will be assessed.

THE URBAN POPULATION MIGRATIONS

Two census reports—those of 1920 and 1970—document landmark changes in the 20th century urban population migration, as the population expanded and shifted its location in response to economic and social forces. Due to changes in industrial and agricultural production systems, a substantial part of the population was no longer needed on the farm to provide to nation's food and clothing.

By 1920, for the first time in history, more than half of the nation's population resided in urban areas. Though the definition of urban areas used by the Census Bureau included all places having over 2,500 residents—many of which were not located in metropolitan areas—these figures marked a significant change from the predominantly rural society of the past. Continuation of this trend gave rise to a new kind of American civilization and paved the way for the massive migration to the cities that occurred in later decades.

In addition to the increase in central city and suburban population in existing metropolitan areas, more areas became metropolitan as their total populations increased. There were 44 metropolitan areas in 1910; 97 in 1930; 168 in 1950; and 242 in 1970. As of January 1974, the Census Bureau reported that 268 areas met the criteria for designation as Standard Metropolitan Statistical Areas (SMSAs).[1]

The 1970 census report documented the extensive growth of urban populations beyond the legal limits of the central city. This outcome was virtually inevitable because the structural adaptations available to the expanding central cities—annexation or merger with the adjacent territory—proved to be too inflexible to expand central city borders as rapidly as the population grew. This was not a totally negative development because many metropolitan areas are too large to be governed by one central unit. Especially since the 1960s, large cities have been trying to find ways of decentralizing their authority in order to be more responsive to citizen preferences.

More precise growth and migration information is contained in Table 1-1, which shows that the 1970 population was heavily concentrated in the nation's SMSAs. Within those metropolitan areas, *for the first time*, the population residing outside central cities exceeded the popula-

---

[1] According to Office of Management and Budget, *Statistical Reporter*, No. 72–6, December 1971, p. 97, the following criteria are used to define metropolitan areas and SMSAs:

A metropolitan area is considered a SMSA if it has a county or contiguous counties with: (a) one city with 50,000 or more inhabitants, or (b) a city having a population of at least 25,000 which, with the addition of the population of contiguous places, incorporated or unincorporated, having a population density of at least 1,000 persons per square mile and constituting for general economic and social purposes a single community with a combined population of at least 50,000—provided that the county or counties in which the city and contiguous places are located has a total population of at least 75,000. A contiguous county will be included in a standard metropolitan statistical area if (a) at least 75 percent of the resident labor force in the county is in the non-agricultural labor force, and (b) at least 30 percent of the employed workers living in the county work in the central county or counties in the area.

TABLE 1–1
Geographic distribution of population
(in millions)

	1960*		1970†	
	Population	Percentage of total U.S. population	Population	Percentage of total U.S. population
Inside SMSAs				
Inside central city	58,004	32.4	63,797	31.4
Outside central city.	54,881	30.6	75,622	37.2
Total inside SMSAs	112,885	63.0	139,419	68.6
Outside SMSAs				
Nonmetropolitan	25,706	14.3	26,318	12.9
Rural	40,732	22.7	37,475	18.5
Total outside SMSAs	66,438	37.0	63,793	31.4
Total population	179,323	100.0	203,212	100.0

* U.S. Bureau of the Census, "U.S. Census of Population: 1960," vol. 1, *Characteristics of the Population,* part 1, U.S. Summary, section 1 (Washington, D.C.: U.S. Government Printing Office, 1964), p. 1–27.

† U.S. Bureau of the Census, "U.S. Census of Population: 1970," vol. 1, *Characteristics of the Population,* part 1, U.S. Summary, section 1 (Washington, D.C.: U.S. Government Printing Office, 1973), p. 1–261.

tion living in central cities. Of the total U.S. population in 1970, 31.4 percent lived inside the central cities, while 37.2 percent lived *inside* metropolitan areas but *outside* of central cities. The arrival of *The Suburban Era* had been statistically confirmed.

The noncentral city metropolitan residents live either in suburban municipalities or in the unincorporated areas of counties. Some of these counties also contain the central city while others do not. These two kinds of metropolitan counties can be classified as urban or suburban counties. Both types of counties will be discussed in Chapter 7. For purposes of this book, counties containing any suburban population will be considered suburban counties. In addition, rural areas in suburban counties will also be considered as suburbs if they are within one hour's driving time of the central city.

PERSPECTIVE ON SUBURBANIZATION

The trends of recent years represent the outcome of an acceleration of forces that have been influencing urban growth for a century. Although the Census Bureau did not collect data on the growth of suburban rings until 1910, there is considerable evidence that suburbanization has been occurring throughout most of the nation's history. As early as 1823, a Brooklyn newspaper included the following realtor advertisement touting the advantages of suburban living and open space just across the Brooklyn Bridge from lower Manhattan:

> Situated directly opposite the SW of the city, and being the nearest country retreat, the easiest of access from the center of business that now remains unoccupied; the distance not exceeding an average fifteen to twenty-five minutes walk including the passage of the river; the ground elevated and perfectly healthy at all seasons. . . . Gentlemen whose business or professions require their daily attendence in the city, cannot better or with less expense, secure the health and comfort of their families than by uniting in such an association.[2]

At about the same time, similar kinds of suburban development were also taking place in Chicago, Cincinnati, and other cities. However, only a very small proportion of the population was able to live in the suburbs. In his study of three Boston suburbs, urban historian Sam Bass Warner, Jr., theorized that the main reason for this was the cost of transportation.[3] Because public transportation was nonexistent prior to 1850, a suburban resident had to own a horse and carriage if he needed to travel frequently to the city. To some extent this situation was alleviated when the horsedrawn trolley was introduced in a number of cities during the late 1850s. Further mobility resulted from the development of the electric streetcar between 1885 and 1900. Since the streetcar was faster than the horsedrawn trolley, residential areas now could be settled at a greater distance from the central core. Due to the availability of more advanced public transportation systems, a larger geographic area became physically accessible. Unfortunately, the unplanned development of the outlying areas contributed to the suburban sprawl that now exists.

The data on selected cities offers strong evidence supporting Warner's theory. Boston extended a mere two miles outward from its center in 1850 and there were only a few wealthy suburban communities beyond this limit. With the introduction of the horsedrawn trolley, the area of settlement soon extended to four miles. The limit was pushed to six miles when the electric streetcar was put into service. The population of the 3 suburban communities Warner studied increased from 60,000 in 1870 to 277,000 in 1900.[4] Similar rapid increases in suburban population occurred with the introduction of the electric streetcar in Milwaukee and Norfolk.[5]

The two greatest surges in suburban growth took place in the decades

---

[2] Dennis P. Sobin, *The Future of the American Suburbs* (Port Washington, New York: Kennikat Press, 1971), p. 127.

[3] Charles N. Glaab and Theodore A. Brown, *A History of Urban America* (New York: Macmillan, 1967), p. 154.

[4] Sam B. Warner, *Street-Car Suburb: The Process of Growth in Boston* (Cambridge: Harvard University Press, 1962).

[5] Glaab and Brown, *History of Urban America*, p. 155.

beginning in 1920 and 1940. The importance of the 1920s in the suburban growth process becomes even more apparent when three facts are considered:

1. During that decade suburban growth rates, as shown in Table 1–2, exceeded those of the nation's central cities for the first time.
2. The construction of highways in the suburbs triggered the beginning of metropolitan sprawl.
3. For the first time suburban growth rates along the railroad lines were exceeded by the growth rates in other suburban areas.[6]

TABLE 1–2
Increases by decade in U.S. population 1900–1970
(in percentages)

Type of place	1960–70	1950–60	1940–50	1930–40	1920–30	1910–20	1900–
Total U.S. population	13.3	18.5	14.5	7.2	16.1	14.9	21.0
All metropolitan areas	16.6	26.4	22.0	8.4	27.5	25.9	32.5
Central city	6.4	10.7	13.8	5.5	24.2	27.9	37.1
Satellite areas	26.8	48.6	34.2	13.4	33.2	22.0	25.6
Areas outside metropolitan area	6.8	7.1	6.1	5.5	6.0	6.7	13.6
Number of metropolitan areas at the end of the decade	242	212	168	140	97	58	44

Source: Warren S. Thompson, *The Growth of Metropolitan Districts in the United States: 1900–19* (Washington, D.C.: U.S. Government Printing Office, 1948), p. 45; and calculations from U.S. Cens *Number of Inhabitants: United States Summary* (Washington, D.C.: United States Government Printi Office, 1970), p. 180.

Previous suburban growth had been primarily along the transit lines radiating from the central cities, leaving considerable open space between these radial corridors. Since the 1920s these open spaces have been subject to rapid development. It is difficult to generalize, however, about the pattern of suburban growth because individual metropolitan areas vary in size, age, and other characteristics. Amos Hawley documented the influence of these contingencies in his study, *The Changing Shape of Metropolitan America*, which covers the suburban growth process during the first half of the 20th century.

Hawley's analyses revealed that a number of factors are related to differential suburban growth rates. Throughout the period of his study, suburban growth was found to be a function of central city growth. Suburban areas tended to grow most rapidly in metropolitan areas with

[6] Ibid., pp. 155–156.

a central city of 500,000 to 1,000,000 population and lowest in metropolitan areas with a central city populaton of less than 100,000. Hawley also found that the following 6 other central city characteristics were associated with high levels of suburban growth: a sea or lake location, the location of other central cities within 50 miles, a high proportion of the labor force employed in manufacturing, deconcentrating industry, location in the North, and a low annual rate of central city growth. Of the 168 cities in Hawley's study only 13—Baltimore, Boston, Buffalo, Chicago, Cleveland, Galveston, Milwaukee, Philadelphia, Pittsburgh, Reading, San Francisco, Wheeling, and York, Pennsylvania, possessed at least 5 of these 7 characteristics. The only city of the 13 having such characteristics that did not have a high suburbanization rate was York. The other 12 had by far the highest suburban growth rates of all the cities in the study.[7]

Hawley's study suggests that suburban growth rates vary according to the characteristics of the metropolitan area's central city. Yet, it is misleading to discuss suburbs in the aggregate, since the characteristics of central cities vary widely and since so many different combinations of these factors are possible. For example, Hawley did not consider a significant central city characteristic—the relative usage of annexation. This factor alone accounted for most of the growth of some central cities. Without annexation, the suburban growth would have been even greater in some metropolitan areas.

THEORIES OF SUBURBAN GROWTH

A number of attempts have been made to explain the underlying reasons for the rapid growth of suburbs in the 20th century. In 1963 William Dobriner developed a four-dimensional typology of these studies that still is useful in the 1970s.[8] His four explanatory models of suburban growth are based on: (1) the social psychology of the suburban personality, (2) the value-orientation view, (3) the social movements approach, and (4) the structural view.

Proponents of *the suburban personality* school of thought maintain that suburbanites have a unique personality structure that distinguishes them from the central city population. The key elements of this suburban personality structure are the desire for privacy, a drive for independence, and an affinity for nature and outdoor life.[9]

---

[7] Amos H. Hawley, *The Changing Shape of Metropolitan America* (Glencoe, Illinois: The Free Press, 1956), pp. 161–68.

[8] William M. Dobriner, *Class in Suburbia* © 1963, p. 79. Reprinted by permission of Prentice-Hall, Inc., Englewood Cliffs, New Jersey.

[9] Harlan P. Douglas, *The Suburb Trend* (New York: The Century Co., 1927) and George A. Lindberg, Merra Komarovsky, and Mary Alice McInerny, *Leisure: A Suburban Study* (New York: Columbia University Press, 1934).

The second approach, *value orientation*, explains suburban growth in terms of the rational acts of individuals. It postulates that migrants choose their place of residence on the basis of self-interest, as defined by their personal values and goals. This view differs from the first one in that suburban residence is considered a conscious personal choice rather than the common natural yearning of a distinctive group. Advocates of this view maintain that suburban migrants believe that suburbs are more suitable than the city for raising a family, that they are less congested, and that they possess a desirable level of racial and ethnic homogeneity.[10]

The *suburbia as a social movement* approach recognizes the value orientation dimension, but sees it only as a conscious manifestation of a general discontent with modern society. According to this view, the value orientation of migrants is a rationalization for a flight from the industrial order, the competition, the impersonality, and the complexity of the city. William Whyte and David Riesman attribute this movement to a basic change in the American value system, namely a shift away from the Protestant work ethic and its emphasis on self-denial and productivity, to a social ethic that emphasizes personal gratification and consumption.[11] Robert Wood believes the suburbanite, eager to be part of a grass roots democracy, is searching for a community in which he can become involved and which he can control.[12]

The fourth mode of suburban growth, *the structural approach*, emphasizes factors that are external to the individual. Its proponents feel that influences such as the automobile, rising prosperity, a liberal FHA and VA mortgage policy, inadequate housing opportunities, and the degree of maturity of a central city are the important factors in suburban growth. Acknowledging that individual desires exist, the structuralists claim they are not the basic determinants of urban growth. Suburbanization seems to be the inevitable outcome of the operation of certain structural forces. Accordingly, Leo Schnore and Colin Clark argued that the continued economic growth of central cities caused an inflation of land values that inhibited the construction of cheap housing.[13]

Dobriner attempts to explain suburbanization by synthesizing these

---

[10] Dobriner, *Class in Suburbia*, pp. 66–67; Wendell Bell, "Social Choice, Life Styles, and Suburban Residence," in William M. Dobriner (ed.), *The Suburban Community* (New York: G. P. Putnam's Sons, 1958), pp. 225–47; and William T. Martin, "The Structuring of Social Relationships Engendered by Suburban Residence," in Dobriner, *The Suburban Community*, pp. 95–108.

[11] David Riesman, "The Suburban Sadness," in Dobriner, *The Suburban Community*, pp. 375–408; William H. Whyte, *The Organization Man* (New York: Doubleday and Company, 1956).

[12] Robert C. Wood, *Suburbia, Its People and Their Politics* (Boston: Houghton Mifflin, 1958).

[13] Leo F. Schnore, "The Growth of Metropolitan Suburbs," *American Sociological Review*, April 1957, pp. 165–73; and Dobriner, *Class in Suburbia*, pp. 76–77.

four theoretical models. Skeptical of the suburban personality approach, he combines the other three factors and concludes:

> In the final reckoning, conscious evaluations, social movements, and technological-economic forces constituted a hierarchy of the determinants involved in suburban growth. The migrants must have "reasons" and a "definition of the situation." The source of their strains, needs, and hopes lies, at least in part, in the ideologies of modern society. But the development of new "definitions of the situation," of new ideologies, rests in some significant degree upon the structural dynamics of institutions within the total societal matrix.[14]

The researchers who developed these models used various methodologies. The suburban personality and value orientation theorists used survey research methods to obtain information from suburban residents. Suburbanites most frequently claimed that they moved because the suburbs were better for raising children and were less congested than the central city. In developing the social movements approach, case studies of individual suburban communities and an intellectual analysis of trends in the total society were used. Unfortunately, such studies focused largely on upper middle class suburban patterns. Since suburbia has always consisted of different types of communities, and is becoming even more heterogeneous in the 1970s, there are some serious questions about the reliability of the conclusions based on such data.

The structural theorists used different research techniques. They evaluated growth in terms of the occurrence of characteristics associated with the highest levels of suburbanization. Hawley used this technique in isolating the fact that suburbanization was most rapid in northern metropolitan areas sharing a number of common characteristics. Schnore took this research one step further and compared suburban growth between 1800 and 1950 in 99 metropolitan areas that had a population over 100,000 in 1950.[15]

Establishing as a criteria for decentralization three successive decades in which suburban growth rates exceeded those of central cities, Schnore concluded that decentralization occurred prior to 1920, but that it was limited to only ten cities. More importantly, he found that only 3 of the 94 cities that reached a population of 50,000 after 1850 began decentralizing before they reached that population level. Most of these began decentralizing within 4 decades after reaching the 50,000 mark.

The Schnore study supports a hypothesis relating suburbanization to metropolitan maturity. Sixty of the 99 cities he studied reached the decentralization stage for the first time between 1920 and 1940. He

---

[14] Ibid., p. 79.

[15] Leo F. Schnore, "The Growth of Metropolitan Suburbs," *American Sociological Review*, April 1957, pp. 165–73 and "The Timing of Metropolitan Decentralization," *Journal of the American Institute of Planners*, November 1959, pp. 200–206.

concluded that there is probably a relationship between metropolitan maturity and historical structural factors such as prosperity, transportation systems, congestion, lack of adequate housing, and rapid population increase.

All these factors were important in increasing the rate of suburbanization in the 1920s. The post-World War I economy underwent a rapid expansion that created prosperity throughout the nation, especially in the urban centers. The First World War also resulted in a temporary curtailment of foreign immigration, but induced large scale migration from rural areas to meet the demand for labor in the cities. The federal government built highways to transport war materials, which later facilitated this movement to the cities. In the 1920s, mass production techniques and economies of scale lowered the unit cost of production of automobiles, making them available to the general public. The total impact of these four factors reduced the cost of suburban living, increased the individual's financial ability to live in the suburbs, made the suburbs more accessible, and, at the same time, raised city land values and congestion levels.

The high levels of suburbanization since World War II can be described in terms of similar structural factors. The three decades following World War II were characterized by general economic expansion, a high level of migration, and rising prosperity. World War II triggered massive migrations. Many defense workers and military personnel married women they met where they were stationed. Instead of going home, many moved to areas they had seen while traveling in the service or working for the defense industry. In addition, there was a postwar economy boom, especially in housing, due to the pent-up wartime demand for industrial products and the sharp increase in marriages delayed by the war.

Federal policy was an important contributor to the post-World War II suburban growth. The GI Bill and the FHA helped make money available to finance the mortgages needed for the expansion. The interstate highway system approved by Congress in 1956 had a major impact on central city-suburban transportation patterns during the 1960s. It not only provided alternative intercity transportation, but also led to the development of metropolitan beltways, which have become so crucial to intersuburban transportation.

The net effect of these dramatic structural changes was to make suburban living feasible for larger numbers of Americans than ever before. Individual motivations proposed in the suburban personality, value orientation, and social movements theories were all important contributing factors to the rate of suburbanization.

The preceding discussion tends to support the Dobriner and Schnore models, suggesting that a number of structural elements are involved in the suburbanization process. Considerable uncertainty remains, however, about their relative importance and their interrelationships. The relationship between individual motivation and social structure is also unclear. On the surface, it appears that individual motivation is real, but less important to suburbanization than the other factors. However, there is much evidence that the suburban migrants of the 1960s and the 1970s were especially influenced by a desire to avoid integration in the city. Another significant factor ignored by Dobriner is the influence exerted by suburban leaders who established an environment that attracted populations responsive to the values they projected. "Snob zoning," requiring, for example, large building lots or specified architectural designs, was often used to draw the upper class residents while locking out the economically disadvantaged.

SUBURBAN DEMOGRAPHY AND
SOCIAL DIFFERENTIATION

Having assessed possible reasons for suburban migrations, researchers addressed the question of whether this new suburbanism, as a way of life, constitutes a distinct set of behavior characteristics. Various case studies of suburban communities have suggested that it does not.[16] However, there is substantial evidence to suggest that, in the aggregate, suburbia is a distinctive kind of demographic community. Therefore, while suburbs as a group differ from the central city in significant ways, individual suburbs are not necessarily homogeneous and some actually may have more "central city" than "suburban" characteristics because of the nature of their populations.

Duncan and Reiss maintain that suburbs must be viewed as specialized areas within a larger economic entity rather than as independent cities. They point out that the characteristics that distinguish central cities and suburbs are not merely a function of size, as might be the case in a comparison of small and large cities. Their findings indicate that both suburbs and small cities outside metropolitan areas differ from central cities in terms of characteristics related to family organization. Their data show that, as contrasted to central cities, suburbs and small cities outside metropolitan areas have higher fertility ratios, higher percentages of married residents, lower percentages of separated residents, higher percentages of primary families, and a lower percentage of women in the labor force.[17]

---

[16] Herbert J. Gans, "Urbanism and Suburbanism as Ways of Life: A Re-evaluation of Definitions," *People and Plans: Essays on Urban Problems and Solutions* (New York: Basic Books, 1968) pp. 34–52.

[17] Otis Dudley Duncan and Albert J. Reiss, Jr., "Suburbs and Urban Fringe," in Dobriner, *The Suburban Community,* pp. 45–66.

With regard to economic characteristics, both the suburbs and small cities outside metropolitan areas differ significantly from central cities. However, they differ in directly opposite ways since the "suburban labor force has higher socioeconomic status, with higher median income than that of central cities, whereas the smaller urban places differ from the urbanized areas in having lower medium incomes and a labor force of a generally lower socioeconomic level."[18]

A close look at the aggregate demographic information on suburban residents suggests a number of other unique suburban characteristics. The fact that suburbs have a disproportionate number of primary families and a younger population with higher incomes and higher levels of education, reinforces the myth that the American suburbs are predominantly middle class. Commentators on suburban growth following World War II generally took this position in describing suburbs as largely middle class dormitories. However, case studies of individual suburbs written by Gans and Berger, as well as the 1970 data on the migration of industry to the suburbs, suggest that, in the aggregate, the suburbs are generally less homogeneous than the earlier data indicated.[19]

Leo Schnore's research moves beyond aggregate statistics and stresses that the distinctions between the central cities and suburbs are not the same in metropolitan areas that differ in size, age, and growth rates. For example, instead of using aggregate measures of socioeconomic class, Schnore set up 8 levels of educational attainment and applied them to 200 metropolitan areas. By using the imbalances between central cities and the suburbs in the distribution of the various educational classes, he classified the data into five basic types of relationships:

Type 1.   Highest educational classes overrepresented in the city and underrepresented in the suburbs (Tucson, Albuquerque).
Type 2.   Both the highest and lowest educational classes overrepresented in the city (Los Angeles).
Type 3.   Lowest educational classes overrepresented and highest educational classes underrepresented in the city (Baltimore, New York).
Type 4.   Intermediate educational classes overrepresented in the city (Miami).
Type 5.   No systematic variation (Memphis).

The pattern represented by Tucson and Albuquerque is the opposite of the expected city-suburban relationship, while that of Baltimore and New York (Type 3) corresponds to the expected central city-suburban

---

[18] Ibid., pp. 62–63.

[19] Bennet M. Berger, *Working Class Suburb* (Berkeley and Los Angeles: University of California Press, 1960) and Herbert J. Gans, *The Levittowners* (New York: Pantheon, 1967).

pattern. But the most interesting outcome of this analysis is that Type 2—in which both educational extremes are overrepresented in the city—rather than Type 3, is the most frequently occurring pattern.

These findings suggest that, in some cases, the age of the community translates into socioeconomic differences between central cities and suburbs. Schnore described this sequence in the following fashion:

> (1) smaller and younger central cities in the United States tend to be occupied by the local elite, while their peripheral, suburban areas contain lower strata; (2) with growth and the passage of time, the central city comes to be the main residential area for both the highest and lowest strata, at least temporarily, whereas the middle classes are over-represented in the suburbs; and (3) a subsequent stage in this evolutionary process is achieved when the suburbs have become semi-private preserves of both the upper and the middle strata, while the central city is largely given over to the lowest strata.[20]

Clearly, there is a need for further study of the socioeconomic differences between central cities and suburbs. Regional location tends to inject an age factor that must be considered. It also should be expected that the differences between the kinds of cities and suburbs would be even greater and more predictable if race were taken into account. Further, where a city has engaged in extensive annexation of areas that would otherwise fall into the suburban category, many of the central city-suburban distinctions would be obscured.

These findings have potential implications for future planning and development decisions. If, as they suggest, the suburbanization process involves certain inevitable stages, it will be very difficult to control and direct growth. This raises serious questions about the potential effectiveness of efforts to create socially balanced communities, like the new towns that were heralded as the ideal model for future urban growth. The New Towns program is discussed in detail in Chapter 12.

The Schnore theories also may be overtaken by new demographic trends. The 1970 census indicates that some of the differences between cities and suburbs are narrowing substantially. This appears to be due to changes in urban-suburban migration caused by the increased availability of multiple dwelling units, the opening up of the suburbs, and employment pattern changes.

Five specific changes in suburban demography already can be catalogued. First, more young people are moving to the suburbs and setting up households both independently and in groups. This is occurring not only in former single family dwellings and in the increasing number of apartments in the suburbs, but also in the new condominiums. In

---

[20] Leo F. Schnore, *Class and Race in Cities and Suburbs* (Chicago: Markham Publishing Co., 1972), p. 72.

metropolitan Washington, for example, 10,200 of the 37,000 new housing units approved in 1973 in the major suburban counties—Montogmery and Prince Georges in Maryland and Arlington and Fairfax in Virginia—were condominiums.[21] Many of these units have been occupied by single individuals rather than by families. In Montgomery County there were 21,000 singles households in 1970. This constituted 14 percent of the 1970 total and represented a 243 percent increase since 1960.[22] Continuation of these trends will necessitate substantial changes in the assumptions of suburban planners regarding age levels and number of children per housing unit.

Second, mobile middle class blacks and younger blacks in the family formation stage increasingly are moving to the previously segregated suburbs. The increase in black migration to the suburbs during the 1960s was greatest in Atlanta, Cleveland, St. Louis, and Washington.[23] There are now even predominantly black suburbs in some metropolitan communities such as Glen Arden and Seat Pleasant, Maryland; Compton and East Palo Alto, California; Kinloch, Missouri; and East Chicago Heights, Illinois. This migration also is well illustrated in high-income Westchester County, New York, where the nonwhite population increased by 39 percent between 1960 and 1970, and in Montgomery County, Maryland, where the increase was 85 percent. Though the rate of increase in the number of blacks in the suburbs is actually greater than that of whites, the disproportion in the base figures has been so great and the numerical increase of whites is still so large, that it will be decades before the black proportion of the suburban population increases substantially.

Third, people in high income brackets are being attracted back to the city by the new highrise apartments and town houses being built in urban renewal areas, such as southwest Washington, or restored areas, such as Georgetown and Capitol Hill in Washington. This movement is not likely to reduce substantially the income differential between central cities and suburbs. The increasing proportion of elderly persons who rely upon relatively fixed incomes and who are locked into city residence will offset the higher income of suburbanites returning to the city. Meanwhile, the exodus to the suburbs of black families, as well

---

[21] Thomas W. Lippman, "Condominiums Bring Bigger Profit," *Washington Post*, May 27, 1974, p. A. 24, and telephone interview with Bruce Steele, Washington Metropolitan Council of Governments, July 22, 1974.

[22] Fact Research, Inc., *Beyond the Mid-Million Mark, Life, Change, and Government in Montgomery County, Maryland*, prepared for the Office of the County Executive, April 1974.

[23] Reynolds Farley, "Migration Trends among Blacks," *Newsletter, Southern Regional Demographic Group*, June 1974, pp. 20–23, and U.S. Bureau of the Census, *City-County Data Book* (Washington, D.C.: Government Printing Offices, 1972) pp. 222 and 330.

as singles of all races and childless couples with good incomes, will contribute to the widening of the per capital income gap between city and suburban inhabitants.

Fourth, a recent study by Bennett Harrison, an urban economist, raised substantial questions concerning the assumption that increasing suburban job opportunities are undermining the central city economy.[24] Central city employment growth appears to be tied more directly than suburban growth to business cycles. Since the mid 1960s, central city employment actually has increased in some places, although the increases are lower than those in the suburbs of the same metropolitan areas. Furthermore, in some of the cities Harrison reviewed, most of the new jobs in the central city were for unskilled or semiskilled workers. Harrison suggested that the economy of central cities would have to be reviewed throughout several business cycles before the assumptions about central city economic problems could be proven. At least his findings confirm that suburban-central city employment patterns are highly complex and that some central cities may not be economic disasters in all respects.

Finally, there is a popular model of urban political integration that assumes "that suburban areas rely upon strategies of homogeneous and complementary population groupings to achieve their objectives of protecting life-style values at variance with those in central cities."[25] As Vincent Marando has summarized it,

> the theory further suggests that the greater the life-style differences between the city and suburban areas in favor of the suburbs, the more likely will the suburban area resist political integration; the reasoning being that suburban residents will not want to subject their life-styles to a consolidated government that must also respond to city residents with different life-styles. This, of course, implies that consolidated governmental control of such relevant policy areas as zoning, planning, and public housing would threaten and perhaps modify suburban life-styles.[26]

However, Marando's research on 24 city-county consolidation votes suggests that:

1. There is no firm basis for the assumption that city-suburban area life-style distance will cause suburbanites to vote against consolidation for life-style reasons.
2. City-county consolidation occurs at a point in time when housing

---

[24] Bennett Harrison, *Urban Economic Development* (Washington, D.C.: The Urban Institute, 1974), pp. XIII, 14, 52–53, 103.

[25] Vincent L. Marando, "Life-Style Distances and Suburban Support for Urban Political Integration," *Social Science Quarterly*, June 1972, p. 155.

[26] Ibid.

patterns and land development (primary urban functions that affect life-styles) have in the main been established. . . .

3. Those who have most to fear from life-style threats (upper and middle status whites) have many methods of protecting themselves before and irrespective of consolidation.[27]

SUBURBAN ECONOMIC DEVELOPMENT

The population movement has been accompanied by a parallel movement of economic activity from the central city to the suburbs. Even where central city economic activity has continued to grow, it has been at a slower rate than previously and much slower than in the suburbs. When David Birch compared the growth of 75 metropolitan areas in terms of major economic activities of central cities and suburbs, he found that, as early as the period from 1958 to 1963, suburban development rates exceeded central city rates in retail and wholesale trade as well as in manufacturing. In the retail trade sector, central cities actually experienced a net decrease in employment activity, while suburban job activity increased by 11.4 percent.[28]

Many suburban areas have overtaken their central city as the predominant location of both metropolitan employment opportunities and metropolitan housing.[29] According to census figures, the 15 largest metropolitan areas experienced a radical shift in employment between 1960 and 1970. The number of jobs in the suburbs increased by 3 million or 40 percent, while the 15 central cities lost 800,000 jobs, a 7 percent drop. In the Los Angeles, Philadelphia, Detroit, Washington, and Boston metropolitan areas, there are now more jobs *outside* than *inside* the central city. Washington was the only one of the 15 central cities that did not experience a net decline in the number of jobs in the city. This was primarily due to the employment stability offered by federal agencies and the federal policy to maintain Washington's economic strength.

Census figures show that 71.4 percent of all retail trade in the United States occurs in SMSAs. In future years, an even greater proportion of sales probably will take place in suburban counties and municipalities, especially those of the larger SMSAs. From 1958 to 1967, there was a steady increase in the suburban share of SMSA sales. By 1967, the suburban share of all metropolitan sales had increased from 36 to 45 percent. In the 33 SMSAs with populations over 1 million, the suburban sales

---

[27] Ibid., pp. 159–60.

[28] David L. Birch, *The Economic Future of City and Suburb* (New York: Committee for Economic Development, 1970), pp. 7–10.

[29] U.S. Bureau of the Census, *Census of Population and Housing*, General Final Report PHC (2)-1 United States (Washington, D.C.: U.S. Government Printing Office, 1971), Demographic Trends for Metropolitan Areas, 1960–1970.

growth went from 41 percent to 52 percent of the total metropolitan sales. Seventeen of the 33 largest SMSAs showed more suburban than central city sales.[30]

Table 1–3 lists the most concentrated central city and suburban sales patterns. Even the central cities that still held a dominant position were losing out to the suburbs. Over the entire 10-year period, 31 of the 33 largest central cities lost sales relative to their suburbs. The only exceptions were Portland, Oregon, and San Jose, California, each of which showed a slight improvement between 1963 and 1967, but not enough to offset their losses between 1958 and 1963.[31]

TABLE 1–3
The expanding suburban share of retail sales 1958–67
(in percentages)

Metropolitan areas where central city dominates sales	1958	1967	Metropolitan areas where suburbs dominate sales	1958	1967
Houston	84	75	Pittsburgh	62	66
Dallas	78	68	Newark	70	79
Tampa-St. Petersburg. . . .	76	66	Boston	61	70
New Orleans	82	65	St. Louis	51	67
New York	73	65	Washington, D.C.	48	66

Source: *Urban Transportation Factbook,* American Institute of Planners and Motor Vehicle Manufacturers of the U.S., Inc. 1974, Part I, Table 1–30.

These statistics imply that the functional economic relationships of many metropolitan areas are changing drastically. The metropolitan area is no longer just a two-part arrangement of center and ring in which the center dominates the economic activity of the entire metropolitan area. Instead, the pattern involves interdependent subareas as well as a center, because specialization of functions is increasing within and between the various suburbs.

METROPOLITANISM: THE MULTINUCLEATED METROPOLIS

The migration of population to the suburbs, the pattern of economic activity, and the relative expansion of suburban employment during the 1960s all indicate that these decentralizing tendencies are stronger now than ever before. As a result, the nation's metropolitan areas are developing into multinucleated territories in which the center is less

[30] U.S. Bureau of the Census, *Census of Business, 1958–67* and *Retail Trade: United States Summary, 1958–67.* (Washington D.C.: U.S. Government Printing Office 1961–1970.)

[31] Urban Transportation Factbook, American Institute of Planners and Motor Vehicle Manufacturers of the U.S., Inc. 1974, Part I, Table 1–30.

dominant. The increased level of metropolitan complexity constitutes a distinct form of urbanism that is often referred to as "metropolitanism." Clearly, the "concentric ring" theory of metropolitan growth no longer provides a sufficient explanation for existing growth patterns.[32]

Suburbanization and metropolitanism have serious implications for public policy and for local government. For years, experts have called for coordination and cooperation between central city governments and suburban jurisdictions. Now, due to increasing suburbanization, the jurisdictional jumble requires more cooperation among suburbs and between suburbs and their counties.

An analysis of metropolitan Washington's public transit system provides a good example of this need for coordination. As in many other areas throughout the nation, the unskilled labor force lives primarily in the inner city. However, the demand for unskilled and semiskilled employees has increased in suburban areas while it has remained static in the central city. Eighteen percent of the Washington residents now work in the suburbs. This presents difficulties because the Washington transportation system, like most public transportation systems, is primarily designed for peak hour auto and bus movement between suburban residential areas and the central business district.

Many low income Washingtonians seeking suburban employment do not own automobiles, and so are not served by the major suburban-central city highway system. Many Washington residents who own automobiles are discouraged from seeking employment in the suburbs by the cost of a lengthy daily round trip for a low-paying job. Mass transit is not only expensive but is often too time consuming to use since it may involve two or three separate buses. For this reason, several cities, including Boston, St. Louis, and Kansas City, have operated experimental subsidized bus transportation direct from inner city areas to suburban industrial parks during rush hours. The results of these experiments have been inconclusive as it appears that the poor, like the middle class, prefer to use cars whenever possible.

Washington has not tried to use such a tailored bus system, but the new Metro Subway System in Washington will aid the central city resident who commutes to the suburbs. Since a rail system requires continuous round trip routing, the subway will be more valuable to reverse commuters than the rush hour express buses designed to travel primarily toward Washington.

There is a new element of complexity from a metropolitan standpoint, however. The problem now extends to intersuburban as well as city-suburban transportation. In metropolitan Washington, for example, 40

---

[32] See R. D. McKenzie, *The Metropolitan Community* (New York: McGraw-Hill Co., Inc., 1933), pp. 197–98; and Ernest W. Burgess, "The Growth of the City", in R. E. Park et al. (eds.), *The City* (Chicago: University of Chicago Press, 1925).

percent of the suburbanites commute to other suburbs to work.[33] Even an effective central city-to-suburbs transportation network would not help the new suburbanites get from one suburb to another.

The extent of the change in the flow of commuter traffic is reflected in the national statistics on reverse commuting. According to the Census Bureau, about 845,000 residents of the 15 largest central cities worked in the suburbs in 1960; by 1970, the total for commuters increased 75 percent to 1.46 million. The 1970 total for commuters from the suburbs *to* those 15 cities was 3.3 million, an increase of only 13 percent since 1960.[34]

Another problem related to inadequate public transportation system is that of inadequate or insufficient housing in the suburbs for the low income worker employed there. For example, in the last decade, Prince George's County, Maryland, the largest of Washington's suburban counties, has had a dramatic increase in low income population, much of it composed of blacks migrating from Washington. Prince George's County does not have sufficient jobs for these residents and commuting to neighboring counties is very difficult. In response to this problem, the Metropolitan Washington Council of Governments developed a program of "fair share" housing that would enable low income people to obtain housing in the more affluent suburbs closer to where the jobs are located.[35] This program began as the U.S. Department of Housing and Urban Development was suspending or reducing its subsidized housing programs, and coupled with the politically sensitive nature of the program, this factor precluded serious implementation.

If the housing, transportation, and employment systems are not better coordinated in metropolitan areas, the disparities that now exist between central cities and suburbs probably will increase. Further, similar disparities will develop among suburbs as they grow larger. In metropolitan Washington, for example, Alexandria and Arlington, Virginia, are rapidly taking on the characteristics of central cities. Consequently, their representatives to metropolitan commissions and councils are beginning to appreciate the problems of Washington, D.C., and are more receptive to metropolitan approaches to areawide problems.[36]

This increased interdependence highlights the most important implica-

---

[33] Michael Kernan, "Escalating Suburban Sufficiency," *Washington Post*, August 19, 1973, p. K-1.

[34] U.S. Bureau of the Census, *Census of Population and Housing*, 1960 and 1970, *Census Tracts*, Final Reports PHC (1).

[35] Metropolitan Washington Council of Governments, *Housing: Policies and Programs for Metropolitan Washington* (Washington, D.C., MWCOG, 1971) and *Fair Share Housing Formula* (Washington, D.C.: MWCOG, 1972).

[36] Washington Center for Metropolitan Studies, "Washington Area's Real Central City Now Includes Arlington and Alexandria, Key Indicators Show," *Metropolitan Bulletin*, January 1974, no. 12.

tion of suburbanization. As its population increases, much of suburbia is likely to be confronted with problems it will not be able to resolve alone. Some of them will be the same ones that central cities now face: suburbs are already feeling the effects of crime, pollution, and inadequate public transportation. Poverty is also a serious problem in the suburbs, where 40 percent of the nation's metropolitan poor are located. Other problems will be unique to the suburbs. For instance, sprawl is a more serious issue in the suburbs than it ever was in the more compact central cities.

In his book, *The Future of the American Suburbs*, Dennis Sobin concludes that today's suburbs will soon be replaced by "citified suburbs that will be places where the young and old, rich and poor, black and white will live, where there will be local jobs, afterwork activities . . . where high rise buildings, multitype mass transit, industrial development and 'downtown' shopping areas will be common place."[37] As metropolitan growth continues to extend toward the hinterlands, some of these suburban communities will, in effect, become new central cities.

SUMMARY

Population growth and migration have played a major role in transforming 20th century America within six decades—first, from a rural to an urban society and then, to a society with more population in its suburbs than in either the central cities or the rural areas. This rapid transition has fostered some false notions about the degree of homogeneity and the economic levels of suburban communities.

Continued suburban growth has spurred the decentralization of population, economic activity, and employment. Many metropolitan areas quickly are becoming multinucleated territories in which the central city no longer is totally dominant. There is an increasing need for more collaboration among suburban cities, counties, and central cities to coordinate policies affecting functional matters such as transportation, utilities, water, and solid waste disposal.

The percentage of minority and young unmarried residents living in the suburbs is also likely to increase. Suburbs will be marked both by increased population densities and by economic and social heterogeneity. These demographic trends and increasing suburban problems have serious implications for the types of public services suburban governments will be expected to provide. In time, fewer and fewer suburbs will qualify as places to go to avoid central city problems. These changes might encourage the development of new kinds of suburban political leadership.

---

[37] Dennis P. Sobin, *Future of American Suburbs*, pp. 127–29.

These political and governmental changes are occurring at the same time the suburbs have become the most populous sector in America. The new trends might result in increased suburban influence over local, state, and national elections and policy decisions. However, the available data suggest that the assumptions regarding homogeneous suburbs are *not* substantiated and that the "suburban political bloc" is more a theory than a reality. The implications of these trends will be explored in the chapters that follow.

2

Emerging suburban political power

It is no longer unreasonable to suggest that suburban political power will affect future federal, state, and metropolitan decisions. This potential power did not develop automatically. A substantial number of political and constitutional barriers stood in its way. However, now that these obstructions have been removed, the suburban population is in a position to assert itself.

The first barrier impeding the emergence of suburban political power was the position of state governments in the federal system. As formerly sovereign bodies united to form the federal government, states retained control over certain significant government functions. At first states had total control over establishing the qualifications for voters. Eventually, Congress set some basic national standards that states were required to follow in applying criteria for voting eligibility. It specifically outlawed poll taxes and mandatory literacy tests, which had been used in some states to disenfranchise numerous voters.

The states, however, still retained the power to establish the boundaries of their congressional districts as well as those of districts for the lower and upper houses of their state legislatures. This power enabled the dominant group in the state legislature to control the districting of seats in the federal and state legislatures to enhance its own political power. Since the legislatures were almost all rural-dominated, the rural legislators used districting to hold onto seats that should have been reassigned. This practice resulted in a system of malapportionment of state and federal legislative districts in which the rapidly growing urban areas had far less representation than their population justified. Because of this disparity, the rural areas continued to be the dominant force in most state legislatures long after they had become a minority of the population.

This conscious and deliberate attempt by rural legislators to exclude urban representation in state legislatures was attacked for decades. But the federal court system refused to deal with it, ruling in *Colegrove* v. *Green* (1946) that it was a political legislative rather than a constitutional issue and, therefore, outside the Court's jurisdiction. Finally, in response to the dramatic urban migration of the post World War II period, the Supreme Court intervened in the 1960s to establish the one man-one vote principle in state and local legislative systems, as well as in elections for the U.S. House of Representatives.

The achievement of an equal vote for residents of urban areas was hailed as a great victory for the cities. However, the decision had been delayed for so long that, by the time it occurred, the growth rates of many major central cities had already passed their peaks. Consequently, the real beneficiaries of the Supreme Court's actions were the suburban areas, where populations now were growing faster than in the central cities.

Even so, the implications of reapportionment for the suburbs are not yet totally clear. The Supreme Court's decision insured the suburbs substantially more representation than they previously had. Yet, simply having a large number of votes does not guarantee that a group will be powerful. It must have seniority and interests to which it can apply those votes. So far, few suburban communities have been able to define a coherent set of policies they would like the state and federal legislatures to enact. This should not be surprising. Suburban interests are much more diversified than those of central cities because, as a group, suburbs are much more heterogeneous than most central cities. Consequently, suburban legislators frequently split their votes, reflecting the different interests of the suburbs they represent.

"Suburban power" remains a paper tiger, but it has the potential to exert great influence. This chapter will summarize the reapportionment and redistricting cases and then focus upon the general question of the foundation and the magnitude of suburban political power. It will highlight the factors that encourage or thwart the formation of a suburban political power bloc at the metropolitan, state, and national levels.

THE REAPPORTIONMENT REVOLUTION

As noted above, suburban influence at the state and federal levels was suppressed for many years by underrepresentation in the state legislatures and in Congress. This was the result of the *deliberate overrepresentation of rural interests*. The rural dominated legislatures maintained this imbalance by redistricting spasmodically and by assigning more legislative seats to rural areas than their population would justify.

Tennessee, one of the states pursuing this policy, was the target of a law suit that resulted in a drastic alteration of the districting practices of state legislatures. By 1961, 60 years had passed since the Tennessee legislature had been reapportioned. Domination by the rural areas was evident in that 27 percent of the voters could elect a majority of the upper house and 29 percent could elect a majority of the lower chamber. But Tennessee was not the worst offender. According to Andrew Hacker: "In California, 11 percent of the voters could elect 51 percent of the State Senate; in Florida, 12 percent could elect the majority. In Kansas, 19 percent of the electorate could select more than half of the state's lower house; in Vermont, it took only 12 percent of the voters to choose the majority."[1]

By the 1960s, malapportionment was so widespread that the U.S. Supreme Court intervened. The Court concluded that an important constitutional question existed that deserved consideration. The question was whether the Tennessee legislature was denying its citizens equal protection of the law as required by the 14th Amendment to the Constitution. In 1962, Justice Tom Clark's majority decision in *Baker* v. *Carr* charged that "Tennessee's apportionment is a crazy quilt without rational basis. . . ." and further that "Tennessee is guilty of a clear violation of the State constitution. . . ."[2]

Although the decision directly affected only Tennessee, it served as a warning to states with unequal legislative districts. *Baker* v. *Carr* ended an impasse in the legislative-political sphere of government that, in the words of Justice Clark, was responsible for the fact that a "majority of voters were caught up in a legislative straitjacket."[3] A majority of Tennessee voters could not change the system, since their votes did not count as heavily as those of the rural minority which controlled the state legislature. Even the governor, whose constituency included the whole state, had not taken a strong stand on the issue. Reform could come only from the legislators themselves.

Baker v. *Carr* brought state apportionment laws under the jurisdictional protection of the federal courts by virtue of the "equal protection clause" of the 14th Amendment. Within 20 months of this decision, most states were facing civil suits challenging the districting schemes used for the seats in their state legislatures. Some states reapportioned

---

[1] Andrew Hacker, *Congressional Districting: The Issue of Representation*, rev. ed. (c) 1964 by the Brookings Institution, Washington, D.C.

[2] *Baker* v. *Carr*, 369 U.S. 186 (1962), pp. 254–59.

[3] Ibid., p. 259.

voluntarily to comply with the Supreme Court's ruling and the others eventually were forced to do so.

One of the fundamental questions left unanswered by *Baker* v. *Carr* was whether the "fairness" test required other kinds of voting districts, such as congressional, county board, or city council districts, to be "equal" in population. The Court answered that question with respect to congressional districts in *Wesberry* v. *Sanders*. In the majority opinion, Justice Hugo Black interpreted the language of the Constitution as supporting the principle that "as nearly as practicable one man's vote in a congressional election is to be worth as much as another's."[4] Therefore, state legislatures were required to draw new lines for congressional districts so that they would include essentially equal populations.

The 1964 case of *Reynolds* v. *Sims* further clarified the concept of "fairness" by repudiating the notion that the "little federal system," which characterized the basic structure of many state legislatures, was a valid approach to representation. The case involved the 60-year old apportionment plan of Alabama, under which Alabama's 35 counties, ranging in population from 15,000 to 635,000 people, each elected one senator to the Alabama Senate. This system resembled the representation pattern of the United States Senate, where each state is constitutionally guaranteed two senators. The Supreme Court asserted that the one man-one vote principle must be applied to both houses of a state legislature and that the obvious population disparities in the Alabama Senate had to be redressed.

The decision also made it clear that any analogy between county representation in state government and state representation in the Senate was fallacious. In Congress, Senate representation favors small states whereas House representation, based on population, favors the larger states. The Supreme Court's ruling that states could not legally use the same approach for county representation in the state Senate was very controversial. However, there is an important difference between the position of counties in the states and of states in the federal system. Unlike states, counties are creatures of the state rather than sovereign entities that joined together to form the national government.

A key passage of Chief Justice Warren's majority opinion stated:

> . . . the fundamental principle of representative government in this country is one of equal representation for equal numbers of people, without regard to race, sex, economic status, or place of residence within a state. . . . Legislators represent people, not trees or acres. Legislators are elected by voters, not farms, cities or economic interests. . . . Our constitutional system amply provides for the protection of minorities by means other than giving them majority control of state legislatures. . . . The complexions of societies and civilizations

---

[4] *Wesberry* v. *Sanders*, 376 U.S. 1 (1963), p. 531.

change. . . . A nation once primarily rural in character becomes primarily urban. Representation schemes once fair and equitable become archaic and outdated. But the basic principle of representative government remains. . . . —[that] the weight of a citizen's vote cannot be made to depend upon where he lives. . . .[5]

Another significant Supreme Court decision concerning one man-one vote involved county governing boards. Many counties traditionally had permitted overrepresentation of their less populated areas, at the expense of their cities. This favored the growing suburban interests as well as the rural voters in the county. In some cases, cities that had the majority of the county population had a minority voice in the county board. The 1969 decision in *Avery* v. *Midland County, Texas,* ended this practice by extending the one man-one vote principle to county governments.[6]

ONE MAN-ONE VOTE AND THE STATE LEGISLATURES

It is possible to make a preliminary assessment as to whether the increase in the number of urban and suburban legislators, in previously rural-dominated state legislatures, has had any significant effect in determining policy outcomes. Patterns in California, Arizona, and New York offer some indication.

According to several measures of malapportionment used to rank states in terms of equality of representation, the California Senate was the least equitable of all bodies. In 1965, both state houses underwent court-ordered reapportionment according to equal population standards. There were relatively slight changes in the Assembly, but the changes in the Senate were dramatic. About 15 seats shifted from rural northern areas to metropolitan constituencies in southern California and the San Francisco Bay area. Most observers reasoned that metropolitan areas would gain influence in the state legislature at the expense of small town, agricultural, and forestry interests in the state.

The 1965 reapportionment of the California legislature had a significant impact on policy outcomes. In general, the voting changes benefited policies favorable to metropolitan areas, farm labor, civil rights proponents, consumer interests, mass transit, and highway construction. These changes were not direct or immediate. In most instances, three or more legislative sessions passed before the changes occurred. To analyze the changes in the California legislature between the time of reapportionment and 1970, Alvin Sokolow compared bill introduction and enactment patterns in seven policy areas before and after reapportionment. Significantly, the number of bills and the percentage of enactment in most of the areas remained constant. The areas with the highest bill enactment

---

[5] *Reynolds* v. *Sims,* 377 U.S. 533 (1964).

[6] *Avery* v. *Midland County, Texas,* 88 S. Ct. 1114 (1968).

rates in both periods were agriculture, highways, and air pollution; the areas with the lowest rates were labor, equal employment, mass transit, and general consumer protection.[7]

The reasons for the delay between reapportionment and real output are not entirely clear, but Sokolow theorized that the delay can only be understood by examining the internal characteristics of the legislature. He characterized the legislature as "change resistant" in that it took several legislative sessions after reapportionment to enact bills that might have been acted upon shortly afterward. To quote Sokolow:

> The legislature is change-resistant because of such institutional character-
> istics as policy pluralism, ongoing leadership, leadership control of com-
> mittee membership, and rapid socialization of new members to the norms
> of conformity and loyalty. The influx of a very large number of new
> legislators can upset these patterns of stability, but only if the new
> members can effectively replace the leadership or otherwise revise pat-
> terns of legislative control. It took more than two years for the new
> California senators to reach this point of effectiveness, a process that
> involved growing criticism of the leadership and its traditional norms
> and slow development of a bipartisan coalition, with support from a
> few veteran members.[8]

Reapportionment also gave more power to metropolitan interests in Arizona. The Phoenix-Maricopa County metropolitan area realized substantial gains due to redistricting; however, Eleanore Bushnell wrote that as of 1969, "the translation of urban sentiments into legislation has not occurred in massive proportions."[9]

Bushnell noted that urban interests may have been suppressed "because the major anti-urban interests—the mines, cattlemen, and land speculators—have not only maintained their strength in the legislature but have mounted propaganda campaigns to sell the urban dweller on the merits of the anti-urban interests' position." For example, "cities have failed thus far in their major aims: to get a meaningful air pollution control bill (opposed by the mines) and a reallocation of funds for the construction of urban streets and freeways."[10]

One of the most significant results of reapportionment in Arizona was the effect it had on party politics within the state. It appears that reapportionment served as a catalyst to unleash Republican strength that had been dormant for some time. Whereas Democrats had at least

---

[7] Alvin D. Sokolow, "Legislative Pluralism, Committee Assignments and Internal Norms: The Delayed Impact of Reapportionment in California, *Annals of the New York Academy of Sciences*, November 9, 1973, p. 302.

[8] Ibid, p. 308.

[9] Eleanore Bushnell, *Impact of Reapportionment on the Thirteen Western States* (Salt Lake City: U. of Utah Press, 1970), p. 67.

[10] Ibid., p. 67.

a five to one superiority in voter registration in the recent past, Republicans now dominate. The Republicans have found that, unlike the pattern in many other states, they are the dominant party in urban Arizona and that the Democratic strength is in rural areas.

A summary of the initial effects of reapportionment in Arizona would include the following points: (1) it allowed the urban areas to elect a majority of the legislators; (2) it gave the Republicans control of the legislature; (3) it produced a very limited body of urban-oriented legislation; (4) it prompted mining and cattle interests from rural areas to change their tactics and; (5) it opened up the possibility of changes in the representational bodies that allocate water and other resources.[11]

New York is a third example of state adaptation to the changes wrought by redistricting on the one man-one vote basis. Four separate geographic interest groups exist in the legislature: the rural areas, New York City, New York City suburbs, and the upstate metropolitan area. Table 2–1 shows that, prior to redistricting, the suburbs were underrepre-

TABLE 2–1
Apportionment of New York legislative seats by region

	1954–64		1965		1966		Citizen population
Assembly							
New York City	65	43%	74	45%	68	45%	45.7%
New York suburbs*	16	11	29	18	26	17	17.5
Upstate metropolitan†	29	19	36	22	34	23	22.1
Remainder of state	40	27	25	15	22	15	14.8
Total seats	150	100%	165	100%	150	100%	100.1%‡
Senate							
New York City	25	43%	30	46%	26	46%	45.7%
New York suburbs*	7	12	12	18	10	18	17.5
Upstate metropolitan†	14	24	16	25	13	23	22.1
Remainder of state	12	21	7	11	8	14	14.8
Total seats	58	100%	65	100%	57	101%‡	100.1%‡

* Nassau, Suffolk, Westchester, Rockland.
† Erie-Niagara, Albany-Rensselaer-Schenectady-Saratoga; Broome; Monroe; Oneida-Herkimer; and Onondaga-Madison-Oswego.
‡ Deviation due to rounding.
Source: Richard Lehne, *Reapportionment of the New York State Legislature* (New York: National Municipal League 1972), p. 5.

sented in both the New York Senate and Assembly. As a result of redistricting, the size of the rural Assembly delegation dropped from 40 to 22 seats, the New York City suburbs increased their representation from 16 to 26 seats, New York City's remained almost constant, and

---

[11] Ibid., p. 68.

the upstate metropolitan areas scored a slight increase. As a consequence, control of the Assembly passed to the Democrats.

In addition to representational inequities, legislative processes and procedures also influence the distribution of power. In New York, the increase in suburban legislative seats resulted in an increase in suburban legislative power. At first this power was not obvious in the state Senate because the Republicans, who captured some of the new Senate seats, dominated that body both before and after the redistricting, and so controlled the legislative committees. In 1962, rural Republicans held 36 percent of the key committee positions in the Senate, compared to 15 percent held by suburban Republican legislators. By 1968, this relationship had switched; the suburban Republican senators held 33 percent of the prime assignments and the rural senators 19 percent.[12]

However, more new suburban seats were created in the state Assembly than in the Senate, most of which were captured by Democrats. The result was that the Democrats took control of the Assembly from the Republicans. This changed all the committee power structures, but the new suburban legislators had no seniority. Meanwhile, the suburban Republicans who had seniority were no longer in line for these positions since, unlike in the Senate, the Republicans had lost control.

The increased suburban representation within the New York legislature influenced policy outcomes. Richard Lehne analyzed the reaction of legislators to various types of state aid in New York, including highway aid, welfare and medical assistance, and aid to education. Highway funds are very important to suburbanites as they affect their daily travel to and from work, as well as their personal travel patterns. Aid to education is also a priority issue for suburban residents who consider it essential to their children's success in life. On the other hand, welfare and medical assistance are more important to central city residents than to suburbanites due to the higher concentrations of low income residents in the cities.

Because of these suburban interests, one would expect suburban legislators to exert their influence to *limit* allocations of state funds for welfare and medical assistance, while seeking to *increase* highway and education allocations. For diverse reasons such as logrolling tradeoffs and party-line voting, the suburban portion of highway aid actually decreased from 1963 to 1970. However, highway funds allocated to New York City and its suburbs constituted roughly 50 percent of the total, compared to less than 33 percent prior to the one man-one vote era. Expenditures for rural highways actually were reduced. Apparently, suburban influences were exercised to reduce the rural total, and to support the major city road systems that are heavily used by suburbanites.

---

[12] Richard Lehne, *Reapportionment of the New York State Legislature: Impact and Issues* (New York: National Municipal League, 1972), p. 5.

Although New York City contained 43 percent of the state's population, from 1963 to 1970 it received only 29 to 31 percent of the aid to education. The suburban areas surrounding the city had approximately 18 percent of the state's population, but received from 23 to 25 percent of state aid to education. The rural area's portion also remained essentially the same over the seven year period.

Lehne's study concluded:

> . . . the 1970 halt in the increase of welfare costs can be partially attributed to the increase of suburban representation accompanied by reapportionment. This also provided part of the resistance to a greater decline in the educational portion of the total state aid package. . . . From this perspective, reapportionment stimulated slightly more vigorous support for educational aid, especially to suburban areas, and strengthened somewhat the opposition to social welfare costs. . . . In sum, reapportionment accomplished the redistribution of about 100 million dollars in New York State aid. Even though the basic contours of New York politics were not altered, the influence of reapportionment is evident.[13]

The impact of the new districting has been felt in New York, although not in the revolutionary way many political commentators predicted. Now that representation must reflect the location of population, the relative power of suburbs in the state legislature will continue to increase. It has been projected that by 1985, suburbanites will outnumber city dwellers by almost two to one. The potential for the exercise of suburban political power in state legislatures clearly is growing.

Reapportionment had a significant effect for several reasons. First, representation was moved from the poorest areas of the state to the most affluent areas. Second, according to Lehne, redistricting increased representation in areas where intraparty conflict is greater and interparty competition more heated. In short, New York state legislators must adhere to the wishes of constituents more closely, since the voters are more sophisticated and the races more competitive than ever before.[14]

One of the most important byproducts of reapportionment is that, in most cases, the elected representatives will be held more accountable for their actions than they have been in the past. To that extent, suburban and metropolitan area residents will feel the benefits of receiving a fairer share of representation than ever before. How significant this increased representation will be in bringing about real changes in metropolitan and suburban areas still remains to be seen. It is clear that, in order to bring about meaningful change in favor of urban and suburban areas, the legislators from these areas must secure influential positions on committees.

---

[13] Ibid., pp. 25–35.
[14] Ibid., p. 12.

In addition to these three cases, further data relevant to evaluating the impact of reapportionment is suggested by the pre-reapportionment analysis of David Derge, who concluded that urban interests in Illinois and Missouri were hampered more by policy disagreements among the metropolitan state legislative delegation than by rural interests.[15] Likewise, Brett Hawkins and Cheryl Whelchel studied the post-reapportionment Georgia legislature and noted that "gains in total urban membership in Georgia's General Assembly have not been matched by proportionate gains in influence positions."[16] They attributed this result to the increased diversity in the expanded metropolitan delegation.

Harlan Hahn's research on urban-rural conflict in state legislatures classified states in terms of the distribution and density of their populations and their legislative reactions to urban issues. His conclusions stress the impact of interest groups on these decisions in different states as follows:

> The same groups that traditionally have shaped the development of politics in many states have retained their strong positions in modern lobbying efforts. In both rural and transurban states, for example, the major pressure groups represented business and agricultural interests that frequently have acted in concert rather than in conflict with each other. On the other hand, agricultural or labor organizations have ebbed sufficiently in midurban or preurban states to give business interests preeminent influence. In the industrialized states, however, labor unions have challenged business organizations to a contest that has been relatively moderate in suburban and metropolitan states and strong in proto-metropolitan states.[17]

The question of how reapportionment has affected suburban influence on legislative outcomes, then, is very complex. Samuel Patterson sums up the diverse factors involved in an article on the political cultures of the American states. He refers to factors such as political style, basic attitudes toward tolerance of nonconformity, political identification with the state, degree of political participation, level of political socialization, socioeconomic characteristics, and even historical influences.[18] Ira Sharkansky has argued that, on the whole, increased representation

---

[15] David R. Derge, "Metropolitan and Outstate Alignments in Illinois and Missouri Legislative Delegation," *American Political Science Review*, December 1958, pp. 1051–65.

[16] Brett Hawkins and Cheryl Whelchel, "Reapportionment and Urban Representation in Legislative Influence Positions: The Case of Georgia," *Urban Affairs Quarterly*, March 1968, p. 75.

[17] This excerpt from, *Urban-Rural Conflict: The Politics of Change* by Harlan Hahn, (c) 1971 is reprinted by permission of the Publisher, Sage Publications, Inc. p. 259.

[18] Samuel Patterson, "The Political Culture of the American States," *Journal of Politics*, vol. 30 (1968), pp. 187–209.

of suburban interests has not necessarily led to increased levels of expenditures for those issues and programs affecting the suburbs.[19] Sharkansky
attributed this to the impact of incrementalism in the budgetary process.
It is true that the public will not tolerate great fluctuations in the level
of spending for public concerns. For example, public expenditures for
education generally are not allowed to vary greatly from one year to
another. The constituents who pay for these services expect security
and continuity in exchange for their tax dollars. They want to know
that the standards of education which have been established for their
children will not be jeopardized by a sudden withdrawal or decrease
in state funds. Similar expectations apply to virtually every category
of spending in a state budget. Great political pressures are generated
when even moderate changes occur in the allocation of public
expenditures.

Sharkansky also notes that incrementalism in the budgetary process
will continue to retard suburban impact on policy outcomes because
of the sheer size of public budgets. Because the complexity and techni-
cality of a state or federal budget precludes reevaluating all its contents,
the preceding year's budget generally is viewed as a legitimate basis
for beginning the evaluation of the new budget. Such a process, of
course, reinforces those external pressures for budgetary rigidity. Further, the budget for any one year must be prepared over a year in
advance so it cannot possibly reflect current spending needs. Thus, not
only are appropriations delayed reflectors of changing social needs, but
the very nature of the budgetary process constrains broad and rapid
social changes.

However, Sharkansky appears to exaggerate the influence of budgetary incrementalism as a factor contributing to the failure of the suburbs
to reorient state spending. Even within incrementally changing budgets,
there is room for increasing some suburban-related expenditures. However, the Arizona, California, and New York cases demonstrate that
this kind of response was slow to develop.

A more important factor explaining the unresponsiveness of state budgets to the suburbs has been the failure of the suburbanites to agree
on positive programs that would affect them. Often they find it easier
to rally in opposition to central city programs than to adopt comprehensive suburban programs. As part-time legislators, often without real ties
to the county or suburban officials, the suburban state legislators are
not able to cope with the situation. This diversity of suburban interests
and the leadership vacuum within the suburban delegation is the most
compelling explanation for what appears to be a slow response to suburban interests.

---

[19] Ira Sharkansky, *Spending in the American States* (Chicago: Rand-MacNally
and Co., 1968).

SUBURBAN POLITICAL POWER IN THE U.S. HOUSE OF REPRESENTATIVES

Article 1, Section 2, of the U.S. Constitution requires that Congress apportion congressional seats to the states on the basis of the population count of each official ten-year census. The state legislatures then must decide how the apportioned seats will be distributed within their borders. Until *Baker* v. *Carr* the rural state legislators also gerrymandered congressional districts to enhance the power of their constituents in Congress. This helped to create safe rural and southern districts whose representatives held a disproportionate share of committee chairmanships.

When legislative districts are redistricted only once in ten years, the residents of the most rapidly growing area will become underrepresented in the intervening period. Table 2–2 shows the discriminatory effect on

TABLE 2–2
Equity of congressional representation by type of district in 1962*
(in percentages)

Ratio of actual size to the population norm for a district†	91 urban districts	52 suburba districts	181 mid-urban districts	102 rural district	All districts
Overrepresented (under 85)	20	13	17	49	25
Equitable (85–115)	61	35	60	45	54
Underrepresented (over 115) . . .	19	52	23	6	21
Total	100	100	100	100	100

Source: *Congressional Quarterly Weekly Report*, February 2, 1962.
* Population composition was based on the 1960 Census of urbanized areas, with districts classified as follows: urban 60 percent or more urban population; suburban, 50 percent or more urban-fringe population; rural, 90 percent or more nonurban population; and mid-urban, all other districts.
† Districts having 85 to 115 percent of the number of voters included in the average congressional district (national population divided by 425 seats in the House of Representatives) were categorized as "equitable." Districts with less than 85 percent of the population of the average district were disignated overrepresented and those with more than 115 percent of the population were classified as underrepresented.

suburbs of using the 10-year census as a basis of representation following the growth that occurred in the 1950s. Fifty-two percent of the suburban districts and only 6 percent of the rural districts were underrepresented at the time of the *Baker* v. *Carr* decision. At the same time, 49 percent of the rural districts and only 13 percent of the suburban districts were overrepresented.

Following the voluntary and court-directed redistricting of the 1960s, the power of the suburbs in Congress has been gradually increasing. In 1966, 92 congressional districts were more than half suburban, an increase from 52 in 1962. By 1974, there were more districts classified suburban (131) than rural (103) or urban (102). This numerical superiority, however, has not resulted in a coherent voting bloc. There are apparently three basic explanations for this. First, some districts include part of a central city or even rural areas. Second, the Democratic party controls Congress and of the 131 suburban congressmen in 1974, 73 were Republicans and only 58 were Democrats.[20] Finally, and most importantly, the suburbs as a group are extremely heterogeneous and not well organized.

In predicting changes that would occur from reapportionment, many analysts assumed that suburban and urban constituencies had compatible interests. However, as was suggested in the introduction, suburban homogeneity is a myth; different types of suburbs have different needs and make different types of demands upon their government and their legislators. It is not surprising that suburbs would elect different types of congressmen to represent their various constituency interests or that these congressmen would fail to develop a common agenda for congressional action.

Even suburban congressmen of the same party differ widely. For example, Prince George's and Montgomery Counties are predominantly "suburban" Maryland counties bordering Washington, D.C. Although both congressmen representing these counties in the early 1970s were Republicans, they had very different political philosophies. Larry Hogan of Prince George's County, which has a large black population and a lower per capita income than Montgomery County, consistently voted the conservative position, while Gilbert Gude of Montgomery County usually voted like a liberal Democrat. Although Montgomery County has one of the highest per capita incomes in the nation—which would normally foster a conservative orientation—a large portion of Gude's constituents are high ranking federal employees, who are more liberally oriented than nongovernment employees at the same economic levels.

Despite the diversity among suburban constituencies, a study of 1973 congressional votes on eight major issues with substantial rural or urban overtones suggested that some general patterns of suburban voting behavior can be identified. The study compared the votes of congressmen from three categories of districts: urban, suburban, and rural, as summarized in Table 2–3. Only districts having 60 percent of their population in one category were included in the study. Eighty-eight of the 258 districts included were suburban and 57 of those suburban districts were represented by Republicans.[21]

On two of these votes—one permitting use of highway trust fund money for mass transit and one limiting farm subsidy payments—the

---

[20] Alan Ehrenhalt, "Suburbia Gains Plurality in House, But Not Influence," *Washington Post,* April 28, 1974, Section H, p. 3.

[21] "Suburbs: Potential But Unrealized House Influence," *Congressional Quarterly,* April 6, 1974, pp. 878–80.

TABLE 2–3
Selected 1973 voting studies and key votes in house
(predominant district characteristics*)

	Urban All (78)	Urban North Dems. (52)	Urban South Dems. (12)	Urban Reps. (14)	Suburban All (88)	Suburban North Dems. (28)	Suburban South Dems. (3)	Suburban Reps. (57)	Rural All (92)†	Rural North Dems. (17)	Rural South Dems. (30)	Rural Reps. (45)
Urban-rural key votes‡ (percentage voting in favor)												
1. Permit use of highway trust fund for mass transit	77	98	27	46	72	88	100	63	7	27	0	5
2. Authorize funds for mass transit operating subsidies	79	100	73	29	49	93	67	27	24	75	31	0
3. Increase funds for community comprehensive planning grants	81	100	44	33	44	83	67	24	24	36	36	12
4. Increase funds for urban renewal	70	93	25	8	28	73	67	6	12	64	4	0
5. Increase minimum wage for farm workers	77	100	50	21	51	93	67	28	23	76	4	14
6. Require spending of impounded rural environmental assistance program funds	69	84	80	14	34	85	67	8	79	100	96	60
7. Limit farm subsidy payments	79	90	45	71	80	80	100	80	36	50	7	51
8. Phase out farm program over three years	28	12	27	86	80	42	100	98	29	12	4	51
Group ratings§ (average rating score)												
Americans for Constitutional Action (ACA)	27	10	36	76	51	17	26	70	56	22	54	70
Americans for Democratic Action (ADA)	63	79	50	16	40	79	70	19	27	68	23	14
AFL-CIO Committee on Political Education	78	96	67	20	50	93	72	27	42	94	49	18
National Farmers Union (NFU)	79	93	82	25	50	89	77	29	68	97	82	49
Conservative coalition¶	27	11	43	75	52	17	35	70	67	30	72	77

* Based on district populations 60 percent or more in one category.

† Includes Speaker Albert's 3rd district of Oklahoma, which was omitted in percentage tabulations.

‡ CQ vote numbers and 1973 Weekly Report page references for key votes 1–8 are: CQ vote 66, p. 949, 366, p. 2682, 189, p. 1774, 190, p. 1774, 118, p. 1468, 10, p. 310, 229, p. 1912, 234, p. 1912.

§ 1973 ratings, Weekly Report p. 813.

¶ CQ conservative coalition voting study, Weekly Report p. 198.

Source: "Suburbs: Potential But Unrealized House Influence," *Congressional Quarterly*, April 6, 1974, p. 880.

urban and suburban representatives virtually voted as a bloc. In each case, a large majority of suburban Republicans and Democrats voted the same way. However, on two of the votes—one to phase out the farm program and the other to require the president to spend impounded rural environmental assistance appropriations—there was a party difference. Suburban and urban Democrats voted with the rural representatives, while the suburban and urban Republican congressmen strongly opposed the rural position. For example, on the impoundment vote, 92 percent of the suburban and 86 percent of the urban Republicans voted against the rural position. Only 16 percent of the suburban Democrats and 17 percent of the urban Democrats opposed it.

Generally, these figures, (especially votes 1, 3, 4, and 8), suggest that suburban Democrats are more conservative than urban Democrats, and (votes 1, 3, and 5) that suburban Republicans are normally more liberal than either urban or rural Republicans. On votes 2, 3, 4, 5, 6, and 8, suburban Democrats tended to vote more like urban Democrats than like suburban Republicans. Suburban Republicans also were closer to their party brethren in the city than to their fellow suburbanites of the other party.

Despite the increase in the number of congressmen representing suburban districts, a strong suburban bloc has not emerged. Power in the congressional legislative process involves more than just the number of seats representing a region or a particular cluster of population. Committee power and legislative or parliamentary skill are also factors. If legislation is sent to a hostile committee, it can be buried or drastically amended before being sent to the floor. It takes time to acquire parliamentary-legislative skills and "positions of influence" within the congressional committee structure. Therefore, seniority still plays a significant role.

However, incumbency rates of suburban congressmen indicate that many of them do not get the chance to develop such skills and seniority. Again, the influence of the type of suburban constituency has an impact on the congressman. Generally, greater heterogeneity of interests and parties within suburban congressional districts results in a higher turnover of congressmen than in central city or rural districts where one party usually is dominant.

In short, more equitable distribution of congressional seats has increased the numerical strength of the suburban areas in Congress. However, the diversity of interests among suburbs, competition among suburban congressmen, clashes in political philosophies of different suburban districts, a legislative system that rewards seniority, and constituencies that deny suburban congressmen the level of seniority enjoyed by their rural and central city peers, all inhibit the formation of a viable suburban voting bloc within Congress.

Increased representation for suburban areas as a result of the one man-one vote principle provides the potential for gaining policy outcomes desired by suburban voters. However, the future suburban political landscape will continue to be marked by the conflicting demands of highly diverse interests, which suburban congressmen will have difficulty reconciling. Only when clearly suburban issues are identified, as they were in the 1974 votes on rapid transit and on the farm subsidy program, will the suburbs be able to express their collective interests and mobilize suburban political power in Congress.

INTRAMETROPOLITAN SUBURBAN POWER

Due to the increasing population of the suburbs, their changing demographic profile, and the effects of one man-one vote reforms in translating that population increase into political power, the impact of future population shifts on public policy outcomes will be more difficult to predict. Future political changes will be more subtle and will be shaped by the total environment peculiar to a given metropolitan area. Different types of suburbs will provide a different context for public policy decisions and political campaigns.

Most small villages and cities use the nonpartisan system, which is not an appropriate vehicle for expression of suburban political power on state and national issues. The suburban power base is more effectively mobilized when it is related to the county political scene. This is one reason for the increasing importance of the suburban counties that are large enough to influence decisions at the state and national levels. These jurisdictions have had partisan political traditions and their decisions touch the lives of all the suburban residents. Their elections serve as a means of expressing voter reactions that will be heeded by Democrats and Republicans at the state and federal levels.

"County power"—which very often means suburban county power—is one of the major lobbying influences at the national level. The National Association of Counties is one of the strongest motivating forces behind the formation of a suburban bloc. The association represents the interests of counties at the federal level. Since virtually all major counties belong to it, it is in a position to encourage Republican and Democratic congressmen and senators representing suburban areas to unite in support of suburban interests.

Other increasingly powerful forums for expanding suburban influence are the metropolitan planning commissions and the councils of governments (COGs). These forums are discussed in detail in Chapter 9. However, it seems clear that as these multifunctional and voluntary organizations formed by local governments take up metropolitan and regional issues, the power of central cities will become less decisive. In the past, central cities have established regional facilities, such as airports, high-ways, and sports stad:ums, without regard to the rest of the metropolitan area. Few central cities still have such unilateral power. Suburbs now are participating in decisions about where to locate the metropolitan solid waste treatment facility or the regional airport. This has been one of the indirect effects of federal funding of urban projects.

A good example of the functional consequences of subjecting local decisions to the less partisan interests of the entire metropolitan area was the 1972–75 battle over location of an airport for metropolitan St. Louis. The city of St. Louis owns Lambert Field, the current regional airport, located west of the city of St. Louis County. As the demands upon the airport began to exceed its capacity, a decision had to be made concerning the location of a new one.

St. Louis County desperately wished to retain the new airport because of its beneficial impact on commerce and employment. However, to receive federal funds, it was necessary to have a recommendation from the East-West Gateway Coordinating Council, the metropolitan area's council of governments, concerning the airport's location. The Gateway Council debated the issue and voted to place the airport east of St. Louis in St. Clair County, Illinois. The vote in the Council resulted from an alliance between the city of St. Louis and the Illinois jurisdictions of the metropolitan area, formed to thwart St. Louis County and the other Missouri counties that wanted the airport in their jurisdiction.

The federal authorities may accept or reverse this recommendation. The point here is that, before the establishment of the COG and the federal requirement for metropolitan clearance, the city of St. Louis could have made a bilateral deal with any county in which it wanted to locate the airport. Also, the suburban counties could have allied against the city of St. Louis to block relocation of the airport in an area unacceptable to them. Since the process now requires participation by almost every jurisdiction affected by the decision, the suburbs and central city had to declare where they stood. In this case, the suburbs were able to see that their interests were in opposition to each other rather than to those of the city of St. Louis.

VOTING BEHAVIOR OF THE NEW SUBURBANITE

Most of the early suburban areas tended to support the Republican party candidates in local, state, and national elections. Political analysts assumed that the large scale post-World War II migration of central city voters, who presumably had been Democrats, would overturn this Republican dominance of suburban politics.

This did not occur. In fact, the 1952 election generally is viewed as a landmark because it was the first time in a quarter of a century that a Republican was elected to the White House. The initial reaction to this victory was to attribute it to Dwight Eisenhower's great personal popularity. However, when Eisenhower was reelected in 1956 with an even larger majority than he received in 1952, many analysts began to suggest that the popularity of the much-admired general could not explain the overthrow of the successful Democratic electoral coalition originally organized by Franklin Roosevelt. Then, in 1960, John F. Kennedy, despite his charisma, won by only a small margin over Richard M. Nixon. Even though Kennedy won, Republicans slightly increased their numbers in Congress. This further suggested that the Eisenhower image was not a sufficient explanation for the electoral shift of 1952. Something more profound and fundamental apparently was taking place within the American political system.[22] Several theories were offered to explain this phenomenon.

One theory is that when the central city migrants became homeowners in heavily Republican, middle-class suburbs, their voting patterns changed. Homeownership generally is equated with conservatism and concern over property taxes, fiscal responsibility policies, low taxes, and balanced budgets. These orientations commonly are associated with Republican rather than Democratic governments. In addition, these new suburbanites may have been subjected to some social pressures that made them feel it was useless to vote for Democrats when they consistently were outvoted by Republican peers.

The statistics from the presidential elections of 1952, 1956, and 1960 seemed to substantiate this "conversion" theory. Yet some skeptics argued that, rather than converting from the Democratic party, these new Republican voters may have been expressing the same political sentiments but in a different locale. That is, instead of "becoming" Republicans *after* arriving in the suburbs, they had been Republican voters in the cities all along. This view has been labeled the "political transplantation" theory.

A third theory is that the new suburbanites were not so much "con-

---

[22] The extensive literature on suburban voting motivations and political party ties includes the following: Eugene Burdick, *The Ninth Wave* (Boston: Houghton Mifflin, 1956); Louis Harris, *Is There a Republican Majority?* (New York: Hager and Brothers, 1954); Herbert Hirsch, "Suburban Voting and National Trends," *Western Political Quarterly*, September 1968; Samuel Lubell, *Result of the Moderates* (New York: Hager and Brothers, 1956); Richard Scammon and Ben Wattenberg, *The Real Majority* (New York: Coward-McCann, 1970); Timothy Schilty and William Moffitt, "Inner-City/Outer-City Relationships in Metropolitan Areas," *Urban Affairs Quarterly*, September 1971; William H. Whyte, *The Organization Man* (New York: Simon and Schuster, 1956); Fred Wirt et al., *On the City's Rim* (Lexington, Mass., D.C. Heath and Co., 1972); Robert Wood, *Suburbia* (Boston: Houghton Mifflin, 1958); and Joseph Zikmund II, "Suburban Voting in Presidential Elections: 1948–1964," *Midwest Journal of Political Science*, May 1968 and "A Comparison of Political Attitudes and Activity Patterns in Central Cities and Suburbs," *Public Opinion Quarterly*, Spring 1967.

verted" to Republicanism as they were "predisposed" to the symbols of status, one of which is the Republican party label. Advocates of this "predisposition" theory hold that upwardly-mobile citizens were anxious to shed all identification with a working-class past. Physical movement *away* from the city partially fulfilled that need. But, the longing for acceptance also required subordination to the dominant culture of the suburbs, and voting Republican is one way to demonstrate this deference in many suburbs. Such behavior often is attributed to a deep-seated dislike for the city, an identification of the Democratic party with city life, and a transfer of city-associated hostilities to the Democratic party.

All these theories assumed that the 1952, 1956, and 1960 national elections manifested a change in American voting behavior. However, it is difficult to calculate the influence of other factors, such as the potential one-time impact of a war hero candidate (Eisenhower) and the negative impact of a Catholic Democratic candidate (Kennedy). Further, a number of suburban political studies have weakened support for all three of the change theories.

In his 1960 study, *Working Class Suburb*, Bennett Berger found that the new blue collar suburbanites who moved out from San Jose, California, were 81 percent Democratic and 11 percent Republican.[13] Another study, *First Tuesday*, by David Wallace, found "no support in Westport, Connecticut, predominantly a middle class suburb, for any conclusion that present suburban voters are becoming any more Republican than their parents."[24] Finally, as Gans concluded in *The Levittowners*, his study of suburban Willingboro, New Jersey, "people's lives are changed somewhat by the move to suburbia, but their basic ways remain the same. They do not develop new life-styles or ambitions for themselves and their children."[25]

In any case, the impact of suburban growth on the politics of the state and nation, as well as on the suburbs, will be felt only to the extent that suburbanites participate in politics. A host of factors determine the type and degree of participation in suburban politics. Social and environmental factors are at least as important for participation as some of the legal factors surrounding redistricting. Occupation, education and per capita income are the strongest demonstrable correlates for voting behavior.[26]

Despite suburban diversity, some degree of unity and relatively high

---

[23] Bennett M. Berger, *Working Class Suburb* (Berkeley: University of California Press, 1960).

[24] David Wallace, *First Tuesday* (Garden City, New York: Doubleday, 1964), p. 113.

[25] Herbert Gans, *The Levittowners* (New York: Pantheon Books, 1967), p. 409.

[26] Thomas Dye, *Politics in States and Communities* (Englewood Cliffs, N.J.: Prentice-Hall, Inc., 1969), pp. 65-70.

levels of participation can be inspired by certain types of issues. Questions dealing with public schools, housing, and taxes are the most sensitive ones for suburbanites. They influence their family affairs, their chosen life-styles, and their bank accounts. The suburban responses to these issues differ only in degree, depending upon the circumstances surrounding them. Any suspicions of suburban apathy and unwillingness to become "involved" in such issues would be quickly dispelled by a review of controversies over school busing in the 1970s. This single issue has had far-reaching effects for many political careers and underlines the potential of suburban political power to shape and alter the course of public policy at every level of government.

Another factor that influences the nature of suburban voting behavior is the mass media. The network media and the metropolitan press are very effective in sensitizing voters to state and national issues and candidates. This may be one reason why, despite the low participation rate in local suburban politics, the suburbs have a rather high turnout for state and federal elections. Further, while some big-city papers have gone out of business in recent years, numerous suburban papers have been created. These papers are expanding their coverage of state and national as well as local elections.

The levels of voter participation in the gubernatorial and congressional elections of the past decade also reflect a distinct influence of region upon voting behavior.[27] The aggregate distribution of voter participation by states varied considerably for different types of elections. Most of the states with low turnouts were heavily rural southern states. New England states, except for Maine, had a relatively high voter turnout. On the other hand, some western rural states including the Dakotas, Montana, and Utah also had high turnouts. Suburbs generally had a relatively high level of voting participation but reflected the regional differences.

In discussing levels of suburban political participation, one must take account of the various factors that influence voter participation. Generally, nonvoting is associated with low levels of education, nonskilled jobs, and areas most distant from the city. Since suburbs exhibiting these characteristics presumably will have proportionately less participation than other suburbs, it is difficult to generalize about suburban voting participation, much less about how suburbanites will vote.

Part of "the suburban myth," as Scott Donaldson describes it, is that the suburbs are homogeneous in terms of socioeconomic variables.[28]

---

[27] Lester Milbrath, "Political Participation in the States," cited in *Politics in the American States*, Herbert Jacob and Kenneth Vines, eds. (Boston: Little Brown and Company, 1965).

[28] Scott Donaldson, *The Suburban Myth* (New York: Columbia University Press, 1969).

The suburbs, as the legend goes, serve almost as a second "melting pot." Motivated by common interests—to escape from the city, its problems and its taxes; to own a home; to provide a good education for one's children, as well as a proper environment in which to raise them— individuals of different social rank, background, and outlook have come together to establish a green paradise beyond the city's asphalt and soot.

Homogeneity, the assumption underlying most suburban literature, must be carefully qualified. While most suburbs tend to be internally homogeneous, suburbs in the aggregate are heterogeneous. Virtually all suburban counties are also heterogeneous. This is due to their substantial populations and the fact that they may contain a number of suburban cities, as well as unincorporated areas, which rely upon the county for most of their services. Consequently, any discussion of suburban political power must be related to the size of the constituency involved. As will be suggested in the next chapter, appeals to community and homogeneity are important in electing a suburban mayor. However, since the election of a county executive or a congressman involves a large geographic area and population, heterogeneity and broad-based appeals are likely to be the key to victory.

SUMMARY

The emergence of suburban political power has been discussed in the light of the history of malapportionment of state legislatures. The U.S. Supreme Court decisions during the 1960s deprived the rural legislators of the power to keep urban areas under-represented in state legislatures. As a result of the one man-one vote principle established by the Court decision, suburban residents now receive more representation in state legislatures than ever before.

Despite increased suburban and metropolitan representation in the various state legislatures, it is not clear that the increased numbers have been translated into political powers for the suburbs. The increase in the number of state legislators from suburban areas has not significantly altered the rurally oriented decisions of the Arizona legislature. The California legislature enacted changes reflecting the increased number of members from metropolitan areas, but the changes were not immediate. The most significant changes occurred in New York, where about $100 million in state aid was redistributed as a result of reapportionment. Even there, however, the increase in highway aid was lower and welfare programs were not as adversely affected as had been anticipated.

The most important results of reapportionment to date are that the legislatures are more representative of all the citizens of the states and that state legislators are more accountable to the voters than ever before.

There have been no dramatic changes in the voting behavior of the majority of state legislators, as metropolitan governmental officials had hoped. Instead, suburban legislators often team up with rural legislators to thwart central city programs. In addition, they have not developed programs of their own.

The myth of suburban homogeneity has been disproved by the behavior of congressmen representing suburban areas. Different suburbs have elected representatives who reflect their diverse wishes. This helps to explain why the strong suburban delegation in Congress has not caused more dramatic changes. There simply is no clear suburban bloc interest on most issues. Where such interests have been identified, as in the 1974 votes on mass transit and farm subsidies, the suburban delegations have shown they can act as a unit.

Until suburban political leaders and the people they represent can mobilize their political power for suburban agendas, numbers of legislators alone will not result in suburban power. In addition, suburban legislators will be unable to overcome powerful lobbying efforts of special interest groups whose impact might be antisuburban. To exert their influence at the state and national levels, people and groups must be able to define their common interests and priorities. There is a need for suburban leaders to cooperate with central city officials in an effort to secure their common metropolitan goals.

One area in which the suburbs have displayed some unity is in their reaction to the central city. This factor shows up in city-county consolidation roles as well as in the level of support suburban representatives provide metropolitan planning bodies and councils of governments. However, even here the interests of suburbs with different geographic relationships to the central city can lead to unlikely alliances, as in the case of the St. Louis airport location controversy. Clearly, the suburbs must have better leadership to contribute effectively to the determination of metropolitan policies.

3

Grass roots suburban politics

THIS CHAPTER will focus upon political behavior within the bounds of individual suburban cities. An examination of the patterns and levels of suburban political activity is important because it forms a substantial part of the total political life in the United States. Further, the belief in "local control" and "grass roots democracy" has always been a strong and pervasive component of the American approach to government. However, a number of scholars and commentators have questioned whether local government is as open as other levels of government, an issue to be examined in the pages that follow.

The chapter is divided into three parts. The first part concerns some of the sources of suburban political conflict. The second section focuses upon the local political official, his recruitment, behavior, and orientations as a member of the city council. This is crucial since the style of a city government and the nature of its decision-making process is largely determined by the city council. The final portion of the chapter is concerned with the participation of the citizen himself, through voting, direct contacts with local officials, and organizational affiliations. An assessment of citizen attitudes toward their local government and suburban levels of trust and support also is included.

SUBURBAN POLITICAL CONFLICT

No two towns or cities are quite alike in their patterns of conflict and conflict resolution. Some are rife with conflict, while others seem

50

to avoid it. For some it is but a temporary occurrence that is undergirded by substantial consensus, while some are perpetually and deeply divided. Some cities divide over basic policy issues, while others seem to argue about personalities or styles of politicians. This is why James Coleman, in his study of community conflict, wrote that "communities differ in the degree to which community life is important enough to argue about."[1]

There are four general areas in which incidents of conflict arise. The first involves economics and normally exists between workers and management in economically self-contained towns. Most suburbs do not have purely economic cleavages. Therefore, most suburban conflict is rooted in the three other major areas—questions of power and authority, cultural values, and personal attitudes. People living next to each other often have radically different views due to: (1) mobility; (2) population waves resulting in a wide range of age groups; and (3) widespread commuting, which thwarts the local socialization process and the maintenance of a "range of tolerance."

Questions of power and authority involve such matters as working class disagreement with the mayor or city manager as to what the community's priorities should be. Cultural values or beliefs can lead to conflict regarding such matters as educational expenditures, segregation or religious issues. Finally, attitudes toward certain persons, individuals or groups, are a personalistic source of conflict.[2]

However, Bryan T. Downes has argued that suburban political conflicts are not based upon economic, class, religious, or personalistic issues. He asserted that disagreements arise concerning (1) the nature and seriousness of problems, (2) estimates of the best way to solve them, and (3) the role government, at each level, should play in the solution.[3] Downes, paraphrasing Coleman, states:

> If these changes and the problems they create touch upon important aspects of people's lives and also affect people differently, the stage may be set for controversy and conflict. This would be particularly true if some people felt actions could be taken that cope with or solve problems brought about by change. . . . Of particular importance is the way in which residents and their political leaders respond to conflicting demands for policies designed to solve problems.[4]

---

[1] James Coleman, *Community Conflict* (Glencoe, Ill.: The Free Press, 1957), pp. 3–14. This section relies heavily on this work.

[2] William Gamson, "Rancorous Conflict in Community Politics," in Terry N. Clark (ed.), *Community Structure and Decision-Making: Comparative Analyses* (Scranton, Pa.: Chandler Publishing Company, 1968), pp. 197–212.

[3] Bryan T. Downes, "Problem Solving in Suburbia: The Basis for Political Conflict," in Louis Masotti and Jeffrey Hadden (eds.), *The Urbanization of the Suburbs* (Beverly Hills: Sage Publications, 1973), pp. 281–302.

[4] Ibid., p. 288.

Three general types of problems give rise to conflict. First are physical or material problems, such as pollution, the condition of housing, street maintenance, and police or fire facilities. Second, human problems originate in the needs of people. These include issues such as health, public welfare, and variations in the level of city services from one area to another. Finally, problems arise concerning development decisions in newer suburbs and redevelopment of aging communities.[5]

Suburbs have generally adopted negative policies in problem solving, choosing to do nothing if they can avoid taking action. Part of this failure is due to lack of jurisdiction, part is due to the lack of consensus on the seriousness of the problem, part is due to the inability of government to affect change, and part is a preference to maintain the status quo.

Suburban governments are much more likely to initiate problem solving action when a problem seems vital to the basic nature of the city. This is particularly true in cities oriented to certain basic values, such as growth or urban amenities. If a city perceives that a proposed project could threaten its life-style, action will be taken almost instantly. However, in dealing with such human problems as discrimination or the physical problem of housing stock, cities with a less cohesive life-style cannot claim such consensus. Some compromises may be effected, but basic issues may still remain unresolved. But even in less cohesive cities, if a clear physical problem can be isolated, it usually is resolved.

Of course, a great deal of problem solving in suburbia is noncontroversial and the dominant mode of suburban political behavior is consensus, so that city councils can often take direct action on a range of topics with little or no conflict and without expressions of citizen support. Even if the annual budget has significant divergences from past policies—expanded police coverage, reduced maintenance, or a proposed VD clinic in the health department—there often will be little public reaction.

Until fairly recently, the issues at stake in suburban politics were modest or even trivial. However, this situation has changed dramatically in the past few years. Suburban political issues are now more closely related to national issues. For instance, several cities held referenda on whether to support the U.S. action in Southeast Asia in the late 1960s. Although these efforts were not effective in changing national policy, they indicated that the local policy had become tied politically and socially to the national government.

Lately, urban problems have become suburban problems as well. Drug usage and venereal disease are widespread in the suburbs. Older

---

[5] *Ibid.*, pp. 292–93. In some cases, suburbs prefer not to make formal decisions. See Peter Bachrach and Morton Baratz, "Decisions and Non-decisions: An Empirical Framework," *American Political Science Review*, September 1963, pp. 632–42.

suburbs close to central cities are faced with deteriorating housing and heavy expenditures for police and fire protection in their relatively dense populations. The energy crisis has placed a premium on public transportation in both the central city and suburbs. Court orders for school integration, which have sometimes divided entire metropolitan areas, have thrust a critical political question into suburban laps.

Not only have national issues impacted the suburbs, but suburban political issues have become more important at the national level. As individual problems, suburban issues may have relatively little weight, but they can add up, suburb by suburb, to a significant impact on national policy. An example is the recent spate of local attempts to enact "no growth" policies. With each success at the local level, pressure increases for national action on the issue.

Furthermore, the way that suburbs, as well as all other local units of government, adjust to federal initiatives determines the speed at which innovations spread. Current major examples of policy questions that have been initiated by federal action include affirmative action involving women, racial and ethnic minorities, government employee unionization, revenue sharing, and school integration. The jury is still out on many of these questions, but clearly such issues have given local action a national significance.

Local politics are also crucial since they can affect the quality of public life. Cities can decide whether or not to increase the amount of park area within their boundaries, to support a first class library, or to build community pools. Decisions such as these provide additional options to many citizens but also raise questions as to priorities and how to raise the revenue. Environmental decisions on water quality and municipal sewage disposal are crucial to public health. Local social policies may provide public housing for the aged or enforce open housing ordinances to help eliminate discrimination. Some cities provide bus systems to supplement the private transportation sector. Although these services cannot be easily quantified, almost everyone would agree that they represent an increase in the quality of urban life. Similarly, it is generally assumed that keeping streets clean and attempting to lower the crime rate also contribute to community well being.

These traditional services, as well as nontraditional amenities, often deal with issues a city alone does not control. The cleanliness of streets may be a function of through traffic in town, and the crime rate, a factor of the number of juveniles and the level of poverty in the population. More money spent on street crews or police patrolmen may not significantly affect these problems. It is not clear what a city should do in cases such as this, and it is not even certain that better measures of performance would suggest the proper policies. Since most cities are chronically short of money, policy makers are beginning to question whether more expenditures for traditional services will indeed affect the quality of life.

One increasingly common practice is to ask citizens how they evaluate the quality of public services and life in their community. Without claiming that citizens always are the best judges of public services or their own well-being, it can be argued that their opinions are very relevant. Recent studies comparing citizen satisfaction with suburban police services and citizen satisfaction in similar central city neighborhoods indicate that suburban citizens generally rate their police departments higher than do residents of central cities. This suggests that a feeling of "community control" in a suburb is an important element in evaluating services.[6] Another recent study compared citizen evaluations of public services in new planned communities with those of "less planned" suburban communities which "just grew" at about the same time. While most ratings were highy favorable, the overall rating in excellence was only 5 percent higher for planned communities than for less planned communities.[7] These findings suggest that federal policy to encourage "new towns" may not significantly affect the quality of life. In evaluating both police services and new towns, then, citizen opinions are an important variable.

Although local governments bear the responsibility for the quality of life in the community, they often do not control the functions vital to maintaining it. Nothing could be more important than decisions concerning transportation, shopping convenience, health, or recreation facilities, yet these areas generally are not under the full control of city or county governments. Some of these decisions are made in the private sector or by regional groups. To a large extent, schools are a local function, but usually not of city or county government. However, citizens will continue to hold local government responsible for the condition of their neighborhoods and communities. For this reason local political action now is receiving considerable attention, particularly since the "New Federalism" is emphasizing decentralization and local decision making. Effective local action could increase local influence over urban policymaking at other government levels in future years. This will depend on the quality of the elected political leadership in local government and, ultimately, on the expectations and behavior of the average citizen in local units. These matters are the concern of the balance of this chapter.

---

[6] Elinor Ostrom and Gordon Whitaker, "Does Local Community Control of Police Make a Difference? Some Preliminary Findings," *American Journal of Political Science*, February 1973, pp. 48–77. See chapter 6 of this book on suburban delivery systems for an expanded discussion.

[7] "Evaluation of New Communities, Selected Preliminary Findings," proceedings of a National Science Foundation Seminar (Chapel Hill: Center for Urban and Regional Studies, University of North Carolina, March 1974), p. 38.

THE POLITICAL BEHAVIOR OF LOCAL
ELECTED OFFICIALS

While suburban governments are responsible for public policies, these policies are made at any one point of time by specific sets of elected legislators. Their political behavior, the ways in which they are recruited and elected, and the way they perform their legislative duties has a substantial effect on the decisions that are made.

Local councilmen are "elite" in a very real sense. Better educated and usually male, they are of much higher socioeconomic status than their fellow citizens. Table 3-1 compares three demographic studies of

TABLE 3-1

Demographic information on city councilmen from three studies (in percentages)

	Illinois	Southeast Virginia	San Francisco Bay
Nonwhite	1.7	4.8	Under 1.0
Male	93.0	95.0	95.0
Religion		n.a.	
Protestant	60.0		64.0
Catholic	33.0		34.0
Other, *n.a.	7.0		2.0
Over 12 years of education	97.0	74.0	95.0
Age at election			n.a.
Under 40	26.0	26.0	
40–50	39.0	53.0	
Over 50	35.0	21.0	
Years of city residence			n.a.
Under 10		19.0	
Under 15	32.0		
10–20		14.0	
16–25	26.0		
Over 20		22.0	
Over 26	42.0		
Since birth		45.0	

*n.a. = not available.

Sources: John Rehfuss, "Political Recruitment—The Case of Illinois City Councilmen," a paper presented to the American Political Science Association Annual Convention in New Orleans, September 1973; Manindra Mohapatra, "An Empirical Study of Legislature Behavior in American Local Government," *Quarterly Journal of the Local Self Government Institute*, Bombay, India, January–March 1973; and Kenneth Prewitt, *The Recruitment of Political Leaders* (Indianapolis: Bobbs Merrill, 1972).

local city councilmen in the San Francisco Bay area, in Illinois, and in the Norfolk, Virginia, area. The San Francisco study included interviews with councilmen from all 88 cities except San Francisco; while the Illinois sample included councilmen in 65 randomly selected cities, of which about half were suburbs; and the Tidewater, Virginia, cities included suburban areas as well as the central city of Norfolk. Over 90 percent of all Councilmen are male. Ninety-five percent of the councilmen from higher socioeconomic areas have high school educations. This figure is even higher for some of the wealthy suburbs where all councilmen are college graduates. A strong majority of councilmen are Protestants, and minority religions are notably missing from councils. The relatively low age of councilmen is perhaps surprising—26 percent are under 40 years of age and the mean age is in the early 40s. Regardless of age or sex, most councilmembers have resided for long periods of time in their suburban cities.

Political recruitment

There are two general views of how individuals are recruited to run for public office. One suggests that persons seek out public office for a variety of personal reasons such as a concern for city problems, a drive for power or prestige, or an honest motivation to serve the community. However, the final determinant is the conclusion reached by the potential candidate after he has calculated his changes, his resources and the opportunities for success. Gordon Black argues that the political structure shapes the ambition of men who rationally calculate their chances for election. Examining two major features of the political system in the San Francisco Bay area, he suggest that the size of the community and the degree of competition in community elections have a major impact on personal calculations and the costs of campaigning.[8]

The other view of the local electoral process generally holds that the party, interest groups, friends, and neighbors "pull' most candidates into office seeking. Most people require some strong stimulus to commit themselves to a campaign, and this stimulus is usually the urging of a party, the "call" of a city caucus, or the encouragement of friends and neighbors.[9] Two actual studies seem to suggest that environmental stimuli are crucial to encouraging candidacy. About two thirds of all councilmen from the Illinois and San Francisco Bay Areas indicated that some group or individual was involved in their decision to run.

These views are oversimplified, as there are at least four broad routes to local suburban political office, each of which tends to attract a certain type of candidate. Kenneth Prewitt emphasized two "pathways" to political office, including apprenticeships in community and civic associations

---

[8] Gordon Black, "A Theory of Political Ambition: Career Choices and the Role of Structural Incentives," *American Political Science Review*, March 1972, pp. 144–59.

[9] Lester Milbrath emphasizes the need for some strong stimuli to commit the potential candidate to run for office, in *Political Participation* (Chicago: Rand McNally, 1965).

and also certain occupational patterns.[10] The former is a "community service" route emphasizing church leadership, school and neighborhood activities, and, depending upon the city, organizations such as Rotary or Kiwanis Clubs. Thus, the little league manager, head usher, and Kiwanis president prepare themselves for local political roles without even knowing it. The second pattern is through high status occupations as local businessman, lawyer, banker, and other occupations that are at the center of the community communications network. Since these people are involved in local affairs and in roles closely related to those of councilmen, the transition often may seem natural.

Another route to local political office is the "partisan activist" route. Persons on this "track" are found in suburbs with partisan activity or at least strong local parties. They also may become active at the local level as a result of party activity related to state and federal politics. These people give money, work for candidates, attend candidate selection meetings, and may solicit funds for candidates. Finally, they become candidates themselves.

The last type of candidate is the "self-starter." Generally having little or no previous activity, he seems to be "pushed" into candidacy by personal orientations. The Illinois study indicated that about 31 percent of all councilmen had not been involved previously in any political activity short of running for election. Some of the "self-starters" with no previous experience are no doubt the civic notables picked by caucuses or by parties as "blue ribbon" candidates. But most of them are simply persons who decided that they wanted to run for office as a reaction to local problems and to try out their own ideas.

The study in metropolitan San Francisco indicated that many councilmen seem to observe an "ethic of volunteerism."[11] Prewitt found that electoral control over city councilmen was severely limited by the following events: (1) only about one third of the citizens voted, so that members often were elected by small numbers of voters; (2) nearly 24 percent of all councilmen initially had been appointed to their seat (the Illinois sample showed 12 percent); (3) incumbents rarely were defeated, with over 80 percent successfully standing for reelection; and (4) many councilmen plan to retire voluntarily after one or two terms. These factors form an ethic of volunteerism that undermines the importance of elections and of electoral accountability.

---

[10] Kenneth Prewitt, *The Recruitment of Political Leaders* (Indianapolis: Bobbs-Merrill, 1972), found that only 32 percent of all councilmen did not link their recruitment to other persons, while Rehfuss found that 66 percent of all councilmen indicated some external stimuli (party, group, friend, etc.). John Rehfuss, "Political Recruitment—The Case of Illinois City Councilmen," a paper presented to the American Political Science Association in New Orleans, September 1973.

[11] Kenneth Prewitt, "Political Ambitions, Volunteerism, and Electoral Accountability," *American Political Science Review*, March 1970, pp. 5–17.

The attitude of "I serve for nothing; I will follow my conscience rather than citizen demands" prevails, with obvious consequences for electoral accountability. Prewitt found that the members of those councils with the greatest degree of volunteerism were most likely to acknowledge voting against majority public opinion. They were also the least likely to involve constituencies in policymaking or to sense demands from the public. He cited other studies that suggested that the combination of trusteeship in representation, ritualism in elections, and volunteerism is potentially dangerous to democratic control at the local level. Popular controls are certainly weak when councilmen exhibit volunteerism, behave as trustees acting in a paternalistic fashion "for" the citizens, and are elected at ritualistic elections with small turnouts where incumbents almost always win.

These findings are disturbing because they could lead to policies seriously out of touch with popular desire or with changes in the nature of the city. They seem to contradict the conventional assumption that city councils are excessively amenable to citizen pressures. Prewitt correctly ends his article by indicating that it is a research task of significance to discover what, if anything, establishes democratic controls over legislators who were somewhat immune from electoral sanctions.

Councilmanic behavior

Most councilmen are likely to assert strongly their independence from popular pressures, yet many observers note that they are extremely sensitive to public criticism or opinions. Three commonly identified roles are those of the "trustee" who is primarily concerned with the best long range interests of the city, regardless of what the citizenry may favor in the short run; the "delegate" who is mandated to vote for what his constituency favors; and the "politico" who enjoys political life for itself and who often plays a legislative broker role.[12]

This presents a paradox in that councilmen can feel independent yet not always act independently. Perhaps these roles are operative only at certain times or under certain conditions. The situational nature of local or suburban politics helps to explain this disparity. In most cases, there is relatively little citizen demand placed on legislators and the local council exercises its own set of values. Since even some complex issues may not be controversial, councilmen may engage in "problem-solving" without a great deal of citizen input. Further, controversial

---

[12] These are specifically mentioned in Heinz Eulau and Kenneth Prewitt, *Labyrinths of Democracy: Adaptations, Linkages, Representation and Policies in Urban Politics* (Indianapolis: Bobbs-Merrill, 1973), p. 407, in their analysis of San Francisco Bay Area councilman. For an earlier work on roles of state legislators, see John Wahlke, Heinz Eulau, William Buchanan and Leroy Ferguson, *The Legislative System: Explorations in Legislative Behavior* (New York: John Wiley and Sons, 1962).

matters may polarize large sections of the community and create off-setting pressures, so that a councilman may take any position he pleases. Conversely, when complex or unsettled issues arise and substantial or expert citizen participation develops, the councilman is likely to defer regardless of his professed intention "not to feel the weight of voter responsibility."

Community homogeneity is another explanation for council behavior. Since most suburbs are individually homogeneous, the councils are selected as "like-minded" men who can be trusted to carry on city business in the tradition of the suburb. Under these conditions, councilmanic and citizens values are not likely to diverge substantially. Thus, councilmen can be trusted to make important decisions in the best interests of citizens. Conversely, citizens who oppose council decisions or who demand action that councilmen consider inimical to city values are likely to be seen as unrepresentative, as isolates, or even as illegitimate. It is not difficult for a councilman to reject these demands. He can claim that he is making up his own mind when, in fact, he knows that his position is likely to have substantial support in the community.

A supporting explanation is the citizen's feeling that "friends and neighbors" rule. This explains citizen support for councilmen in terms of friendship and social approbation rather than attributing it to a sharing of values. Although similar values probably exist, they are not as crucial as friendship ties, since one can forgive his friends for errors of judgment or differences of opinion. The result is the same as for "like-minded" men—the councilman may exercise his own judgment, free from substantial citizen pressures and secure among his friends in the electorate. It should be noted that a councilman chosen either as a "friend" or as a "like-minded" person cannot be consistently at odds with the dominant community consensus. The ability of the councilman to feel free to do as he pleases without offending community values rests on a relative scarcity of divisive issues. A community full of conflict is not likely to elect councilmen who adopt a trustee view toward council behavior.

A basic element of the local official's life is a lack of privacy while making public decisions that are often both complex and controversial. He is not as isolated as a state legislator or congressman. On display every other Monday night, his words appear in next morning's paper and his telephone is listed for the instant access of interested parties. While most councilmen do not receive much pressure on most issues, intense pressure is generated on specific issues such as zoning cases and the possibiity of such pressure exists at all times.

This intense exposure can have a number of results, some contradictory. Some councilmen tend to say little or nothing during a meeting, assuming that anything said may be used against them. Others posture outrageously to the audiences. Councils often wish to meet privately or semipublicly so that members can speak off the record to hammer out consensus. This presents difficulties, since most states prohibit local governments from holding meetings closed to the public, except in cases involving personnel or matters such as land acquisition where the public interest would be damaged by open discussion. Consequently, personnel matters often are interpreted very broadly in order to provide an opportunity for closed meetings. As a general rule, however, local decision-making occurs in a "goldfish bowl" atmosphere. This has a significant effect on the style and substance of local council decisionmaking.

Both the "friends and neighbors" policy and this intense public exposure can foster a somewhat antiprofessional attitude on the part of councilmen. Uncomfortable in this public role, their instinct is to fall back on an amateur way of conducting public business. This pattern is strengthened by the support councilmen receive in their role as friends and neighbors, who could hardly be expected to act as professional politicians. Any mistakes made in the public eye partially can be excused since they are amateurs as well as friends. After all, a friend judging a zoning case can be trusted more than an expert who may not understand how people feel in River City. He may make mistakes, but his heart is in the right place.

Council orientations

In maintaining this support level, councilmen have to adopt some form of group orientation toward problems they encounter. The patterns vary from city to city. Councils as a group have dominant orientations that differ from those of any individual councilman. Some members may defer to the group, while others may not. Disagreement sometimes is tolerated, sometimes discouraged, and, in certain circumstances, perhaps encouraged. Nevertheless, councils tend to utilize three broad and general orientations in dealing with municipal problems: maintaining, adapting, and programming.[13] While not completely distinct from each other, the identification of these roles makes it possible to generalize about the political roles that councils as a whole play. To the extent that these roles remain consistent over time, one can predict the style, and some of the outcomes of political questions.

---

[13] Eulau and Prewitt, *Labyrinths of Democracy*, chapter 8, particularly pp. 153–61. Eulau and Prewitt identify these orientations by asking individual councilmen their views on the job of a councilman and then generalizing their views to councils as a whole. While this has both practical and theoretical weaknesses, it is probably the only way, short of extended observation of all 88 councils in the Bay area, to develop overall generalizations. These orientations, at any rate, do not seem far from the way that observation suggests councils seem to operate. In many cases, we have expanded the orientations beyond what the authors specified.

The first orientation, maintenance, involves protecting the status quo of the city against the threat of unwanted change or increased urbanization. This is the dominate view of most typical smaller and homogeneous cities. The maintenance orientation also reflects a limited view of governing, that of caretaking or administering rather than problemsolving. The good councilman, then, plays the role of a steward who takes meticulous care of that with which he is entrusted and who does not take it upon himself to suggest any radical departures or even modest adaptations. Maintenance councils exhibit a strong interest in preserving the quality of traditional services such as fire protection, the police force, and street maintenance, although the specific level and type of service emphasized will vary from city to city. Museums and expensive libraries could reflect maintenance orientations in a wealthy amenities city, while underfunding even the most traditional police and fire services may mark the same attitudes in a caretaker city.

Many cities are faced with rapid growth or are threatened with external forces such as a freeway or land development, which could affect traditional community values. The maintenance role generally demands a strong resistance to such changes. Because maintenance councils implicitly believe that the present city is the best mix of taxation and services, they tend to resist urbanization or modernization.

Other councils are oriented toward adapting the city to community wishes or to unavoidable changes. This orientation involves a willingness to make changes in traditional patterns of governance or in city policies if citizens or groups demand such changes. In adapting to changes, of course, the council will attempt to maintain the existing life-style of the suburb or to modify it as little as possible. For example, in 1971 the Highland Park, Illinois, City Council had the choice of opposing a decision to expand an existing sewage disposal site in the city, or of agreeing with the expansion on terms that would guarantee odor control and visual screening through issuance of a conditional use permit. Since resistance probably would have involved them in unsuccessful litigation, they chose to adapt and retain some control over the installation. Thus, the single family nature of the community was damaged as little as possible.[14]

Programming the city's future is the most policy laden orientation of councils. Programming councils adopt the roles of policymaking, of directing the city's actions, of planning for the future, and of acting as a board of directors. Long range planning, developing a master plan,

---

[14] This decision, incidentally, became extremely divisive and resulted in a heavily contested mayoral race and proposals for a ward system to protect areas from intrusions such as sewage plants. However, the point is that the council choose an "adaptive" strategy and played such a role in contrast to simple opposition to change. The latter would have been closer to a "maintenance" orientation.

and evaluating the effect of proposed land uses are a crucial part of the programming function. As policy makers, however, councils tend not to interfere in administrative details, which are best left to appointed officials who are hired for their technical expertise.

The programming and maintenance task orientations are least likely to encourage citizen participation. Both programming and maintenance require group consensus among council members, which is likely to be weakened by citizen demands. Maintenance is often associated with a paternalistic image of the council vis-à-vis the city. Programming requires extensive study and evaluation of alternate developmental plans. Both, then, are less comfortable with group demands than are adaptive councils, which rely more on citizen input.

The programming orientation is most likely to rely heavily on the expertise of professional staff. However, because they see themselves as policy directors, councilmen are not likely to let the manager or department heads develop substantial discretionary powers.

Staff power is generally greater in cities with councils having maintenance or adapting orientations. Maintenance councils are more likely to trust and defer to the staff, since all that is required is maintenance of the status quo, with few policy judgments to review. Adaptive councils regard the staff as a specific kind of interest representing administrative concerns.

CITIZEN PARTICIPATION IN SUBURBAN POLITICS

Compared to programming or maintenance councils, adaptive councils are more likely to be receptive to citizen demands. This does not mean that heavy and vociferous group and individual pressures on the council are particularly common. While rather infrequent, citizen participation is still a crucial element in local politics. Generally, suburban living is not associated with high levels of political activity.

With the exception of very high status locations, suburbs are not "beehives of political activity." Suburbanites participate in politics even less than central city residents when social status is ignored. Verba and Nie found that suburbs have the lowest overall participation rates of any of six types of cities: isolated villages and rural areas (under 3,000 population), isolated towns (3,000–10,000), isolated large towns and small cities (nonmetropolitan, over 10,000), small suburbs (under 25,000), large suburbs (25,000–150,000), and core cities. Participation in small suburbs was particularly low and consisted primarily of efforts to influence social issues in less partisan settings.[15] These low levels of activity seem to be due to the lack of strong local ties since residents

---

[15] Sidney Verba and Norman Nie, *Participation in America, Political Democracy and Social Equality* (New York: Harper and Row, 1972), pp. 229–48.

identify with the neighboring metropolis rather than with the local community. Verba and Nie suggest that their data confirms the "decline of community" hypothesis of urbanization, which holds that participation declines when the citizen moves from the smallness and intimacy of town or village to the city, where politics is more complex and impersonal.

Alford and Scoble found that local political involvement, which includes voting, attending meetings, and paying attention to political phenomena is heavily associated with social status, organization membership, and home ownership. Political involvement is not related to ethnicity, religion, political alienation, or community attachment.[16] The connection between social status and political activity is consistent with most findings. More significant is the association of home ownership and organizational membership with local political activity. Home ownership develops tax awareness, and generates a feeling of social and psychological stake in the community, which demands civic action. Similarly, membership in an organization exposes the citizen to a flow of new political information and to political events involving the organization. Home ownership, organizational membership, and high social status are mutually reinforcing. That is, higher status communities have more organizations and residents are more likely to own their homes. Of course, this does not necessarily mean a greater commitment to a specific community, since high status persons would probably own homes and belong to clubs wherever they lived.

Consistent with the Verba and Nie study, Alford and Scoble conclude that:

> The fact that neither mobility, residence, nor subjective attachment is significantly related to local involvement suggests that "traditional" ties to the community have lost whatever significance they might once have had. . . . Similarly, the trivial role played by neighborhood sociopolitical environment indicated that people "carry around" with them their predispositions to participate, and are not significantly influenced by "immediate" sociopolitical milieu.[17]

If it is true that today's suburbanite "carries around" his predisposition to participate, it surely suggests that the community is not the source of involvement. Rather, people participate for a variety of reasons which are, at best, incidentally related to the community in which they reside. Suburbs comprised of wealthy home owners appear to have extraordinary levels of activity—but this is due to the nature of the citizenry rather than to the suburb itself.

---

[16] Robert Alford and Harry Scoble, "Sources of Local Political Involvement," *American Political Science Review*, December 1968, pp. 1192–1207.

[17] Ibid., p. 1205.

One specific study measured the high status suburb of Radnor, near Philadelphia.[18] Its findings indicated that participation in local political events is related to age, income, education, and occupation, confirming that social status is highly related to political activity. Also, men participated as much as women, and commuters as much as noncommuters. Political activity in Radnor was associated with feelings of political efficacy and community involvement, contrary to the findings of Alford and Scoble. The high income nature of the city may be responsible for this finding. Perhaps the extent to which feelings of political efficacy and community involvement foster political activity varies among different socioeconomic levels. Members of the highest income group may not participate if they feel distrustful or alienated, and may participate as their commitment to the community increases. Regardless of possible variations in political activity by class, it is clear from most research that political activity in Radnor is due to social status, home ownership, and the values people hold, rather than to Radnor's suburban role.

As we noted, organizational membership is highly associated with local political involvement. Group memberships introduce the individual to differing viewpoints, alert him to community problems, and develop the political crosspressures that discourage precipitous and extreme political action by the individual. The greater the number of local organizations to which a person belongs, the more likely he is to be politically integrated into his community.

A study of Montgomery County and Dayton, Ohio, indicated the range of interests in organizations in the metropolitan area. Generally, suburban area residents were members of more child-centered organizations and purely social and hobby groups, while central city residents were involved in more church-related groups and community service organizations. Again, holding social status constant, there was little difference in participation levels between suburb and central city.[19]

A more recent survey indicated that within the central cities, blacks generally exhibit a proportionately greater degree of organizational involvement. Abelbach and Walker found that blacks have relatively more memberships than whites in every kind of community organization except business and professional associations. This is particularly true of churches, labor unions, civil rights groups, PTAs, and fraternal groups.[20] Blacks seem to be more likely to participate actively in most organizations to which they belong, although there may be a class distinction—

---

[18] Joseph Zikmund II and Robert Smith, "Political Participation in an Upper Class Suburb" *Urban Affairs Quarterly*, June 1969, pp. 443–58.

[19] John Bollens, *Metropolitan Challenge* (Dayton, Ohio: Metropolitan Communities, Inc., 1959).

[20] Joel Abelbach and Jack Walker, *Race in the City* (Boston: Little Brown, 1973).

lower class blacks may be more active than lower class whites, but higher class blacks may be less active than higher class whites.[21]

Voting

Voting is the most common form of local political activity and probably the most significant. As has already been indicated, the local political order is not maintained solely, or perhaps even primarily, by local elections. However, voting is a prerogative and a civic duty which is by no means universally exercised. In nationwide summaries of local voting for cities of over 25,000 residents. the mean turnout was 43 percent in elections held concurrently with other elections, usually national, and 31 percent in noncurrent elections.[22] Suburban voting is primarily based on party affiliation, if cues are available. When they are not, as often occurs, then racial attitudes and religion tend to influence voter attitudes and participation.[23]

There are enormous variations in small city voting turnout. In Des Plaines, a Chicago suburb, turnouts at ward elections for councilmen vary from 9 to 49 percent. Close mayoralty contests held at the same time as contested aldermanic elections drew the larger turnouts, while simple uncontested councilmanic elections elicited fewer voters. In Highland Park, another Chicago suburb, the typical turnout for a contested at-large councilmanic election is approximately 20 percent. A close mayoral race drew a 57 percent turnout, large by Highland Park standards, though not by national election criteria.[24] Similar variations occur throughout American suburbs, but turnouts of over 60 percent are very rare. Election turnouts for school districts, county elections, and special district ballot issues generally elicit lower turnouts than city elections. In many special districts, the turnout is often as low as 10 percent.

Nonpartisanship

The low voter turnout for local elections often is attributed to nonpartisanship. Robert Wood's classic study of suburbia lists the results of nonpartisanship in local elections. First, it causes "an outright reaction against partisan activity and an ethical disapproval of permanent group

[21] Verba and Nie, *Participation in America,* establish that blacks, holding socioeconomic status equal, are "over-participators."

[22] Robert Alford and Eugene Lee, "Voting Turnout in American Cities," *American Political Science Review,* September 1968, pp. 796–814.

[23] David Schnall, *Ethnicity and Suburban Local Politics* (Springfield, Mass.: Praeger, 1975).

[24] John Rehfuss, "Political Development in Three Chicago Suburbs," a paper presented to the American Political Science Association at the 1971 Annual Conference in Chicago.

collaboration as a means of settling public disputes." Second, it results in "the suburbanite's acceptance of an obligation for extensive civic participation on the part of the lay constituency." Finally, "most fundamentally, no-party politics implies a belief that the individual can and should arrive at his political convictions untutored and unled; an expectation that in the formal process of election and decision-making a consensus will emerge through the process of right reason and by the higher call to the common good."[25] Wood's three points indicate that nonpartisanship is more than merely the absence of organized competition, either through national or local parties. It is also an ethos of participation, and an insistence upon individual decisionmaking on political matters, accompanied by a healthy respect for the opinions of one's neighbors.

In many upper class communities, an exclusive caucus still may select blue-ribbon candidates who are rarely opposed. However, Wood's view is less true now than when he wrote in 1958. A number of recent studies suggest there is now greater diversity. Leo Schnore compiled governmental data for 300 suburbs located in several major metropolitan areas throughout the nation and found that a partisan ballot was used in over 37 percent of the suburban communities in his sample.[26]

In some suburbs, party competition flourishes between newcomers and oldtimers, commuters and noncommuters, and occupational groups. One classic example is in a high income Chicago north shore suburb of 23,000 population.[27] Local public offices in this community have been contested since 1957 by two locally organized parties. No third party has been created, no independent candidates have run, and virtually all votes cast are for one party slate or another. Both parties publish platforms, distribute handbills, hold public rallies and "coffeeklatches," and have fund-raising dinners. One party, the successor to the original merchant-Chamber of Commerce-noncommuter elite of the town, has a comparatively closed caucus. The other, which originally tended to represent newcomers and commuters, has a wide open caucus and instructs the nominating committee to submit at least two names to the entire caucus. There are no religious, status, geographical, commuter, or partisan reasons for citizens to adhere to either party, but there is some homeowner versus businessman division. Nonetheless, the viable two party system is a source of pride to residents.

---

[25] Robert Wood, *Suburbia* (Boston: Houghton Mifflin, 1958). This and all succeeding quotes are from pages 153–56.

[26] Leo Schnore, *The Urban Scene* (Glencoe, Ill.: The Free Press, 1965), p. 192.

[27] David R. Beam, "Factors Maintaining Local Two Party Competition in a Suburban Community," (unpublished Master's Thesis, Northern Illinois University, DeKalb, Illinois, 1967). This political pattern may have changed recently but was true during the 1960s.

Personal contact with local officials

Another very important form of local political activity is that of contacting public officials. This activity often increases or confirms the feeling of efficacy in the citizen since he may see concrete results in the improvement of city government services.

Contacts with local officials can be loosely divided into two not entirely exclusive patterns—complaining and all other types of direct contacts. Generally, citizen complaints follow patterns of political participation and of voting. Higher income persons are more likely to actually voice objections and homeowners are more likely to complain than renters.[28]

Verba and Nie categorize complaining as "particularized contacting," and find that it is lower in suburbs *and* core cities than in nonmetropolitan isolated cities where citizens know and have access to local officials.[29] Complaining is slightly higher in central cities than in either large or small suburbs. In absolute terms, however, there is plenty of citizen complaining to officials. A study of three Chicago suburbs indicated that a very high percentage of elected and administrative officials (councilman, city manager, and certain department heads) receive at least one citizen contact per day.[30] Of those interviewed, 41 percent in Des Plaines, 78 percent in Elgin, and 44 percent in Highland Park reported at least one or more citizen contacts per day. The newly elected mayor of Elgin reported about five complaint calls per day. A councilman who had lost the election to him reported that he received no more than a complaint or two per month. The councilman referred complaints to the city hall staff, but the mayor apparently relished them.

Citizens can use contact with public officials as a form of control over them. Personal contact seems to be regarded by most elected officials as the most effective means of participation in local affairs. One study of suburban elected officials in Illinois and New York found that they ranked personal contact as the most effective way of citizen participation in any area of local affairs. It ranked ahead of (1) forming an *ad hoc* group, (2) working through an established organization. (3) voting, and (4) working through a political party. These rankings were almost identical between the two states and between types of suburbs within states, regardless of their growth rate.[31]

---

[28] This and the following findings on complaints are from John Bollens, *Exploring the Metropolitan Community,* pp. 445–47. This is from St. Louis data in 1960–61.

[29] Verba and Nie, *Participation in America,* pp. 237–39.

[30] Rehfuss, *Political Development.*

[31] Steve Parker, "Access to Suburban Decision Makers: A Comparative Analysis of Illinois and New York," a paper presented at the annual meeting of the Midwest Political Science Association, April 1974, Chicago.

The effectiveness of direct personal contacts is attested to in the San Francisco Bay area study, although such contact seems to be more important in medium sized and small cities. Small city councilmen rated contact with council colleagues, friends and acquaintances, the general public, influential citizens, work associates, and people at council meetings as the most important decision influences. Medium sized city councilmen rated city staff and people in the neighborhood as the more important contact points. The tendency of large city councilmen to communicate through "intermediaries," such as newspapers and organizational leaders, is inevitable since they cannot rely as much on informal, personal contacts. Conversely, these personal linkages seem to make up the very web and fabric of small city political contacts.

City commission membership

One minor but important way of participating in local government is by serving on a city commission. City commissions are generally advisory to the city council, and include such bodies as planning commissions, human relations commissions, police and fire commissions, and park and recreation commissions. In smaller communities, they may be extremely important in studying issues or municipal functions, especially if technical city staff is not available. In larger communities, certain commissions such as the planning commission, can determine and implement priorities. Consequently, membership is competitive and is often a springboard for council membership, particularly when the municipal "ethos" is strongly pro-planning. In Elgin, over 140 citizens were appointed to commissions in 1971, an average of 2.5 citizens per 1,000 populaton. Excluding youth and nonactive citizens, one out of 200 politically aware Elgin adults have been on a city commission. Highland Park's rate per 1,000 population was even higher than Elgin's.[32]

Citizen attitudes toward suburban government

Citizens' attitude toward their local government is closely related to the extent to which they participate in it and understand it. Positive feelings by the citizenry will normally be related directly to greater participation and should lead to higher citizen support for the city government, enabling the city to initiate new programs or maintain existing ones. Finally, higher levels of support and trust should serve as one point of evaluation for city performance. Conversely, low levels of trust and support would suggest that the city's programs are not considered

---

[32] Rehfuss, *Political Development.*

useful or satisfactory, or that citizens have general doubts about their ability to affect government. Under such circumstances, citizen participation will be severely reduced or will manifest itself in aggressive and negative behavior at the ballot box or in personal interaction. A final possibility is that persons may go through the motions of participating in political life but may not feel that their actions really mean anything.

The latter two attitudes appear to be increasingly common. A June 1974 Harris poll indicated that alienation was at the highest level since the yearly surveys began in 1966.[33] Seventy-nine percent of all persons sampled agreed that "the rich get richer and the poor get poorer"; 78 percent agreed that "special interests get more from the government than the people do"; and 63 percent agreed that "the people running the country don't really care what happens to you." Those agreeing with the latter statement were up from 26 percent in 1966. The biggest increases in alienation have taken place among suburban residents, up from 22 to 58 percent and among people under 30, up from 24 to 62 percent.

One might argue that the suburbanite is not alienated from his local government, but from the national government or from society in general. Under this rationale, increases in suburban alienation, merely reflect the suburban resident's response to a national mood. There is no way of disproving this argument, particularly since these Harris poll questions did not apply to local government. However, a 1973 Harris poll found that only 35 percent of suburban residents "felt that local government affects your life personally." This result was 3 percent less than that of all respondents. Only 26 percent of them had a "great deal of confidence in the people in charge of running local government."[34] There is also some additional evidence that central city citizens as well as suburban citizens hold local governments in somewhat lower regard than the national government.[35]

In the United States, most of the attempts to reduce alienation have taken the form of administrative or political decentralization. These programs attempt to decentralize power to the neighborhood level by shifting resources to the residents, by increasing their influence in decision-making, by creating alternative institutions such as little city halls, or

---

[33] Reported in the *Chicago Tribune,* June 25, 1974, pp. 62, 80.

[34] Subcommittee in Intergovernmental Relations, Committee on Government Operations, U.S. Senate, *Confidence and Concern: Citizens View American Government, A Survey of Public Attitudes* (Washington, D.C.: U.S. Government Printing Office, 1973).

[35] Some surveys actually show that people trust the national government more than local government and that they consider local government to be dominated by considerations of patronage rather than merit. See David Sears, "Political Behavior" in Gradner Lindzey and Elliott Aronson (eds.), *The Handbook of Social Psychology* (Reading, Mass.: Addison-Wesley, 1969), pp. 315–458. While this may not extend specifically to suburban government, it seems likely that it does.

by increasing information services to the residents.[36] There are three broad ways in which these decentralization moves can reduce alienation. First, the citizens' control over government could increase through their increased participation in decentralized institutions. Second, even if participation does not increase, alienation may decrease through local awareness of decentralization attempts. Finally, while neither of the above may occur, or even if they do occur, alienation may be reduced through the improvement of local services.

These three ways of reducing alienation, all of which aim to bring control of governmental services down to the neighborhood level, have been tried most frequently in central cities. But the efforts to reduce alienation have been based on an implicit "suburban" model. It seems that residents of the central city neighborhood will be less alienated if they gain community control or have greater access to decision-makers—a feat that is more likely in a small independent unit such as a suburb. Consequently, the assumption guiding these efforts seems to be that the neighborhood is to the central city as the suburbs are to the metropolitan area. However, participation levels are not really higher in suburbs and so it may be unrealistic to expect neighborhood residents of larger cities to become politically active. The suburban model may not be as viable as hoped.

Furthermore, as Robert Yin and William Lucas point out, there are reasons unrelated to levels of participation why efforts to decrease alienation may fail. Involving citizens in decisions (the participation hypothesis) does not necessarily reinforce trust. People who believe that they have power to influence political events may feel politically efficacious without feeling greater *trust* toward government.[37] Therefore, decentralization may reduce only one element of alienation, efficacy, without building trust. Evidence linking service improvement to decentralization is nonexistent, which also suggests that decentralization might not decrease alienation.[38]

Variables peculiar to particular areas may account for central city-suburban differences concerning trust in government. One study of a middle class neighborhood in suburban Brookline indicated that efficacy

---

[36] Much of this discussion is taken from Robert Yin and William Lucas, "Decentralization and Alienation," *Policy Sciences,* September 1973, pp. 327–36. Their article covers a good deal of the increasingly voluminous literature in this area. Some of the more significant pieces of literature are: Advisory Commission on Intergovernmental Relations, *The New Grass Roots Government* (Washington, D.C.: U.S. Government Printing Office, 1972); George Washnis, *Neighborhood Facilities and Municipal Decentralization* (Washington, D.C.: Center for Governmental Studies, 1971); the entire issue of the *American Behavioral Scientist,* September/October, 1971; the entire issue of the *Public Administration Review,* September 1972; and Joseph Zimmerman, *The Federated City* (New York: St. Martin's Press, 1973).

[37] Ibid.

[38] Ibid.

and trust were not related in Boston, but that they were in Brookline. In honestly governed Brookline, those few who were distrustful may have felt that they were powerless to change the city practices. The citizens of Boston, historically a corrupt city, may have felt that corrupt practices go hand in hand with attempts of professional politicians to help people.[39]

The information to date on suburban political alienation is far from comprehensive, but it suggests that levels of distrust or powerlessness may be as high in the suburbs as in the central city.[40] It also suggests that, in individual metropolitan areas, there are substantial differences between the central city and suburbs, but that nationally there is little difference between central cities and suburbs in political attitudes toward government. Historical differences in migration, stratification, transportation patterns, and geography have caused differences between central cities and suburbs in given areas; but these differences cancel out in a national sample.

Since the lowest levels of participation are found in small suburbs, any movement toward "neighborhood government" in central cities can be expected to depress civic political participation by duplicating the small suburban pattern of low competition and high homogeneity. The political life of suburbia does not provide a model for decentralization if one wants maximum participation. Rather, if that is the goal, home ownership should be stimulated, educational opportunities and personal income increased, organizational membership encouraged, and communities of medium size established.

SUMMARY

This chapter, covering the wide panorama of suburban political behavior, has focused on activities within the suburban unit and on local political issues. It has emphasized three broad areas. The first has concerned the nature of suburban political conflict and how it arises. Rather than being based on socioeconomic or age distinctions, much urban community conflict can be attributed to differences over the appropriate means to agreed-upon ends. Much urban problem solving involves national issues that affect suburban jurisdictions but upon which local action is constrained or is influenced heavily by national policy. Even when this is not the case, local government must make decisions in cooperation with other jurisdictions.

However effective, and regardless of the extent to which they are con-

---

[39] Edgar Litt, "Political Cynicism and Political Futility" *The Journal of Politics,* May, 1963.

[40] Joseph Zikmund II, "A Comparison of Political Attitude and Activity Patterns in Central Cities and Suburbs," *Public Opinion Quarterly,* Spring 1967, pp. 69–75.

strained by action of other governmental levels, local policies still are made formally by local councils. Local legislatures bear a major responsibility for local policies and sometimes have a free hand in making them.

The background, recruitment, and the group roles councilmembers play was a second theme of this chapter. Councilmen, who are predominately middle-aged males, become councilmen through several different recruitment paths and behave in rather different ways. Generally, however, they act as "groups of like-minded men," who were elected as "friends and neighbors" of their suburban compatriots. Once on the council, they tend to adopt group legislative roles which are oriented toward city policies on the basis of maintaining, adapting, programming, or some combination of these. The role selected has considerable impact on the shape of city policies and the style of political behavior in that city.

The final section of the chapter concerns the methods and extent of citizen political behavior. In general, when social status is discounted, suburbanites generally are "underparticipators" compared to residents of other types of cities. Citizens participate by voting, serving on city commissions, complaining to public officials, and trying in numerous other ways to hold their elected officials accountable. However, alienation and distrust of political institutions seem to be growing, and this lack of support extends to local government.

4

Types of suburbs

VAST DIVERSITY exists among metropolitan areas, between central cities and their suburbs, and among individual suburbs. A driver, approaching any metropolitan area in America, travels through rings of suburbs near the central city. Some of these suburbs have bright neon lights, new construction, and enticements to their minibusiness districts. Others are sleepy marks of a bygone era, passed over by development, retaining a social or political life of the past. Semi-sylvan abodes of the rich, with more acres in open space and golf courses than neighboring juris-dictions have in park land, sit next to nondescript suburbs where houses are distinguishable only by the color of paint. Wholesaling or manufac-turing towns, strung along railroad tracks or highways, represent another type of the seemingly endless variety of suburbs. In the 1960s, yet an-other type of suburb emerged in the form of New Towns or planned communities, such as Montgomery Village in Gaithersburg, Maryland, and "new towns" which became suburbs, such as Reston, Virginia, and Columbia, Maryland.

There is no "typical" suburb, nor is there an "average suburbanite." In an effort to understand better the dynamics of suburbs, social scien-tists have tried to classify them according to their functions, economic levels, governmental service patterns, and types of local government. When compared in terms of these various factors, the suburbs are more easily understood.

ECONOMIC CLASSIFICATION OF SUBURBS

Suburbs can be classified according to their primary economic function, including such general categories as manufacturing, commercial, residential, resort, educational, and governmental. A "balanced suburb" is one which is the site for a mixture of manufacturing, commercial, and residential activities.

Suburban communities with more jobs to offer than there are job holders in their population are considered to be manufacturing or trade oriented. According to the *Municipal Yearbook*, cities with at least 16 percent more jobs than there are residents in the labor force are *employing towns*.[1] Given that a perfectly balanced community has a base score of 100, an employing town has a score of 116. Towns whose score falls between 85 and 115 are considered to be *balanced*, having roughly as many jobs to offer as there are people in the labor force. A suburb with a score of 84 or less has considerably more resident workers than it has jobs to offer and is classified as a *residential* or *dormitory* suburb. While most individual suburbs have more workers than jobs, 72 percent of employed workers living in suburbs also work in the suburbs.[2]

Central cities in most metropolitan areas originally were balanced, as their population tended to live, work, and shop in the same city. In recent years, substantial commuting from the city to the suburbs has increased as trade and industrial jobs have moved into the suburbs. The commuting has been partially offset by the effects of urban renewal, which has sometimes increased the number of professional and governmental office buildings, and thus the number of white collar jobs in the central city.

Manufacturing suburbs are generally blue collar domiciles. Substantial class or economic cleavages often exist in these jurisdictions. This is particularly true in those suburbs most distant from the central city, where the owners and managers of the predominant firms have not yet moved to more fashionable suburbs. In these cases, divisions arise among sections of town and among socioeconomic classes over city improvement, economic issues, and political life. When the business leadership dominates, either economic growth or low taxes become the civic goals, depending upon the needs of management. If the power is more equally distributed between workers and management, the suburb may have no dominant value and the local government may act as an arbiter between groups. If labor is stronger, business may eventually withdraw from the political struggle.

---

[1] International City Management Association, *Municipal Yearbook, 1967* (Washington, D.C.: ICMA, 1968), p. 36.

[2] "Metropolitan Development in the United States," *Studies in Comparative Local Government*, Summer 1971, p. 52.

Some manufacturing or wholesale trade suburbs are virtually deserted at night because they have little or no residential population. Commerce, California, and Bedford Park, Illinois, are good examples of this type of suburb. These towns sometimes serve as tax shelters for their few residents because the domination by industrial uses results in large property tax assessments in a small area while the lack of a sizeable residential population insures that service requirements will be small.

"Reverse commuting" patterns are common in some wholesaling and manufacturing towns. Local residents may travel to nearby towns for white collar jobs, while nonresidents commute into town for service and industry employment. This pattern is becoming more prevalent as industry moves to the suburbs. Since low-income persons in the central city often are unable to obtain or afford suburban living quarters, they are forced to travel long distances to jobs in the suburbs. In 1970, 7 percent of all metropolitan employees "reverse commuted," compared to 4 percent in 1960.[3] It is likely that commuters from the city eventually will move to new suburbs if possible, while many surburban residents will continue to make the trip to professional and business jobs in the core city.

However, the suburb's original "raison d'être" was residential and that is still the most popular suburban land use. These communities are often called "dormitories" because their primary function is to provide housing. The commuter suburbs tend to be socially homogeneous and strive to maintain their residential character.

Generally, community life is rather sedate, centering on the public school and neighborhood life. Only life-style issues like planning or zoning upset an otherwise stable political life in these towns. Of course, there are exceptions, as even dormitory communities may have lively political systems due to a competitive local party system, a division along religious or social lines, or some major issue that arises. In recent years, the issues that have aroused suburban conflict have been plans to construct housing for low income dwellers, the busing of school children, and specific land use or zoning changes.

Retailing suburbs serve primarily as commercial centers for a number of suburbs and have little or no manufacturing activity. The Chicago suburbs of Oak Lawn and Winnetka are in that category, as are Rockville Center, New York, and San Mateo, California. Although these cities are quite diverse in character, they generally have central business districts comprised of retail stores and associated professional buildings that compete with residential interests for attention and services. Service clubs, chambers of commerce, architects, engineers, lawyers, and insurance agents represent these interests. Political life in these suburbs tends to be more pluralistic than in those that are more homogeneous.

---

[3] Ibid.

Some suburbs fall into more specialized categories, but they are few compared to the number of manufacturing, commercial, and residential suburbs. A large military installation or a county seat might make government work the main local industry. There are some towns where most people make their living from resort or tourist trade, such as Virginia Beach, Virginia, Anaheim, California, Scottsdale, Arizona, and Fort Lauderdale, Florida. In still other suburbs, a single institution of higher learning, or a group of them, provide the main source of employment. Coral Gables, Florida, Stony Brook, New York, and Claremont, California, are examples of this type of suburb.

GOVERNMENTAL SERVICES AND LIFE-STYLE ORIENTATION

City and county governments perform certain functions for their residents. These governments generally determine the nature and extent of public services, but citizen attitudes toward the varying mix of services often form stable social orientations toward their suburb. These orientations undergird local political behavior, forming the basis of citizen expectations about the nature of civic and political life. If the orientations are clear, a more distinct image of the prevailing citizens' attitudes should emerge for purposes of analysis and understanding.

Charles Adrian and Oliver Williams categorized four Michigan cities into four general types based on their governmental services orientation.[4]

1. Some cities provide only for the necessities of urban life, but some offer *amenities* by providing comforts as well. These include street landscaping, parks, museums, libraries and other services exceeding traditional services, such as police and fire. The amenities policy is prevalent in residential communities but is rather rare in employing towns. Substantial community expenditures to promote the quality of life are likely if there is a high degree of homogeneity in the population. Therefore, these cities are normally middle and upper class dormitory suburbs or middle size cities dominated by these classes.

2. *Promotion of economic growth* is the chief emphasis of some cities. Government attempts to insure that the city grows and thrives both in wealth and population. Since increased population can promote wealth, it is considered the most important goal. This real estate-banker-businessman view of the community developed when a beckoning frontier and westward economic expansion threatened the actual decline of established cities. Now that national market decisions are less affected by local actions, this orientation turns more to rejecting policies which

---

[4] Oliver Williams and Charles Adrian, *Four Cities* (State College: University of Pennsylvania Press, 1963).

hinder growth. The old suburb must have a good reputation and develop its downtown to compete with outlying shopping centers. It must also maintain a "good and friendly" community profile and provide adequate services, such as water supply and sewage disposal, that are crucial to development.

These first two types of city orientation are monistic, prescribing a single goal for the city government to achieve for its citizens. The next two, the caretaker and arbiter governments, are more pluralistic and do not require the existence of homogeneous citizen values.

3. A *caretaker* government functions to maintain traditional services like roads, law enforcement, and utilities. Most popular among retired homeowners and low income or blue collar workers, this type of government exalts freedom and self-reliance, and determines the values of residents individually rather than communally. The residents of these suburbs often oppose municipal amenities because they cannot afford to pay for them.

4. Finally, there is the *arbiter* community. Here local government serves as the means of resolving conflicts between differing community groups. This sort of government is different from the other three in that it subordinates the function of providing public services. According to Adrian and Williams, every claim is reduced to the level of competing interests whose conflicting demands must be resolved. The governing process is designed to achieve that equilibrium. Homeowner and local business associations, and ethnic groups, are common examples of the interests that compete in such communities.

These four types are not mutually exclusive. Arbiter cities can be found with strong caretaker orientations, since both forms are pluralistic. Amenities and developmental emphases also can occur together. Theoretically, but not practically, an arbiter city could also be amenities and/or developmental oriented. Obviously, caretaker and amenities orientations would not exist together.

Adrian and Williams found that most of the Michigan cities they studied exhibited more than one of these styles. However, further research by Eulau and Eyestone, involving a larger number of cities in the San Francisco area, most of which were suburbs, suggests that many cities are associated primarily with only one of these four typologies.[5]

To characterize these community types further, short case studies of political controversies in two Chicago area suburbs, Elgin and Highland Park, are presented here. Elgin illustrates the arbiter type while

---

[5] Heinz Eulau and Robert Eyestone, "Policy Maps of City Councils and Policy Outcomes: A Developmental Analysis," *American Political Science Review*, March 1963; and John Rehfuss, "Comparative Politics and the Study of American Local Government," *Journal of Comparative Administration*, February 1972.

Highland Park, a high income North Shore commuter center, demonstrates an amenities orientation.[6]

Elgin. Elgin has always been a town of numerous social cleavages, which were particularly agitated by a 1971 public housing issue. Public housing pressure began in 1967 with racial disturbances, which black leaders claim were caused by conflict over fair housing ordinances. City officials appointed a Housing Authority of "liberals" that constructed several housing units for the elderly and selected several sites for low income housing. Controversy arose when one of the latter units was proposed in a newer, high income area. A crowd of 1,800 persons attended one protest hearing at which 2,500 signatures opposing the site were recorded.

A Citizens Committee, composed mostly of area residents and some conservative supporters from elsewhere in the city, was formed in opposition to the Housing Authority, the County Office of Economic Opportunity, fair housing and religious groups, educators, and social workers. After a tense struggle, the Council finally rejected the site. This process was repeated for four different sites until the Housing Authority finally decided to adopt a policy promoting scattered public housing.

Elections for mayor and councilmen in Elgin indicated polarization along public housing lines from 1967 to 1971. While "antipublic housing" candidates did well, a "black vote" emerged among the small number of blacks (5 percent or so) living mostly in 3 downtown precincts. These precincts voted against the most liberal mayoral candidate because he claimed Elgin was not ready for a strong open occupancy ordinance. His opponents were more conservative, but took no position on the issue.

In addition to "anti-public housing" candidates, conservatives and working class candidates have normally run well in Elgin. Prior to 1975, black candidates had not been successful. However, there is some class division. Older and wealthy areas that traditionally vote strongly Republican in national elections did not support a working class Republican conservative for the Council in 1973.

Elgin is marked by the absence of any clear prevailing civic value. Blacks and Chicanos seem to vote their ethnic and racial interests. The white majority tends to project a strong, ideological conservatism with no predominant value except perhaps in respect to economic growth and downtown revitalization. Elgin newcomers tend to be more inter-

---

[6] John Rehfuss, "Political Development in Three Chicago Suburbs," a paper presented to the American Political Science Association annual conference, Chicago, September 1971. This research was done in 1971, and new issues since elections in 1973 have changed the council somewhat, as have the resignations of staff and council members. However, conflict over a range of issues among varying groups remains. The later comments on Highland Park are also based on 1971 observations.

ested in securing a "typical suburban lifestyle" than in becoming involved in community affairs.

Elgin has a number of cleavages, including those between long time residents and newcomers, east and west sides, reformers and traditionalists, black and whites, and upper and lower classes. Even so, by a large majority, the city voted bonds to purchase a private bus system in 1967 and to expand the sewage disposal system in 1971. This suggests that certain issues generally related to maintaining economic viability sometimes command a consensus. The groups divide over most other issues and the city government usually acts as arbiter. Of course, this does not mean that councilmen are neutral, but that various interests find representation through them.

Highland Park.   Unlike Elgin, Highland Park has a dominant political and social theme that supports the upper class, single family nature of the community.[7] A high level of municipal amenities and the preservation of open space reflect this dominant value.

The Moraine Hotel referendum illustrates this ethos. For many years the hotel constituted a nonconforming use of a 14 acre, wooded, Lake Michigan ravine site near expensive single family homes. In 1961, the owner announced that he would develop it through a special use permit into a 40-story apartment and marina. Within two days the Mayor expressed confidence that a referendum could obtain funds to acquire the property for open space or park, even though the city had never previously considered acquiring the property. Various community groups immediately began planning a successful referendum. A Council-selected Citizens Committee "rubberstamped" the referendum while the powerful 500-member League of Women Voters endorsed the bond issue. No alternatives, such as zoning out high rises, were seriously considered. Apparently, the community leadership felt that the land must be retained for open space and that the city's single family pattern would be threatened unless the site was taken over by the community.

In his defense, the developer pointed to an estimated $750,000 in property tax revenues the city would receive from the developed property. He claimed that the site was not suitable for a beach, that a park was not being planned, and that a "yes" vote would mean higher taxes for acquisition costs. He spent three times as much for advertising as the Citizens Committee. The Citizens Committee campaign stressed two issues relevant to the community ethos. There was a "threat to children" argument against development and traffic, while a "pride in your city" emphasis stressed the lovely semi-sylvan nature of Highland Park. The Committee had overwhelming support. Even the developer's spot ad, which attacked the Committee by saying "Vote No—Fight the Establishment," had little effect. The Establishment had more support

---

[7] Ibid.

and its final advertisement, showing a schematic 40-story highrise super-imposed on an aerial photograph of the city, contained nearly 1,000 names urging a "yes" vote.

The final vote on the $1.2 million bond issue was 5,637 to 2,535, a 69 percent "yes" vote, with an unusually high voter turnout of 47 percent. Nearly 60 percent of the registered voters in the old and wealthy precincts along the lakefront turned out and voted over 80 percent "yes." While turnout dropped in precincts further away from the site, the percentage of "yes" votes dropped little. This suggests a very strong civic consensus, although the specific issue was less salient as distance from the hotel site increased.

Four precincts out of 22 voted "no." They were in the lower income downtown areas, consisting mainly of retired homeowners and low income Italian-Americans. The "yes" vote percentage ranged only from 30 percent to 40 percent, but lower turnouts reduced the impact of the negative votes. These precincts usually have voted their "pocket-book," supporting council candidates who argued for lower taxes and, in this case, opposed a certain tax increase.

With the exception of this relatively small area, the picture of an overwhelming civic consensus emerged. Citizens voted over two to one to tax themselves, to give up property tax growth, and for an open space site with no developed plans—all to save the single family nature of the community. Almost all segments of the community, and certainly all of the community influentials, banded together on an issue that challenged the dominant community ethos.

These cases suggest that it is possible, at least in selected communities, to explain political behavior by the existence of aggregate social orientations of citizens.

FORMS OF GOVERNMENT

In addition to economic function and social orientation, another major classification of cities is by governmental form. These forms are prescribed by state law, with certain options made available under specific conditions. All states require a minimum population to incorporate as a city. Communities with less than that minimum must obtain any desired urban services from special districts. Further, cities or counties within certain population ranges may be required to conduct nonpartisan or at-large elections according to state law.

There are three basic forms of local government—the mayor-council, council-manager, and the commission forms. Approximately half of all cities with over 5,000 citizens use the mayor-council form. About 45 percent employ city managers, and 4 percent have a commission.[8]

---

[8] International City Management Association, *Municipal Yearbook, 1973* (Washington, D.C.: ICMA, 1973), p. 4.

The *mayor-council* form is the oldest and the most traditional arrangement of local government. The mayor is the chief elected representative of the townspeople and possesses most executive powers. In small towns, the mayor is a part-time executive, sharing his powers with the council. In large cities, the mayor may be a fulltime official and have at his disposal administrative support, such as a city budget office and administrative assistants who provide professional approaches to municipal operations. In this system, the council acts as a legislative body, and either initiates proposals or acts on those presented by the mayor. The relationship between the mayor and council varies according to the city's charter and its customs.

The mayor-council form is widely employed and can be found in towns quite different in nature. Although it is most common in cities with populations under 10,000 that do not wish to have, or cannot afford, professional government, it is also the predominant form of government in large cities with populations of over 500,000. Many of these large cities have a strong local party system. Since political interests play a dominant role in municipal life, centralized administrative *authority* is not desired, even though professional administrative capability is.

Generally, the mayor-council form is divided into strong mayor and weak mayor forms. The weak mayor form is the traditional form of local government, evolving from early frontier egalitarian times when strong executive leadership from city hall was unnecessary. Under the weak mayor plan, administrative power is fragmented among officials who are often elected separately and are not responsible to the mayor. The mayor rarely prepares the budget and is not usually responsible for administering day to day operations. The council has the dominant role, even if the mayor has a vote and/or a veto, because the mayor is not a key political leader. Nearly two thirds of the small towns with a population between 5,000 and 10,000 have a mayor-council form, and most of them use the weak mayor form (a substantial number of suburbs fall into this category). This form of government is relatively effective in small towns that are merely carrying on routine service functions, and where the citizenry is not demanding higher quality services or some kind of new direction or policy leadership. It is less effective as new or different situations, such as land use changes, enviromental problems or increasing urbanization, begin to affect the city.

The strong mayor-council form resembles the strong executive leadership exercised by the president or a city manager. In its "pure" form, the mayor is responsible for all administrative activities, but shares policymaking power with the council. He appoints department heads and prepares the budget. These powers, even without a formal veto or vote on the council (although he often has these), make him the head of city government and provide him with a policy leadership role. The strong mayor form provides an opportunity for urban leadership and innovation without moving to the city manager form. Many strong mayors in large jurisdictions have an administrative officer to manage the routine affairs of the government. This practice allows the mayor to devote more time to policy questions. The administrative officer can either be a political appointee of the mayor or a career manager.

At one time, the mayor-council was the most widely used form. But, during the era of big city bossism, when politics was deemed the root of local political corruption, the mayor form came under fire. At this time, the *commission* form of government, based on a business efficiency model, was introduced as the first reform structure for local government in America.

A city commission has five or seven elected members. It has both administrative and legislative responsibilities. The commissioners are either directly elected by the voters to specific posts, such as finance commissioner, or the posts are assigned by the commission after election. Similarly, the mayor may be elected directly by the voters or selected from among the newly elected commissioners. The commission approach to local government is somewhat analogous to electing department heads to act in administrative roles and giving them legislative authority as well. There is often a tendency for commissioners to keep their hands off other commissioners "bailiwicks," thus fragmenting governmental action. In this mode of government, the mayor is rarely more than a figurehead or a master of ceremonies. In some commission cities, the office of mayor is rotated among the commission members on a regular basis.

Today the commission form exists mostly in cities that are older and not bent on reform. Most of the evidence indicates that cities retaining the commission form tend to be filled with group and social conflict.[9]

Historically, the *council-manager* form was a reform of the commission system. Whereas the commission form of government is frequently characterized as governance by amateurs, the council-manager form is characterized by the employment of a non-elected professional city administrator. In this model, a council and a mayor are elected, but the mayor is not the chief executive as in the mayor-council form. Though the mayor does have considerable responsibility for representing the city in various ceremonial respects, and often is able to take an active leadership role, he is usually considered just another member of the council.

As a body, the council has the power to hire and fire the manager, who acts as a policy advisor and manages the everyday affairs of the city. The council delegates considerable authority to the manager so

---

[9] A good discussion of strong and weak mayor forms can be found in Charles Adrian and Charles Press, *Governing Urban America*, 3rd ed. (New York: McGraw-Hill, 1968), Chapter 8.

that he can act in both administrative and policy matters. At the same time, the elected body retains control over him since he is subject to dismissal. In theory, this plan maximizes professionalism in governmental administration while maintaining a democratic character.

The intensification of urban problems has been one factor prompting widespread adoption of the city manager plan of government. Because the suburbs, singly and as a group, are now confronting problems formerly limited to the big cities, and since most city manager type governments are located in the suburbs, the manager form of government, more than any of the others, is undergoing rapid change. In turbulent times, the manager's ability to influence policy becomes crucial to his success. Though in theory, city manager government called for a separation of policy and administration, it has proved impossible for the manager's function to be solely administrative. In 1952, the International City Manager's Association (ICMA) changed its Code of Ethics by calling for the manager to be a community policy leader. This was an attempt to more clearly reflect the role of a manager, yet to continue proscribing any politicization of the position.

Present and future city managers are faced with new opportunities as well as new constraints. Since recent federal programs, such as revenue sharing, may reduce grants of money earmarked for particular purposes, managers must play a decisive role in determining priorities for the spending of federal money. Managers must also abide by affirmative action guidelines in hiring women and minorities for city jobs. Further, they must deal with increasingly contentious labor-management issues. At the same time, managers must alter their behavior to serve effectively as grantsmen, experts in intergovernmental affairs, social planners, and calculators of consent among various civic groups. While they perform in these highly-charged political situations, the managers must still maintain administrative control. Success in performing these varied duties may account for the spread of city manager governments in the suburbs.

However, there are substantial variations among managers in their taste for and ability to accomplish these tasks. In addition, many suburban cities do not experience these difficulties. There is some tendency for cities to select different types of managers, depending on their particular needs. Generally, the more complex and controversial a suburb's affairs become, the more likely that managers who relish a challenge will be drawn to that city. Generally, these managers will be somewhat younger, better educated, and more cosmopolitan than managers in more sedate cities.[10]

As suburbs become larger, older, and more beset by problems, it

---

[10] Timothy Almy, "Local-Cosmopolitan and U.S. City Managers" *Urban Affairs Quarterly*, March 1975, pp. 243–72; and Ronald Loveridge, *City Managers in Legislative Politics* (Indianapolis: Bobbs-Merrill, 1971).

is likely that the manager plan will continue to flourish. Eventually, this will result in an almost inevitable dominance of political life, at least in a structural sense, by fulltime professional managers, whether they are politically appointed in nonmanager cities or are required by the city charter in manager cities. The assumption that part-time citizen politicians can continue to administer what are no longer small town problems is being challenged in suburban governments. Thus, it is likely that some sort of professionalization of suburban government will occur regardless of individual suburban political styles.

Professionalism, however, is a "style" rather than a substantive set of policies. Before evaluating professionalization, it should be helpful to examine styles and political effects of the three different government forms. The manager plan is normally businesslike and bureaucratic. The mayor-council plan encompasses many styles, ranging from colorful popular leadership by the mayor to dull problem solving systems in which the council chooses the mayor from its members. However, the real effects of city action do not appear to vary uniformly by structure.

Lineberry and Fowler found that "reformed" cities—i.e., a manager, rather than a commission or mayor; at-large rather than ward elections; and nonpartisan rather than partisan—are considerably less responsive than "unreformed" cities to pressures of conflicting interest groups in terms of spending and taxing policies.[11] Generally, the greater the reformism, the lower the responsiveness. The commission city, the earliest form of the reform movement, was found to be the most responsive to interest groups. Lineberry and Fowler argue that this may be attributed to three factors: (1) it is the most decentralized of the three forms; (2) each legislator is also a plural executive; and (3) the system is more accessible to pressure and input from groups and individuals. Since reducing the effect of interest groups and increasing the efficiency and economy of city government was a goal of the early reformers, Lineberry and Fowler's work suggests that they succeeded. However, their study included only cities over 50,000. It is not clear how these same policies might vary by government form in smaller cities.

Several studies indicate that policy leadership and innovation for major city problems often comes from elected mayors, who are highly visible public leaders. One recent article rejected the "weak mayor" hypothesis by comparing community programs that were adopted with

---

[11] Robert Lineberry and Edmund Fowler found that commission cities taxing and spending practices reflected the presence of social cleavages to a considerably greater degree than did either manager or mayor cities, despite their "reform history." They characterize them as the "black sheep" of the reformists. See "Reformism and Public Politics in American Cities," *American Political Science Review*, September 1967, pp. 701–17, particularly table 2 and footnote 36.

those that were rejected.[12] The probability of adoption in the 93 cities was directly related to the degree of mayoral support for the program. At least in the large cities surveyed, the mayors were neither weak nor restricted to mediating among interests.

Another study of various cities reported similar results. It showed that on the issue of flouridation of city water supplies, a better chance of serious consideration and adoption exists where the local governmental structure has centralized authority—either a city manager or mayor—in a partisan setting.[13] The mayor is a key figure, since adoption occurs over half the time if he supports the measure. He is most likely to support fluoridation when the political system requires him to exert leadership. This usually occurs when there is a strong party system.

Increased professionalism of suburban governments is likely to increase minimum service standards, the relative size of city staffs, and the level of bureaucratization. All of these entail routinization, impersonality, and possibly greater equity, with more intense commitment by specialists. However, professionalism probably does not result in significant policy shifts, such as less spending on police and more on urban renewal. Due to the size and commitments of city staff, it may be harder for elected and appointed leaders to change city priorities in the short run. Ironically, the capacity to innovate, spurred by increased professionalism, may be thwarted by the difficulties of changing a large bureaucratized set of suburban governments.

The classification of suburbs in terms of their economic function, prevailing style, and form of government facilitates an understanding of the suburbs. Examining a particular metropolitan area such as Chicago will help to illustrate suburban diversity.

CHICAGO: A SAMPLE METROPOLITAN AREA

Metropolitan Chicago (Figure 4–1) is typical of many large, old metropolitan areas. While it includes the northwest corner of Indiana, metropolitan Chicago has about 7 million persons in the Illinois portion of which nearly half live in the central city. The balance of the residents live in over 150 suburbs, ranging in size from 79,000 in Evanston to less than 5,000 in East Chicago Heights. The central city of Chicago lost over five percent of its population in the 1960s, while the total metropolitan population increased by 12 percent.

---

[12] Wen Kuo, "Mayoral Influence in Urban Policy Making," *American Journal of Sociology*, November 1973, pp. 220–38.

[13] Donald B. Rosenthal and Robert L. Crain, "Structure and Values in Local Political Systems: The Case of Fluoridation Decisions," *Journal of Politics*, February 1966, pp. 169–96.

FIGURE 4–1
Selected metropolitan Chicago suburbs

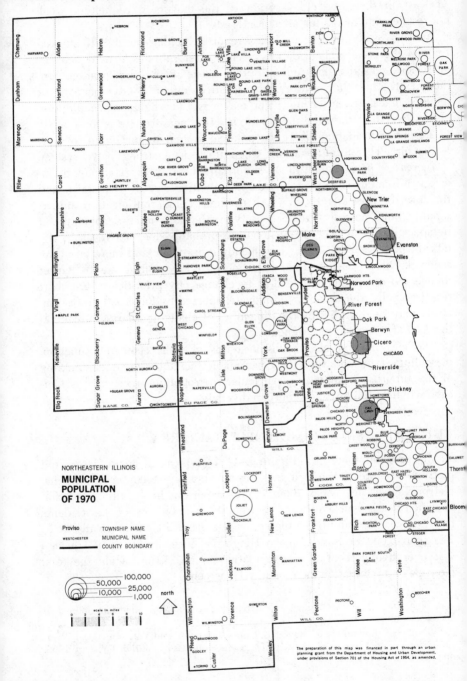

NORTHEASTERN ILLINOIS
MUNICIPAL
POPULATION
OF 1970

Proviso   TOWNSHIP NAME
WESTCHESTER   MUNICIPAL NAME
──────────   COUNTY BOUNDARY

100,000
50,000   25,000
10,000   1,000

north

scale in miles
0 2 4 6 8 10

The preparation of this map was financed in part through an urban
planning grant from the Department of Housing and Urban Development,
under provisions of Section 701 of the Housing Act of 1954, as amended.

With some minor exceptions, the City of Chicago leads the entire metropolitan area as the home of the old, the poor, the black, the blue collar worker, the less educated, and the foreign born. Table 4–1 provides the statistical details.

TABLE 4–1

Comparison of Chicago and its metropolitan area
(in percentages)

	Under 18	Under poverty level	Non-white	White collar	Median school years completed by those over 25	Foreign stock
Chicago.	32.1	10.6	34.4	47.9	11.2	29.7
Suburbs	37.0	3.4	3.1	58.1	13.3	22.6
Total metro- politan area . .	34.5	6.8	18.7	52.9	12.2	26.5

Source: U.S. Bureau of the Census, "U.S. Census of Population 1970," vol. 1, *Characteristics of the Population, Illinois* (Washington, D.C.: U.S. Government Printing Office, 1973), passim.

The exodus from Chicago has been the major cause of population growth in the suburbs. One of the fastest growing suburbs is East Chicago Heights, a small suburb south of Chicago. According to the 1970 U.S. Census, one fourth of its population was under the poverty level, with a median income of $8,169 and median number of school years completed at 9.0, the lowest of all metropolitan Chicago suburbs. East Chicago Heights provides a home for many new suburbanities with large, young families. Fifty percent of the residents are under 18 years of age, compared with a metropolitan average of 35 per cent and a Chicago figure of 32 percent. East Chicago Heights typifies part of the suburban stereotype—it is fast growing and familistic. It violates the remainder of the myth, for it is also poor and 98 percent black.

Flossmoor, ten miles northwest of East Chicago Heights, has almost no nonwhite population (0.7 percent in 1970), one of the highest levels of average school years completed (14.7), fewer residents under the poverty level (1.0 percent), and one of the highest median incomes ($24,898) in metropolitan Chicago. Flossmoor is a good example of the popular conception of the "wealthy suburbs." Yet both Flossmoor and East Chicago Heights reflect the magnitude of the flight from Chicago's problems in their large growth rates—69.7 percent and 52.9 percent respectively in the 1960s.

Table 4–2 compares a number of Chicago suburbs in terms of economic classifications, socioeconomic characteristics, social style, and gov-

TABLE 4–2
A socio-politico-economic comparison of nine selected cities in Chicago suburbs

City	Population and percent change 1960–70	Economic classification	Predominant "style"	Governmental form	Median income	Percent under 18	Percent nonwhite	Median school year completed
Highland Park	32,263 (+26.4)	Residential	Amenities	Council-manager	$20,749	38.1	2.4	14.1
Flossmoor	7,846 (+69.7)	Residential	Amenities	Council-manager	24,898	38.9	0.7	14.7
Evanston	79,000 (+0.7)	Educational	Amenities	Council-manager	13,932	25.5	17.9	13.2
Des Plaines	57,239 (+64.1)	Manufacturing	Promotion of economic growth	Mayor-council	14,056	36.4	0.7	12.5
Cicero	67,058 (−3.0)	Manufacturing	Caretaker	Mayor-council	11,625	25.8	0.3	10.7
Elgin	55,691 (+12.6)	Manufacturing	Arbiter	Council-manager	11,555	30.0	5.3	12.2
East Chicago Heights	5,000 (+52.9)	Balanced residential	Caretaker	Mayor-council	8,169	55.5	98.2	9.6
Oak Lawn	60,000 (+119.5)	Commercial	Caretaker	Council-manager	13,824	38.4	0.3	12.3
Winnetka	14,000 (+5.7)	Commercial	Amenities	Council-manager	28,782	37.4	1.3	16.1

Source: U.S. Bureau of the Census, "U.S. Census of Population: 1970," vol. 1, *Characteristics of the Population*, Illinois (Washington, D.C.: U.S. Government Printing Office, 1973), passim; and International City Management Association *1973 Municipal Year Book* (Washington, D.C.: International City Management Association, 1974), passim.

ernmental form. In addition to the diversity suggested in the Table, there are other significant elements affecting each city. Des Plaines, for example, adjoins O'Hare International Airport. Evanston is the home of Northwestern University. Cicero, the scene of a bloody riot resulting from a Martin Luther King integration march, has a disproportionately large ethnic population of Czechs, Lithuanians, Poles, and Italians. Highland Park is predominantly Jewish and liberal. Elgin is an old manufacturing center 35 miles from Chicago. Oak Lawn and Winnetka are major regional retailing centers.

Of these nine suburbs, six had managers, including the four amenities cities. This suggests that these categories are likely to be found together. Of the three mayor-council cities, two were caretaker cities, and the third was a promoter of economic growth. The only arbiter city, however, was a manager city, and there the manager role has had to be accommodated into a politicized environment.

This implies that while the form of government is associated with the governmental services style or orientation, the relationship is far from consistent. There is even less association between style and economic classification. Each manufacturing city had a different style (growth, caretaker, and arbiter). Of the four amenities cities, two were residential, and the other two were commercial and educational. Of the two commercial cities, one was caretaker and the other was amenities in style. Further, no simple relationship emerges between governmental form and economic classification. Two of the three manufacturing cities had mayor-council governments.

These three dimensions—form, style and economic base—seem to reflect different sets of community characteristics. Only in a very general sense can one aspect, such as form of government, be predicted from another, such as economic function. Even in a sample as small and nonrepresentative as these nine cities, the diversity of suburbs is clear.[14]

SUMMARY

This chapter attempted to delineate three major methods of classifying suburbs so that they could be handled conceptually. Suburbs were classi-

---

[14] There are a number of ways to classify cities, based on factorial or other statistical analyses. Brian Berry and Frank Horton explain the impact of social status and family size of suburbs in "The Factorial Ecology of Chicago: A Case Study," *Geographic Perspectives on Urban Services* (New York: Prentice Hall, 1970), pp. 319–95. An article by Richard Sutton et al., "American City Types: Toward a More Systematic Urban Study," *Urban Affairs Quarterly*, March 1974, pp. 369–401, uses "principal component" scores, and divides all U.S. cities over 25,000 into 8 principal types. Two components, age/ethnicity and socio-economic status, explain 67 percent of the variances, and thus a schematic representation of their 8 groups can be plotted. This article has a good summary of city typologies that have been developed but none of the typologies have purely suburban types.

fied according to (1) economic orientation; (2) service or functional orientation; and (3) form of government. A suburb's economic orientation is most likely to be commercial, residential or manufacturing. Balanced suburbs have a mix of residential, manufacturing, and commercial activities, while dormitory suburbs are primarily residential. When one economic base predominates, the suburb is considered primarily commercial or manufacturing. Finally, specialized categories, such as government or resort trade, dominate a few suburbs.

The second classification is by governmental services style. Many cities can be categorized into one of four types, based on their primary emphasis in delivering public services. Some suburbs, most of which are middle or upper class, emphasize providing amenities in the form of parks, libraries, and museums to their citizens. Others stress the importance of economic growth and vitality within the city by emphasizing growth-related services, such as water supply and sewage disposal. Many suburban governments act as caretakers, keeping taxes low and providing a minimal level of services. The final type is the arbiter city, whose energy and orientations are focused on resolving conflict within the city and acting as referee between competing social groups. Case studies of Elgin and Highland Park, Illinois, were presented as examples of political life in an arbiter and an amenity city, respectively.

The final classification is by government form. The mayor-council is the oldest, and predominates in very large and rather small cities. There are two basic variations of this form, the weak and the strong mayor form. In weak mayor form, the mayor shares executive and legislative powers with the council and exerts little policy leadership. The strong mayor form usually vests administrative power in the mayor. The next form of government discussed is the commission plan, which vests both administrative and legislative power in a group of separately elected commissioners. The last form discussed is the council-manager plan, which predominates in medium sized cities. This form places administrative powers in the hands of a professional manager who is appointed by and accountable to the council. These are the forms best suited for cities emphasizing efficiency and/or adaptation to new situations.

The complexity of metropolitan Chicago was used as an example to illustrate these suburban types. A brief analysis of nine suburbs near Chicago demonstrated that, although some characteristics tend to be associated, such as amenities cities using the manager form, generalizations are difficult. Nevertheless, the following generalizations about suburbs safely can be asserted:

1. There is no typical suburb and no average suburbanite.
2. There is no particular economic function unique to suburbs.

3. Suburbs promote a variety of life-styles for their residents.
4. There is no standard form of suburban government.

Having completed this discussion of suburban typology and the chapters dealing with suburban social and political dynamics, we will now turn to a set of four chapters concerning some specific problems encountered in governing suburbs. Chapter 5 deals with the fiscal patterns and financial problems urban and suburban units face in financing public services, and also examines the potential impact of the federal revenue sharing program. Chapter 6 covers the systems of delivering services on the suburban level and Chapters 7 and 8 examine the roles of county and state governments in financing and delivering services in the suburbs. The final four chapters will deal with the relationship of the suburbs to the metropolitan area and to national policies.

5

Financing suburbia

LIKE OTHER local governments, suburban governments are financed through the collection of compulsory taxes, which are spent to procure or provide public services. However, there are substantive and procedural differences between the tax systems of suburban and other local governments that are of particular interest to the student of suburbia. Suburban governments not only differ from central cities in the amount of revenues raised, they also vary considerably among themselves in terms of taxing and spending. These differences will be explored in this chapter.

GOVERNMENTAL FINANCES IN THE METROPOLITAN AREA

The most basic discrepancies between central city and suburb lie in the differential taxing and spending patterns exhibited by these localities. Almost without exception, central cities tax their residents more heavily than do suburbs. In only 4 of the 37 largest metropolitan areas are suburban taxes as high as those of the central city. According to the 1970 national average, suburbs exerted only about two thirds of the central city tax effort.[1] Central cities spend more heavily on basic

---

[1] William Lilley III, "Revenue Sharing Report/President and the Nations Mayors Shape Delicate Alliance on Funding," *National Journal Reports*. April 3, 1971, p. 738.

services, such as police and fire protection, welfare, and public works, while suburbs spend comparatively more on school systems.

A number of factors force the central cities to spend more on some services than on others. Since central cities are older and contain the central business district of the metropolitan area, they are forced to spend money on services that benefit the suburbs. The central business districts, which service the entire metropolitan area, are used heavily by commuters, visitors, conventioneers, and entertainment seekers. The central cities are also the home of a disproportionate number of the poor, the aged, and minorities. They have considerably more serious crime, illegal drug usage, and vandalism than the suburbs. And, although the need may be greater for compensatory education, per capita expenditures for education are generally lower than suburban totals. The age of the city necessitates endless upkeep to provide a facade of attractiveness to tourists and business people. Therefore, the maintenance and public safety functions of the central city virtually cannot be reduced. Further, overcrowding and the need to maintain social control combine to keep recreation, police and fire protection, welfare, public housing, and hospital expenses high on a per capita basis, as compared to suburbs.

In general, the older and closer a suburb is to the central city, the more it resembles the city in socioeconomic makeup and the more closely its expenditure patterns parallel those of the central city. In its provision of public services, Cicero, Illinois, is more similar to Chicago than it is to Flossmoor, a more distant, wealthier and newer suburb. Thus, in order to assess taxing and revenue variations, suburbs must be considered individually, or in groupings.

These variations partially can be explained by dividing metropolitan area cities into several categories. A broad, but useful division can be made between industrial suburbs, balanced suburbs, residential suburbs, and the central cities. Residential suburbs are usually further distinguished by the level of average family income. Industrial suburbs are defined as those communities in which over 60 percent of the total real property tax base derives from business real estate. In balanced suburbs, 40 percent to 50 percent of the total assessment derives from residential properties, while residential cities obtain more than 60 percent of their revenues from residential properties.

Since most of the property tax base in industrial suburbs comes from business real estate, it is obviously much easier for them to support municipal services than for either central cities or residential suburbs. This is generally the case in many metropolitan areas. In metropolitan Milwaukee, for example, the central city's tax base resembles that of the low income suburbs. Balanced cities are most similar in total tax base to medium income suburbs, but their taxables come from industry and business, whereas the medium-income suburb relies on high residential assessments. High residential assessments explain the comparatively wealthy position of high income suburbs. The industrial suburb owes its financially strong position to heavy industrial assessment.

One of the reasons Milwaukee has such a low per capita assessment is because it has a relatively low industrial base, while its per capita residential assessments are the lowest in the region. The per capita assessed value of property in high income residential suburbs is twice as great as Milwaukee's and that of industrial cities is nearly five times as great.[2]

Given these differences, it is not surprising that Milwaukee has adopted a higher tax rate than any of its suburbs. As Table 5–1 indicates,

TABLE 5–1
Mean full-value property tax rate in mills by purpose among types of municipalities, 1966, in Milwaukee metropolitan area

	Local	School	Total (including county and other levies)
Milwaukee	13.8	16.5	40.7
Balanced	4.2	15.9	29.8
Industrial	1.7	16.0	22.6
Residential			
High income	2.2	18.3	34.6
Medium income	1.9	19.0	29.4
Low income	3.2	18.8	33.9
(Median)	(2.1)	(18.8)	(31.1)

Note: A 40 mill rate corresponds to 4 percent of the total value of property in Milwaukee. Wisconsin, as a state, relies heavily on the property tax for local revenue.
Source: Table from "Metropolitan Disparities and Fiscal Federalism" by John Riew is reprinted from *Financing the Metropolis: Public Policy in Urban Economics,* John P. Crecine, Edit., Vol. 4, UAAR, © 1970, p. 140 by permission of the Publisher, Sage Publications, Inc.

the city's levy is more than 5 mills (about 17 percent) higher than the next highest taxing unit, the higher income residential suburbs. It is nearly twice as high as the average of the two industrial cities.

The aggregate figures document a number of conclusions. First, the similarity between central city and low income suburbs in taxable capacity is not maintained in the actual tax rate, since Milwaukee taxes at a rate 20 percent higher than its low income suburban counterpart. Second, balanced cities tax at very nearly the same rate as medium income residential suburbs. Finally, while all residential suburbs tax

---

[2] Tables from "Metropolitan Disparities and Fiscal Federalism" by John Riew are reprinted from *Financing the Metropolis: Public Policy in Urban Economics,* John P. Crecine, Edit., Vol. 4, UAAR, (c) 1970, pp. 140–142 by permission of the Publisher, Sage Publications, Inc.

property at a higher rate for local educational purposes than do the nonresidential municipalities, the central city taxes itself most heavily for local noneducational functions.

Table 5–2 sheds some light on Milwaukee spending patterns. Industrial and high income residential suburbs are the highest spenders, largely

TABLE 5–2

Mean per capita operating expenditures for selected functions among type of municipalities, 1966, in Milwaukee metropolitan area
(dollars)

	General government	Police and fire	Health and sanitation	Total
Milwaukee	11.9	37.9	16.4	81.3
Balanced	11.2	23.1	10.9	62.5
Industrial	25.0	67.8	21.5	142.9
Residential				
High income.	22.6	42.2	19.4	118.5
Medium income.	10.2	17.0	6.6	55.8
Low income	9.8	15.2	4.6	47.9
(Median)	(11.4)	(19.3)	(9.1)	(63.5)

Source: Table from "Metropolitan Disparities and Fiscal Federalism" by John Riew is reprinted from *Financing the Metropolis: Public Policy in Urban Economics,* John P. Crecine, Edit., Vol. 4, UAAR, © 1970 by permission of the Publisher, Sage Publications, Inc.

because they have the highest tax base. The tax base of industrial suburbs is so strong that they can spend about 75 percent more per capita than the central city, yet, as Table 5–2 demonstrates, they only tax themselves about half as heavily. Because of the valuable manufacturing properties within their boundaries, their expenditures for police and fire protection are the highest in the metropolitan area, resulting in the highest total spending of all classes of cities.

High income suburbs spend at a much higher level, generally in proportion to the extent that their tax base exceeds that of their middle and lower income counterparts. Milwaukee, the central city, has expenditures well in line with the median average of all cities, although its per capita rate for police and fire protection is about double the median expenditure for all cities. With the possible exception of Milwaukee, which taxes itself more heavily than other cities in the metropolitan area, ability to pay seems to be the major criterion upon which local expenditures are based.

In addition to revenues from real and personal property taxes, municipalities or counties have access to intergovernmental revenues. These are often state subventions based on per capita computations such as motor vehicle receipts. When suburban tax levies are low, intergovernmental receipts make up a high percentage of the total. Table 5–3 illustrates this pattern among Milwaukee suburbs that have over 25,000 residents. The smaller suburbs of New Berlin and Brookfield, which

TABLE 5–3
Revenues per capita for Milwaukee suburbs over 25,000 population

			Per capita revenues		
Suburb	*Population 1970*	*Total*	*Property*	*Intergovern- mental*	*Other*
Brookfield	32,140	142	20	80	42
New Berlin.	26,937	70	7	37	26
Waukesha	40,258	353	185	105	63
Wauwatosa	58,676	329	193	98	38
West Allis	71,723	342	241	75	26

Source: Bureau of the Census, *City County Data Book* (Washington, D.C.: U.S. Government Printing Office, 1972), p. 792.

reaches 25,000 by the 1970 census, have much lower revenue totals. West Allis receives over 30 times the per capita property tax of New Berlin. There is less difference between suburbs in the actual intergovernmental revenue per capita, but the percent of their revenue that is intergovernmental does vary among the suburbs. Both Brookfield and New Berlin receive over half of their total revenues from other governments. As revenue sharing monies are received, this ratio will increase further.

Almost all of the tax revenue collected by these suburbs is from property levies, since municipal income taxes are not allowed in Wisconsin and only the very largest cities can levy a sales tax. In other states, local or municipal sales taxes are common. A few states, particularly Pennsylvania, allow municipal income taxes.

VARIATIONS IN LOCAL SPENDING

There are many reasons for the differences in taxing and spending patterns among communities, particularly suburbs, in a metropolitan area. Some of these have already been noted; others include the following:

1. Ability to pay. The wealthier communities are simply likely to make more expenditures. Access to special tax "bonanzas," such as the sales tax from large department stores or the property tax from an industrial plant, enables a city to provide services with relative ease. At the same time, large shopping or industrial centers are likely to generate civic expenses for traffic and crime control, fire protection, and public works improvements. Wealthy cities can decrease or increase revenues by cutting or raising the property tax rates to meet the desired service levels.

2. *Needs sometimes dictate spending.* At the other extreme, needs may determine the nature and level of spending. A study of the Philadelphia area indicated that "for the most part, industrial and commercial wealth is not used in Philadelphia suburbs to finance amenities for local residents."[3] The study found that need rather than wealth was the primary determinant of expenditures, especially in poor suburbs. Depending on the availability of resources, wealthier cities of high social rank demanded high levels of expenditures.

3. *Commitment to various interests.* Over the years, many older suburbs have committed themselves to supporting different interests and a substantial number of traditional services. These support patterns, particularly when the service is "popular," are quite resistant to change. Long established interest groups, ranging from government bureaucracies to private groups, attempt to divide the community's rather small financial resources among themselves. Further, the very longevity of a city necessitates expenditures; civic decay demands spending for revitalization.

4. *Social attitudes.* Finally, social attitudes influence the level of taxing and spending. Some suburbs have a tradition of civic pride and their citizens come to expect the provision of certain types of public goods. Tourist suburbs or upper class traditional suburbs often fall into this class. Amenities suburbs, striving for the "good life," are likely to have parks, bus services, and beautification campaigns.

Caretaker suburbs spend predictably little on most public services. Above the marginal provision of services, such cities try to lower taxes. To the extent that caretaker suburbs are populated by middle or upper class residents, they are likely to be newer and smaller in population and made up of the so-called nouveau riche who are not yet committed to the "gracious" ways of urban amenities.

THE ANATOMY OF LOCAL FINANCE[4]

The property tax

The property tax is the backbone of the local revenue system. During most of the nation's life, it has provided more total revenue than any other tax at any level of government. By 1927, it still composed half of the nation's total tax collections, although it began to decline there-

---

[3] Oliver Williams et al., *Suburban Differences and Metropolitan Policies* (Philadelphia: University of Pennsylvania Press, 1965), p. 134.

[4] This section relies very heavily on James Maxwell's excellent work, *Financing State and Local Governments*, rev. ed. (Washington, D.C.: Brookings Institution, 1969).

after.[5] Now it is only 16 percent of the national total.[6] In 1971 property tax revenues accounted for 32 percent of state and local general revenue, and 64 percent of local general revenue.[7] Property tax collections totalled $37.9 billion that year, providing nearly 85 percent of the tax collections of counties, townships, special districts, and school districts. Cities, which have a wider range of taxing options, including the sales tax, still collected about 67 percent of their taxes from this source.[8] This is an extremely large sum of money to be generated from any one source, particularly one that has been criticized for so long on both economic and administrative grounds. While not without its supporters, the property tax has been badly maligned.

The property tax is levied on real property—land, houses, farm acreage, and commercial and industrial properties—as well as on personal property, including household effects, motor vehicles, and stocks and bonds. Personal property levies made up only 14 percent of the total property tax levy in 1972.[9] Most of this revenue was obtained from industrial or commercial inventories and motor vehicle taxes. For legal and administrative reasons, the tax on intangibles (stocks and bonds, etc.) no longer exists to any significant extent.

Thus, real property is the bulk of total property tax assessments. Approximately 48 percent of total taxes from real estate in 1972 came from residential nonfarm properties, and about 32 percent from commercial and industrial properties.[10] The majority of the remaining amount is derived from farm and acreage properties. Taxes on land are assessed in various ways, such as a certain fixed amount per $100 of assessed valuation, or so many mills (a tenth of a cent) per dollar. The total tax levy is made up of all taxing bodies that have jurisdiction over a given piece of property. For example, Table 5–4 shows the breakdown in Elmhurst, a Chicago suburb.

The rate only appears to be 7.7 percent. Actually, the rate was somewhat under 3.85 percent because property in Elmhurst was assessed at a level somewhat under 50 percent of true or market value. In Illinois, the statewide assessment rate is set at 50 percent of true value, outside of Cook County, but few if any jurisdictions meet this standard. The

[5] Ibid., Table 6–1, p. 126.

[6] Advisory Commission on Intergovernmental Relations, *Financing Schools and Property Tax Relief* (Washington, D.C.: U.S. Government Printing Office, 1974), p. 15.

[7] Advisory Commission on Intergovernmental Relations, *The Property Tax in a Changing Environment* (Washington, D.C.: U.S. Government Printing Office, 1974, pp. 295–98.

[8] Advisory Commission on Intergovernmental Relations, *Financing Schools and Property Tax Relief*, p. 16.

[9] Ibid. p. 25.

[10] Ibid.

TABLE 5–4
Elmhurst tax levy for 1970
(per $100 of assessed valuation)

Grade school district	$2.653
Junior college district.	.131
High school district	1.830
City.	1.230
County	.497
Sanitary district	.374
Fire protection district	.476
Township	.277
Forest preserve	.135
Park	.260
Total	$7.748

Source: State of Illinois, Department of Local
Government Affairs, *Illinois Property Tax Statistics*
(Chicago: Illinois Department of Local Government
Affairs, 1970), p. 3.

actual rate depends entirely upon the ratio of the assessed to real valuation, which is almost always greatly below true value, even when state law calls for true value.

Nationally, ratios ranged from 5 percent to 84 percent in 1967, and averaged about 33 percent of real valuation. At this average rate, a $10 rate would be a true rate of about 3.3 percent, but a rate this high is unusual. In 1971, the average effective tax rate for all states was 1.98 percent, and only 5 states averaged as high as 3.0 percent.[11] On a home with a true value of $40,000, a property tax bill of $1,000 is equivalent to a 2.5 percent rate. Table 5–5 lists the tax rates from some Chicago suburbs; the 1971 Illinois average effective tax rate was 2.15 percent. The municipal rate is only a portion of the total levied by all units of government, including the counties and school districts. Both the municipal and total tax rate vary substantially, except in the states where school and other costs are combined into the municipal rate.

Cities rarely do their own assessing; usually the process is performed by a township or county and includes some sort of statewide equalization to assure equity among jurisdictions. Even with this statewide equalization process, property tax assessment receives considerable criticism since it is often inequitable, administered by amateurs, and subject to manipulation. Inevitably, assessments lag behind increases in values and some "catch up" arrangement is made. Then, either estimates of property values are made without actual examination, or a portion of the county is revalued every few years.

---

[11] Advisory Commission on Intergovernmental Relations, *The Property Tax in a Changing Environment* (Washington, D.C.: U.S. Government Printing Office, 1974), p. 809.

TABLE 5-5
Chicago suburban area tax rates for 1970

City	Valuation assessed	Municipal tax rate	Aggregate tax rate of all units
Elgin	$211,455	$1.062	$6.514
Highland Park	193,398	1.122	7.839
Evanston	357,577	1.242	7.658
Cicero	332,379	.976	5.830
Des Plaines	295,543	.722	7.402
Flossmoor	40,461	1.112	*
Elmhurst	197,099	1.230	7.748
Chicago (central city)	$12,672,457	$2.652	6.890

* Not applicable under 10,000 population.
    Source: State of Illinois, Department of Local Government Affairs, *Illinois Property Tax Statistics* (Chicago: Illinois Department of Local Government Affairs, 1970), pp. 2-3, 26-36.

Another major argument against the property tax is that it is regressive, bearing more heavily as a percentage of actual income on lower income persons. Although some debate surrounds this assumption, it generally is accepted as fact. Further controversy exists concerning the extent to which people increase their housing expenditures as their income increases.[12] A major factor is the federal income tax deduction allowed for mortgage interest and for local property taxes. This results in a significantly lower federal income tax liability for homeowners. The tax advantage, combined with the availability of Federal Housing Authority (FHA) loans for suburban development, significantly contributed to the development of many suburbs after World War II. The annual value of this tax benefit is greater than the total federal, state, and local expenditure for public housing in any year.

With few exceptions, then, these administrative deficiencies and apparent inequities have caused many experts and economists to favor reform of the property tax. However, the tax exists and will continue to be levied because it is generally the only tax that local units of government are allowed to levy.

The local property tax has long been considered the least fair tax; yet, in the two years from 1972 to 1974, public negative reaction has decreased. In 1972, 45 percent of the citizens questioned in a survey conducted by the Advisory Commission on Intergovernmental Relations (ACIR) regarded it as the least fair tax, but only 28 percent regarded it so in 1974. Conversely, 19 percent of the public rated the federal income tax as the "worst" tax in 1972, but 30 percent felt that way

[12] Advisory Commission on Intergovernmental Relations, *Local Revenue Diversification: Income, Sales Tax, and User Charges* (Washington, D.C.: U.S. Government Printing Office, 1974), pp. 16-17.

in 1974. Thus, while neither tax is popular, the public currently is more positively disposed toward the property tax.[13]

There are a number of reasons why the public attitude has shifted. When the first ACIR poll was conducted, the property tax was being denounced by officials at all levels of government and court decisions had created the impression that local property tax was not a good means for financing schools. During the 1974 poll, the property tax was receiving a better press. Further, the use of federal revenue sharing funds and state surpluses for new tax relief programs took some of the burden off the local property tax.[14]

General retail sales taxes

Sales taxes are the largest source of local nonproperty revenues, and their use is increasing rapidly. In 1972, they accounted for about 38 percent of nonproperty taxes.[15] In certain large central cities, such as Los Angeles and New Orleans, the tax brings in over one quarter of the city's total revenue.[16] In the five states where cities levy the tax, many suburbs receive a great deal of the generated revenue. In municipalities blessed with retail shopping centers or large business districts, the sales tax revenues may even exceed those generated by the property tax.

The sales tax varies from state to state. Some localities levy and collect it themselves, while others "piggyback" it on to a state levy. As of January 1973, 3,780 cities and 614 counties in 26 states levied a local sales tax. Most cities were in Illinois, California, Oklahoma, Alabama, Texas, Utah, and Washington.[17]

At present, the sales tax is not the major source of suburban revenue; but it often represents an important "incremental" source of new revenue that could be tapped. Where allowed by law, individual suburbs can hope that proper zoning, selective annexation, and civic inducements will entice commercial developments that bring in sales taxes to locate there. The means are not very different from those employed to encourage industrial development in order to increase the property tax base. Much maneuvering for urban sales tax gain could be avoided by a

---

[13] Advisory Comission on Intergovernmental Relations, *Changing Public Attitudes on Governments and Taxes* (Washington, D.C.: U.S. Government Printing Office, 1974), p. 2.

[14] Ibid.

[15] Advisory Commission on Intergovernmental Relations, *Local Revenue Diversification: Income, Sales Tax, and User Charges*, pp. 31–33.

[16] Maxwell, *Financing State and Local Governments*, p. 93.

[17] Advisory Commission on Intergovernmental Relations, *Local Revenue Diversification: Income, Sales Taxes, and User Charges*, pp. 31–33.

state law that would distribute the total income by population within a region; currently most states distribute revenues based on the point of sale. Attempts to modify this pattern raise objections from those who accidentally have benefited from the existing location of commerce and from those cities that have invested funds to entice business.

The most serious charge against the sales tax is that it is not equitable. It almost always weighs most heavily on those who have the largest part of their income committed to consumption expenditures such as clothing, food, and medicine. This is not a major drawback in most cities. Wealthier city and suburban residents are least likely to object to the tax, while poorer citizens tend to overlook the tax, since only small amounts are paid at a time. To the extent that the state law exempts food, services, or rent, the tax is less regressive than the property tax.

User charges

Local governments are increasingly instituting user charges; only $1.6 million in 1953, they increased to $10.9 billion in 1972. The largest source of user charges are education ($2.49 billion), hospitals ($3.081 billion), and sanitation ($1.24 billion). School lunch sales account for most education charges. Most of the charges for sanitation, housing, and public hospitals cover only from 30 percent to 75 percent of the program costs.[18] These charges are likely to continue increasing as an absolute, and probably relative, share of local revenues, since they accord with the principle of taxing for "benefits received," which most legislators and many citizens favor.

Intergovernmental revenue

Intergovernmental revenue constitutes a very large part of city revenue. It includes categorical grants from the federal government, such as urban renewal funds, health service monies, and law enforcement grants. In most cases, suburbs do not receive significant amounts of categorical grants compared to central cities. The majority of suburban intergovernmental revenues are remitted by the state government, usually on the basis of population. There is some bias in favor of suburbs in the distribution of federal and state formula aid. Direct federal and state aid supports 27 percent of central city expenditures, 29 percent

---

[18] Advisory Commission on Intergovernmental Relations, *Federal-State-Local Finances: Significant Features of Fiscal Federalism* (Washington, D.C.: U.S. Government Printing Office, 1974), p. 12; and James Maxwell, *Financing State and Local Governments*, pp. 176–77 and Appendix A-19.

of suburban expenditures, and 37 percent of all local expenditures in the rest of the nation.[19]

The bulk of state aid to local governments falls into three broad categories: education, welfare, and highways. Education alone comprises nearly 60 percent of the total (See Table 5–6), a share that has remained constant for some time. Aid to education goes almost exclusively to local school districts. Its objective is to "equalize" differences in fiscal capacity among school districts, although this goal frequently is not met. For the last 30 years, states have been forcing consolidation of local school districts that are too small in order to present a broad-based curriculum. The use of financial incentives is an effective way to force or reward compliance.

The second largest portion of intergovernmental revenue is designated for welfare programs. The greatest portion of the money goes to counties or central cities. Some lower income suburbs also have a large number of welfare recipients. Allocations to recipients generally are controlled by state formulas so that localities have relatively little discretion in distributing the funds.

Money for highways, generated largely by vehicle taxes, usually is distributed on a per capita basis to local governments. The use of these funds is often limited to highway-public works functions, such as road maintenance and traffic signals. In 1966 these projects accounted for about 40 percent of all local expenditures for highways.

Federal categorical aid granted directly to local units is less abundant than state intergovernmental aid to local governments. It is directed specifically toward certain functions, although the federal revenue sharing program has changed this substantially. About 18 percent of the federal categorical aid shown in Table 5–6 was channeled directly to local units of governments.[20] All the federal aid to education went to school districts in federally impacted areas. In only a few cases did specific suburbs or independent cities receive considerable sums of money for downtown renewal or individual public housing units. Central cities received the majority of these funds. The same distribution generally applied to grants for waste treatment facilities and airports.

Each state, with its units of local government, makes up a total system with its own balance of taxes, spending, and intergovernmental relations. Table 5–7 indicates some of the parameters of the systems used in Illinois

---

[19] Advisory Commission on Intergovernmental Relations, *Fiscal Balance in the American Federal System*, vol. 2 (Washington, D.C.: U.S. Government Printing Office, 1967), p. 84. See also U.S. Bureau of the Census, *Statistical Abstract of the United States*, 195th ed. (Washington, D.C.: U.S. Government Printing Office, 1974), p. 248.

[20] Advisory Commission on Intergovernmental Relations, *Federal-State-Local Finances: Significant Features of Fiscal Federalism*, p. 91.

TABLE 5–6
Intergovernmental expenditures by selected function,
1971–1972
(millions)

	Government level		
Function	Federal	State	Local
Education	7,941	21,195	53
Highways	5,108	2,633	40
Public welfare	13,251	6,944	190
Health and hospitals	1,312	955	125
Natural resources	624	125	9
Housing and urban renewal	1,981	115	1
Air transportation.	119	34	1
Other.	3,248	4,758	152
Total	$33,584	36,759	571

Source: Advisory Commission on Intergovernmental Relations, *Federal-State-Local Finances: Significant Features of Fiscal Federalism* (Washington, D.C.: U.S. Government Printing Office, 1974), p. 91.

TABLE 5–7
Intergovernmental revenue in suburbs of 50,000 population in the Chicago and Milwaukee areas, 1969–1970

City	Total revenue from state (thousands)	Intergovernmental revenue from federal	Per capita intergovernmental revenue
Chicago SMSA			
Aurora	$ 958	$ 6,000	$ 13.17
Berwyn.	539		10.27
Cicero	442		6.59
Des Plaines.	559	7,000	11.13
Elgin	564	2,000	10.32
Elmhurst.	626		12.38
Evanston.	1,053	202,000	16.54
Joliet	748		9.31
Oak Lawn	557		9.24
Oak Park.	692		11.31
Skokie	557	18,000	23.20
Waukegan	930		14.25
Milwaukee SMSA			
West Allis	$5,320		$ 74.93
Waukesha			105.00
Wauwatosa.	5,625		98.12
New Berlin.			37.00
Brookfield			80.00

Source: John Rehfuss, "Revenue Sharing and Suburban Politics," a paper presented to the Annual Conference of the Midwest Political Science Association, Chicago, May 1974, pp. 1–5.

and Wisconsin, listing actual intergovernmental revenues from the state, both in total and per capital figures. Neither set of suburbs employed federal direct aid to any significant extent. The average state subventions to localities ranged from $6 to $23 in the Chicago area and from $37 to $105 in the Milwaukee area. Obviously, Wisconsin cities receive a great deal more intergovernmental support from the state than Illinois cities. However, Wisconsin cities rely more heavily on property tax revenues than Illinois cities and cannot use a sales tax to supplement them. To maintain an equivalent level of public services, it is necessary to rely more heavily on the state.

Wisconsin traditionally has been a "high tax" state and Illinois a "low tax" state, in terms of total tax effort, based on measures that include both state and local taxes. In 1965, Illinois ranked 44th and Wisconsin third among all states. However, in 1971 Wisconsin was second and Illinois 15th among all states.[21]

The "political culture" of the state, at least as it relates to taxing patterns, has some effect on intergovernmental relations, since a state concerned with maintaining low tax rates is not likely to levy taxes at the state level and then pass them on to another spending level.[22] Illinois traditionally has relied on a sales tax for most of its revenue, while Wisconsin has been strongly committed to income taxation. While these patterns are changing, they have had considerable effect upon levels of intergovernmental spending. It is easier to add one or two cents to a sales tax, allowing local units to levy "piggyback" additions to the base tax, than it is to increase state taxes and send the money to local units.

FINANCES AND POLITICS

Local finance is ultimately a political rather than an economic question. Taxing inequality, poor administration, and an antiquated tax system are valid and significant problems. However, they are often insignificant to the hard-pressed local political leader when compared with his need to increase revenues to meet the ever-increasing demands from citizens and department heads. The increase must be achieved in the face of what usually is perceived as a hostile and antagonistic public attitude toward tax increases and bond referenda. The local politician must face pressures for improved services coupled with the simultaneous demands to keep taxes down.

Basically, local officials avoid raising taxes because it is a politically

---

[21] Ibid., p. 56.

[22] See Daniel Elazar, *American Federalism: A View From the States* (New York: Thomas Crowell, 1966), especially pp. 107–11 for a discussion of state political culture.

unpopular action. In some cases, local officials would like to give greater support to certain public programs, but hesitate to increase the local property tax levy or to put the matter to a public referendum. Being identified as a "taxer" is considered a political liability, whereas being classed as a "spender" is not necessarily a detriment, since tax increases are not always identified with spending programs.[23]

In a 1963 national survey, 50 percent of the people interviewed indicated that they were prepared to pay additional taxes to support 2 or more governmental programs. This same survey found that people favored increased spending but disliked increased taxes.[24] This was consistent with prior surveys. Citizen attitudes toward taxes do not always distinguish between local and state or federal taxes, except when a particular tax, such as a state sales tax, is being proposed. Support for a local referendum in one community may be evoked in spite of opposition to taxes in general, while another community may defeat bond issues because of opposition to a specific nonlocal tax.

Local support also may be a function of overall attitudes toward government. A 1973 survey found that Americans felt local government had the least effect on their personal life and the federal government the most.[25] This was in spite of the relatively greater increase in state and local taxes since World War II. Government receipts rose from 24.4 percent to 31.7 percent of the gross national product between 1946 and 1969. As Table 5–8 indicates, the federal rate of increase was lower than the state and local rate.[26] Perhaps the survey results also reflect lower satisfaction with state and local services. If so, any such dissatisfaction no doubt varies substantially from area to area. For example, Greenbelt, Maryland, a Washington, D.C., suburb, has since 1969 provided voters at local elections with a questionnaire about political attitudes. Citizens have rated the city highest and the federal government the lowest. They have also supported, at least on the questionnaire, higher levels of expenditures for city services.[27] Whether or not Greenbelt resi-

---

[23] Many of the ideas in this section came from the chapter by Arnold Meltsner, "Local Revenue: A Political Problem," in *Financing the Metropolis*, John Crecine, ed. (Beverly Hills, California: Sage Publications, Inc., 1970), pp. 104–35.

[24] Edith Mueller, "Public Attitudes Toward Fiscal Programs," *Quarterly Journal of Economics*, May 1963, pp. 221–28. See John Bollens, *Exploring the Metropolitan Community* (Berkeley: University of California Press, 1961), p. 277 and Morris Janowitz, Deil Wright and William Delaney, *Public Administration and the Community: Perspectives Toward Government in a Metropolitan Community* (Ann Arbor: University of Michigan Institute of Public Administration, 1958), pp. 36–44.

[25] Advisory Commission on Intergovernmental Relations, *Revenue Sharing and Taxes: A Survey of Public Attitudes* (Washington, D.C.: U.S. Government Printing Office, 1973), p. 3.

[26] Advisory Commission on Intergovermental Relations, *Federal-State-Local Finances: Significant Features of Fiscal Federalism* (Washington, D.C.: U.S. Government Printing Office, 1974), p. 5.

[27] Letter from James K. Giese, City Manager, Greenbelt, Maryland, August 28, 1975.

TABLE 5–8

Government receipts as a percentage of the gross national product (GNP)

	1946	1972	Percentage increase
Federal.	18.7	19.7	5.3
State and local.	5.7	12.0	110.6
Total percentage of GNP	24.4	31.7	29.9

Source: Advisory Commission on Intergovernmental Relations, *Federal-State Local Finances: Significant Features of Fiscal Federalism* (Washington, D.C.: U.S. Government Printing Office, 1974), p. 5. (Increase computed.)

dents are typical, however, as demands increase it is clear that local politicians are forced to raise taxes in one form or another.

What groups favor higher taxes

While no citizen or group likes higher taxes, certain groups generally favor projects associated with programs they support. High income groups tend to favor projects or referenda that provide amenities or needed basic public services. Wilson and Banfield term these voters "public regarding." They take the welfare of others and the welfare of the "community" into account as an aspect of their own welfare. To the extent that this group support is for cultural activities such as libraries, civic centers, or city beautification projects, it could be argued that high income people are motivated more by self-interest than by regard for the public, since they use such facilities proportionately more than low income people. However, this "public regardingness" may also extend to programs such as parks and public transit systems which directly benefit lower income persons. In addition to taking the public welfare into consideration, higher income groups seem to have a greater awareness of the connection between the proposed municipal service and the bond proposal.[28]

Lower income groups and nonhomeowners also tend to support many municipal projects. Banfield and Wilson suggest that nonhomeowners have relatively less financial reason to vote against bond issues because they do not pay the corresponding tax increases directly. They also found that ethnicity is a factor; low income blacks are more supportive of expenditures requiring a referendum than low income Poles and Czechs. Overall, however, low income persons in all ethnic groups are more likely to support public expenditures.

---

[28] James Q. Wilson and Edward C. Banfield, "Public Regardingness as a Value Premise in Voting Behavior," *American Political Science Review,* December 1964, pp. 876–87. The concept of "public regardingness" has been controversial among political scientists.

The combination of the rich and the unpropertied interests is countered by what might be termed the "private regarding" ethos, held primarily by middle class voters and ethnic groups such as Poles and Czechs. These groups tend to view public improvements in light of self-interest rather than with regard for public values. For this reason, middle and lower middle income people usually vote against tax increases. A study of Atlanta area bond elections supports this argument. It found that high income voters consistently supported the referenda. Lower income voters also supported the bond issues, although at a lower rate.[29]

In most cases, the greater the voter turnout, the greater the likelihood that the bond issue will be defeated. A small voter turnout is more likely to pass the bond since upper income persons, who normally favor such proposals, ordinarily turn out in larger numbers than other groups. As turnout increases, more middle or lower-middle income persons probably will be voting and the proposal will fail. The very lowest income groups do not usually vote in substantial numbers; yet those that do tend to support such proposals. However, the self-interest argument may assume too much regarding the voter's making a cost/benefit analysis. Certain psychological factors undoubtedly come into play. Alienated and unhappy citizens may vent their frustrations and anxieties by voting against local referenda. In high turnout elections, many of these unhappy citizens are drawn to the voting booth, while in a quieter or less controversial election, they may stay home.

Special interest groups favoring specific programs that would benefit from the tax increase or bond passage constitute another source of support for increased taxes. Groups such as Friends of the Library, Friends of the Zoo, and the Police and Fire Protection League will rally in support of measures that would benefit the public service they promote. In bond issues, these groups take the lead in developing support among their members and friends. Often, these groups take their case to a different political arena, such as the state legislature, to encourage it to levy local taxes in support of their program. In many instances, the state legislature responds by authorizing city or county expenditures for the program. Yet even after securing legitimacy for their programs, these groups sometimes cannot force the local unit to tax for it.

Eliciting support for new taxes

There are some devices and techniques that can be used to decrease opposition to new or increased taxes. User charges are one of these

[29] Alvin Boskoff and Harmon Zeigler, *Voting Patterns in a Local Election* (Philadelphia: J. B. Lippincott, 1964), pp. 46–47. Also see John Horton and Wayne Thompson, "Powerless and Political Negativism: A Study of Defeated Local Referendums," *American Journal of Sociology*, March 1962, pp. 485–93.

devices. As indicated earlier in this chapter, their use is increasing rapidly at both the state and local level. Tolls on state highways are an example of a user charge employed by many states. Consumers are often subject to user charges for the water and electricity provided by municipally owned water systems and electric power plants. Such user charges are identical to those a private owner would make. Occasionally an additional charge to support a project or activity that would not otherwise be possible may be added to the bill. For example, DeKalb, Illinois, adds to the water bill a garbage pickup charge as well as an additional sum designed to retire city hall bonds. While this may raise a few objections, it eliminates the necessity of holding a bond election or adding a sum to the property tax levy to support garbage pickup. Parking meters, animal shelter fees, and transit bus tickets are other examples of user charges.

Another way of eliciting support for new or increased taxes is by associating them with benefits. Many states commit a large portion of specific tax collections to education and welfare. The latter case is a holdover from the Depression, when many states enacted a sales tax to finance public aid. The most widespread earmarking practice is the commitment of all motor vehicle taxes to highway construction and/or maintenance. Federal law requires all collections to be spent on highways, rapid transit, or related highway activities, with rapid transit a permitted expenditure only very recently. In 1967, 28 states had constitutional provisions earmarking highway user funds, nevertheless, many did divert some funds. Conversely, several states placed all highway revenues into the general fund.[30] Earmarking taxes for highway improvements is not as common at the local level.

Local government earmarking of funds is likely to be a verbal or legal commitment to spend certain funds in specific ways, such as committing half the sales tax funds to capital improvements. A common example is the use of special assessments on all benefited properties for local street or sewer improvements. This practice highlights the relationship between taxes and benefits.

Often local interest groups will seek to have the particular function given a separate tax levy or will try to have a certain portion of a tax committed to the program. By isolating the function and associating it with a specific levy, they are likely to secure more money for their function than by having it compete with other functional areas for the limited taxes available. Local legislators are likely to support higher levies in this manner since the particular interest group involved can be blamed for the higher tax.

The public considers some charges legitimate and others an unfair

---

[30] Advisory Commission on Intergovernmental Relations, *State Aid to Local Government* (Washington, D.C.: U.S. Government Printing Office, 1969), pp. 88–89.

nuisance. For example, admission charges to band concerts may raise objections from music interest groups, while charges at the city animal shelter, which are imposed upon unorganized individuals, may not be resisted. Sometimes there is less resistance if the charges fall primarily on nonresidents or on an unpopular group. However, politicians are wary of levying nuisance charges because they irritate many citizens and may encourage resentment toward the taxing system in general or against the local government officials.

As suggested earlier, one of the problems local officials face in attempting to raise taxes or secure favorable votes on referenda or bond issues is that citizens may vote against the local levy out of anger over federal or state taxes. Local referendums are, after all, the only opportunity the individual has to express a direct opinion on financial matters. Citizens do not always comprehend the distinctions between levels of government and sometimes vote in terms of the local benefits to be accrued from the measure. In most cases, local politicians cannot do much about this attitude except stress the relationship between local taxes and local benefits. This strategy does not always work, causing local officials to bear the brunt of dissatisfaction with the taxing actions of higher levels of government.

Results of perceived tax resistance

On occasion, elected local leaders perceive massive citizen opposition to taxes. When this occurs, officials sometimes consider reducing expenditures. But since local governments are labor intensive, major reductions in spending cause a reduction in employment levels. These reductions also generate intense opposition. Officials try to resolve this problem by giving up certain functions to another unit of government or by creating a unit of government that generates its own resources to provide that service. Some states allow the creation of municipal authorities, which provide a legal basis for carrying out ordinary activities through a new authority that is not bound by regular tax and bonding limitations. It is a perplexing process, but it appears to work.[31] Since special districts finance the services they provide from their own sources, taxes for these services are not a political burden on the larger jurisdiction. Special districts for parks and fire protection often are used in this way by suburban communities.

Many municipalities have given up unpopular or expensive public functions to a larger jurisdiction—usually the county, as discussed in Chapter 7. Where large staffs, facilities, and equipment are involved, the transfer must be negotiated; but where the service involves only

---

[31] Harold Alderfer, "Is Authority Financing the Answer?" *Financing Metropolitan Government* (Princeton: Tax Foundation, 1955), pp. 225–26.

a few employees, the switch can be made simply by failing to appropriate city funds. The transfer of functions often is accomplished when a subfunction is rather technical. Technical functions such as criminal laboratories or jail facilities often are performed by the county when the locality withdraws. Even if the transfer is not for the purpose of alleviating tax pressures, it has the same effect. For example, Metropolitan Toronto saved many millions of dollars in bond interest charges by combining small loans into metropolitan-wide loans at a lower rate of interest.

Finally, underspending can occur because citizens misinterpret their need for the services and place little or no pressure on politicians to provide them.[32] Due to insufficient information, citizens often believe that the budget is too large in proportion to the benefits provided. Many politicians, already loath to raise taxes, are especially reluctant to do so for programs that have a low level of visibility.

LOCAL FINANCING IN THE FUTURE

If the current "fiscal crisis" in large cities and many suburbs continues, some reallocations of present taxing/spending patterns probably will occur in the future. Conversely, if the predicament improves or even stabilizes, it is unlikely that drastic changes in the present pattern will occur. Urban and suburban America will muddle along as they have in the past.

Thus, predictions ultimately rely on estimates of the duration and severity of the urban crisis. Unfortunately, experts do not agree and two competing positions can be identified. The first estimate was made by Dick Netzer, a noted urban economist. He projected that state and local expenditure rise would continue despite stabilization of education and highway construction expenditures. Writing in 1967, he foresaw state and local taxes increasing 60 percent by 1975, in addition to a doubling of federal aid. However, these increases would not be sufficient to offset expenditures. The only way to make up the deficit without federal aid would be through increased state/local use of sales and income taxes. Since this seemed highly unlikely, Netzer felt that increased federal help would be necessary to avoid tax resistance and the discouragement of industrial growth due to higher property taxes. He recommended a federal revenue sharing plan.[33]

---

[32] Anthony Downs, "Why the Government Budget is Too Small in a Democracy," *World Politics*, July 1960, pp. 541-63.

[33] Dick Netzer, "State and Local Finance in the Next Decade," *Revenue Sharing and its Alternatives: What Future for Fiscal Federalism?*, Subcommittee on Fiscal Policy of the Joint Economic Committee, U.S. Congress, vol. III, Federal, State, Local Fiscal Projections (Washington, D.C.: U.S. Government Printing Office, 1967), pp. 1332–62.

In 1965, the National League of Cities authorized TEMPO, the General Electric Center for Advanced Studies, to study the future of local finance. The results projected by TEMPO indicated a $262 billion revenue gap in the nation's cities between 1966 and 1975, basically confirming Netzer's projection.[34]

The second estimate on the future of local financing was made by the Tax Foundation. It came to a conclusion diametrically opposed to Netzer's. A report issued in 1966 indicated that two thirds of the increases in state and local expenditures since 1948 were for highways, education, and welfare, and that the first two were due to stabilize. It noted that general revenues would continue to grow with expenditures and that state/local governments would be able to finance growing programs in the next decade. Therefore, the Tax Foundation concluded that a revenue sharing program with federal funds was unnecessary.[35]

Events since 1967 have resulted in continually increased expenditures by state and local governments. Table 5–8 indicates the rapid increase in state and local government spending since 1946, a much greater rate of increase than that of federal spending. The rate of increase has been even greater since the mid 1960s. From 1965 to 1972, state/local spending as a percentage of the gross national product increased from 7.9 percent to 10.0 percent, while federal spending (excluding Social Security contributions) actually declined.[36] During the 1968–72 period, the average annual rate of increase from major taxes was only 6.7 percent at the federal level, compared to 13.6 percent at the state level and 11.8 percent at the local level.[37] During the 1965–72 period, state and local debt increased from just under $100 billion to over $174 billion, an increase of over 74 percent in seven years.[38] Finally, in the period from January 1972 to June 1973, 23 states enacted 40 separate tax rate increases. New Jersey increased taxes on personal and corporate income, motor fuel, cigarettes and alcohol for a total of five increases, while New York increased rates on four of the above. Four other states increased the general sales tax.[39]

Most of these tax increases were levied before the extraordinary inflation of 1973 through 1975, which ate heavily into local ability to finance

---

[34] Robert Weintraub, *Options for Meeting the Revenue Needs of City Governments* (Santa Barbara: Tempo-General Electric Center for Advanced Studies, 1967), pp. 6–8.

[35] Tax Foundation, *Fiscal Outlook for State and Local Government to 1975* (New York: The Tax-Foundation, 1966), p. 11.

[36] Advisory Commission on Intergovernmental Relation, *Federal-State-Local Finances: Significant Features of Fiscal Federalism* (Washington, D.C.: U.S. Government Printing Office, 1974, pp. 6–9.

[37] Ibid., p. 11.

[38] Ibid., pp. 133–34.

[39] Ibid., p. 164.

services. In Kansas City, for example, between 1973 and 1974, price increases included 73 percent for hot asphalt, 170 percent for refuse bags, and 104 percent for a gallon of gas.[40] The effect of increasing demands and increasing costs due to inflation varies substantially by city, but the plight of many is severe, particularly that of the major central cities in the Midwest and East. New York City was saved from bankruptcy by Federal loans in 1975, although the recent inflation was only one of the forces at work. Detroit planned to lay off 1,400 employees in 1975, its income tax collection falling below that of 1974 despite inflation. Atlanta planned to give all employees a five day furlough without pay during 1975. Suburban Westchester County, New York, responded to the financial pinch by freezing all vacant positions.[41]

Contrary to the estimates of the Tax Foundation, it appears that, for economic and political reasons, the state/local tax needs continued to expand and, indeed, accelerated vis-à-vis those of the federal government during the late 1960s and the early 1970s. Neither Netzer nor the Tax Foundation could have foreseen the major inflationary forces beginning in 1973, but hindsight suggests that Netzer's estimates were more realistic.

Congress responded to the pleas of mayors, county executives, and governors in 1972 by passing the General Revenue Sharing bill. Members of the Congress chose to heed past and present difficulties of state and local officials rather than waiting until conflicting views of the future were clarified. It is probably fortunate that they did so because, without revenue sharing, the present inflationary forces would have taxed cities even more severely.

REVENUE SHARING

Serious discussion of revenue sharing began in the 1950s and the first revenue sharing bill was introduced by Congressman Melvin Laird in 1958. It drew support from conservatives, who wanted to eliminate the "strings" on categorical grants and to increase the flexibility of state and local governments. It also was supported by liberals, who saw that spending needs were greater at the state/local level and hoped that a revenue sharing program would increase the total funds devoted to pressing domestic problems. Most opposition came from the natural reluctance of Congress to adopt such a major revision of the intergovernmental system. Some liberals opposed the plan since they distrusted state and local government priorities and many congressmen simply

---

[40] John Urey, "The Finance Director/Problems of Coping with Stagflation," *Public Management*, March 1975, p. 11.

[41] Wayne Anderson and John Shannon, "Slumpflation—Its Effect on Local Finances," *Public Management* March, 1975, pp. 5–7.

did not want to raise federal taxes and then remit the revenues to local officials who did not share the burden of raising the taxes personally. As a result, nothing concrete occurred until President Nixon's 1969 proposal. In 1972, revenue sharing was passed and signed into law.

One appeal of revenue sharing is the degree of discretion that local governments can exercise in spending these monies. In addition, revenue sharing reduced the dependence of local governments on categorical grants, which are infamously associated with "red tape" and compliance with federal requirements. Suburban governments profited little from the categorical aid programs. Local government abhorrence of categorical grants stemmed from the belief that they enabled Washington agencies rather than local governments to set priorities. With the elimination of many categorical grants, monies from the federal government could be spent more freely by local officials on specifically local needs.

While these were the major reasons for the institution of revenue sharing, some other considerations were factors in shaping the final program. There was a conscious attempt to improve the tax effort of state/local governments, which resulted in the tax effort portion of the final allotment formula. Also, the question of the regressive nature of state/local tax systems was raised. Congress rejected a proposal that would have given a tax credit for the use of state income taxes because it was considered too deep an intrusion into state/local tax systems. Apparently Congress felt that the use of revenue sharing monies based on federal income taxes would reduce the regressive nature of the total tax system as applied at the local level. Further, it would do so without invading the sovereignty of state and local affairs. The final act authorized over $30 billion, as illustrated by Table 5–9.

The revenue sharing legislation contained a number of important provisions. First, the funds were to be distributed automatically each year so localities could plan for five years. Second, all units of general

TABLE 5–9
Revenue sharing appropriations
(billions)

Calendar 1972.	$ 5.30
Calendar 1973.	2.99
Fiscal 1974	6.05
Fiscal 1975	6.20
Fiscal 1976	6.35
Calendar 1976.	3.32
Total (rounded)	$30.21

Source: U.S. House of Representatives, *State and Local Fiscal Assistance Act of 1970,* House Resolution 14370, Publication 92-512, 92nd Congress, October 20, 1972.

government were included: states, counties, cities, and townships, excepting special districts or school districts. Third, only very broad requirements relating to legality and propriety were included, and no matching funds were required.

A clearly defined formula for distribution of funds was developed. States would receive one third of the money and local units two thirds. Money would be provided to counties on the same basis as to other local units. Shares for cities, counties, and townships would be computed on the basis of a complicated formula involving tax effort, population, and personal income. While no limits were imposed on state expenditures, local government expenditures are limited to eight specific functional areas:

1. Public safety (police, fire, and building inspection).
2. Environmental protection (includes sewage disposal and pollution abatement).
3. Public transportation (includes transit systems and highways).
4. Health.
5. Recreation.
6. Libraries.
7. Social services for the poor or aged.
8. Financial administration.

Local governments allocated most expenditures in the first two entitlement periods (late 1972 and early 1973) to capital improvements, perhaps because budgets were already established and the money was a "windfall." These capital improvements were made primarily in environmental protection, law enforcement, fire protection, parks and recreation, and street and road repair. An Office of Revenue Sharing study indicated that plans for appropriating later funds primarily included operating and maintenance expenses and social service-oriented capital projects.[42] Later studies suggested that urban governments were using funds for maintenance operations. Conclusions should be tentative, since it is difficult to track down actual expenditures when funds for one functional area replace funds that would otherwise have been spent.

There are a number of important implications arising from the distribution of revenue sharing funds. One very important issue concerns which jurisdictions benefit more from the funds. Suburban jurisdictions have gained relatively more federal funding as a result of revenue sharing. Central cities would benefit more only if payments were based more heavily on needs. Central cities have more poverty (lower per capita income) and usually demand a greater tax effort than other units, and thus, are favored by the formula. However, the increment they

---

[42] *Update*, No. 3 (Washington, D.C.: International City Management Association, November 15, 1973), p. 2.

receive is not sufficient to overcome the disproportionate cost of servicing the poor, elderly, and minorities.

Further, since revenue sharing actually served as a replacement for many categorical grants, they lost additional assistance. Pablo Eisenberg, an opponent of revenue sharing, indicated that many central cities lost much more due to 1973 impoundments, freezes, and program cutbacks than they received from revenue sharing. He notes that Milwaukee's first 3 entitlements totaled slightly over $16 million, while it lost about $75 million.[43] In 1975, the U.S. Conference of Mayors broke the united front of governors, county executives, and mayors and urged that revenue sharing be revised to further favor the jurisdictions with a disadvantaged population.

Statistically significant comparisons between local units are difficult due to lack of data. However, available information suggests that extensive variations exist. In South Dakota, receipts to counties from the early entitlements varied from $32.12 to 4.81 per capita, with an average of $14.31. The five largest South Dakota counties, each with a population greater than 20,000, received less than the average figure; the largest county received only $4.81 per capita. This outcome is partly due to the higher average per capita income of larger counties; but also the per capita expenditures of these five counties were below the mean of all counties in the state. They lost ground both on tax effort and per capita income.[44] The 21 cities in South Dakota received from $4.68 to $18.56 per capita.

One comparison among 19 large cities in or near DuPage County, Illinois (the most populous Chicago suburban area), showed extremely wide variations. The amount per capita ranged from $4 to $25, with the relatively large cities of Joliet and Aurora receiving about $11 each.[45]

However, the implications of revenue sharing ultimately do not revolve around differences between amounts distributed to recipients or perhaps even around the total amount of money appropriated. The significance is the effect on the federal system as a whole. While it is a bit early to evaluate revenue sharing, several interdependent issues seem important. First, revenue sharing became a replacement for many categorical grant programs. Central cities were most severely affected. As Table 5–9 indicates, few suburbs participated in the categorical aid programs.

---

[43] Pablo Eisenberg, "Revenue Sharing: Some Problems and Limitations," *The Grantsmanship Center News*, October 1973, p. 2.

[44] William Farber, "Revenue Sharing: Trick or Treat?," *Public Affairs Report No. 54* (Vermillion, South Dakota: Governmental Research Bureau, University of South Dakota, August 1973), pp. 1–3.

[45] Timothy Wilson, *Local Government Decision Making in Revenue Sharing* (Northern Illinois University, Political Science Department, unpublished manuscript), November 1973, p. 24.

The second major dilemma arising from the distribution of revenue sharing funds concerns how local governments will allocate the funds, since larger percentages are directed toward suburban/metropolitan problems rather than urban/central city problems. There may be more emphasis on highway construction and maintenance, mass transportation systems, recreation activities, and environmental protection, and reduced focus on welfare and health programs. Since expenditures for education by local governments do not qualify as a legitimate use of revenue sharing monies, they are likely to remain relatively constant in dollar terms, while they drop in relation to other expenditures. However, states are allowed to spend their allotments for education, perhaps offsetting some of this reduction. To date, states have spent most of their revenue sharing allotment in this area.

Third, besides uncertainties over the functional areas in which money will be spent, there is the question, raised earlier by the Tax Foundation, concerning whether the money actually is needed. If not, it will be spent on luxuries or marginal public services. This could result in tax reductions and might jeopardize future allocations from Congress. Revenue sharing opponents vigorously exposed the fact that some suburban communities used revenue sharing money to build tennis courts.

Fourth, the extent to which accepting federal money will force broad federal policies upon local government should also be considered. Compliance with equal opportunity laws may be required of all local governments. It is already national policy, but the use of revenue sharing funds makes the recipient government a target for a host of suits not previously envisioned. It is possible that the effect of revenue sharing may be to change federal controls from specific requirements associated with categorical grants to broader, more inclusive, national policies applicable to all state and local governments.

A final consideration is whether revenue sharing is the first step in a process that lodges the tax raising and collecting mechanism at the federal level. If this were so, it would certainly have profound implications for the future of the federal system. It would increase federal dominance, even if the funds collected were disbursed through the state/local decision-making process. Such a movement is not entirely unlikely, because it has proven easier to raise tax rates at the federal level. It is likely that the federal government will gradually assume a larger and larger share of local taxing prerogatives.

SUMMARY

It is very difficult to predict the future of fiscal federalism or the likely future financial position of suburbs. As noted earlier, the divergent projections of financial trends in the mid-1960s were based upon quite different assumptions. The Tax Foundation underestimated demands for state and local government services and the willingness of political leaders to yield to them. Moreover, predictions must account for vastly increased costs for providing public services, and must estimate how much longer Congress will approve revenue sharing, which expires in 1976 unless reenacted.

It seems useless to project state and local spending too far into the future, since assumptions cannot account for rapidly changing conditions. What would happen, for example, if a national collective bargaining policy were attached as a rider to an extension of revenue sharing? This would tend to push up state and local salaries and continue the pressures for increased state and local spending.

However, all projections must acknowledge that public demands will continue and that pressure for state and local spending will not subside. Thus, the property tax is likely to be retained. Revenue sharing monies may be used to prevent further rate increases. There probably will be considerable interest in diversifying the state/local tax base. States without sales taxes or income taxes will be under considerable pressure to adopt them, either to replace other more regressive taxes or to prevent increases. This movement may be accelerated by the federal government if it gives a tax credit for state income taxes or requires them as part of the revenue sharing formula criteria. In 1974, the Advisory Commission on Intergovernmental Relations modified its traditonal position favoring state or federal assumption of additional financial obligations. It now favors strengthening local revenue through income and sales taxes and heavier reliance on user charges. This recommendation also proposes federal withholding of local income taxes to facilitate their collection.[46]

In theory, pressures for tax increases could abate, as the baby boom of the 1960s is absorbed, the birthrate continues to decline, and educational funding needs at the elementary and high school levels thus decline. There may be substantial future redistributions of taxable resources between rural areas, suburban areas, and central cities. This could come as a result of court cases based on state constitutional requirements for equity or from legislative actions. There are some indications of this through court cases in specific states, but the extent to which this will affect every state cannot yet be determined.[47]

---

[46] Advisory Commission on Intergovernmental Relations, *Local Sales and Income Taxes*, (Washington, D.C.: U.S. Government Printing Office, 1974), p. 1.

[47] This happened in *Serrano* v. *Priest*, a California case in which the State Supreme Court used the equal protection clause of the 14th Amendment to the U.S. Constitution to require statewide equalization of school expenditures. The court held, "The California public school financing system, with its substantial dependence upon local property taxes . . . invidiously discriminates against the poor. . . . California Supreme Court, Los Angeles 29829 (1971).

Public assistance demands are still high. Pressures are increasing to make welfare primarily a federal program. This was one of the alternative forms of tax relief proposed in lieu of revenue sharing. President Nixon's Family Assistance Plan of 1969 may have promoted this reform by putting a national floor under welfare payments.

The oil shortage and energy crisis eventually may reduce demands for more highways in rural and suburban areas, although it also could increase the need for inner city mass transit systems. The result may be a trade off, which would not require additional large sums of money.

Finally, the present situation of state/local finance suggests a gradual, centralizing trend with revenue sharing as the first step. Other moves toward centralization would be nationalization of welfare costs and state-wide equalization of aid to public education. Perhaps regional taxes such as pioneered in Minneapolis-St. Paul will be adopted for regional functions such as transportation, solid waste disposal and air and water pollution control. Certainly, more user charges will be implemented wherever possible. Financing suburbia in the future will be difficult and will require many significant modifications of the current system.

6

Suburban governmental services delivery systems

SUBURBS, as has been noted, serve a variety of purposes. Some serve as retreats from the job; others are status symbols; still others are considered good places to rear children. All suburbs, however, are formally responsible for providing public services to their residents. The suburban resident expects, and usually receives, a package of public services, ranging from crucial "life-style" services such as education and police protection to "housekeeping" functions, such as street maintenance and tree trimming. This chapter focuses on the way local governments organize to provide these services, how they respond to citizen demands, and why there are variations in the level of services provided.

Counties, cities, school districts, townships, and special districts are all part of the varied suburban "delivery systems" which exist in the 50 states. These systems will be examined not only from a "purveyor of services" viewpoint, but in the context of their history, social environment and economic capacity. Local control and the methods of political decisionmaking in each unit also will be considered since they influence the policy outcomes associated with each public service.

Table 6–1 lists the major services and the unit of government that provides them. With the exception of education, the services are provided by the county, the suburb, and in many cases, special districts. However, in many metropolitan areas, the urban county furnishes the majority of these services.

120

TABLE 6–1
Major suburban services and the local provider

Service	Sub-urban city	County	School district	Town-ship	Special district
Traditional Municipal Services					
Police.	X	X			
Planning, zoning	X	X			
Recreation, parks, library	X	X		X	X
Fire.	X	X			X
Public works.	X	X		X	X
Highway maintenance					
Sanitation	X	X			X
Education	X	X	X		
Public health	X	X			X
Welfare	X	X		X	
Transportation					
Highway building	X	X		X	
Buses, local transportation.	X	X			X
Airports	X	X			X

Source: Compiled by authors.

TRADITIONAL SUBURBAN SERVICES

Traditional municipal services include police, fire, public works, sanitation; provision of amenities such as recreation, parks, and libraries; and the regulatory and control functions of planning, zoning, building code and subdivision controls. While all of these services are vital to the maintenance of the city, some are more visible than others and very central to the "life-style" or social structure of the city.

These more critical functions generally include the regulation of land use through building and zoning controls. This, to a great degree, is how the physical and eventually the social structure of the suburb is maintained. Another high priority is the police function, which generally mirrors the social norms of the community regarding acceptable behavior in public and sometimes private places.

A crucial "life-style" function is public education, but this service is generally provided by separate school districts and will be considered there.

Since suburban planning and zoning are covered later in this book in Chapters 10 and 12, only a short explanation will be given here. Planning, zoning, building code enforcement and subdivision control comprise a foursome of controls over land use and urban development. Planning is intended to develop and implement a balanced set of physical and social priorities through concerted social and governmental action. Zoning is the use of local police powers over health and safety to control types of land use, population density and building heights. Subdivision controls regulate the design and layout of new residential building as well as assuring the proper installation of streets and public improvements by the developer. Building code requirements prescribe the type of materials used in construction as well as other safety requirements such as exits from public buildings.

These land use and building controls are crucial functions. In upper class communities they may be used to maintain the low density exclusive nature of the community. In caretaker communities there may be, for all practical purposes, no effective planning or zoning and little effective building regulation.

The influence of professional planners on the process varies substantially with the key to high quality planning probably resting with the desires of political leaders rather than the ability of the professional. High quality planning is a necessary but not sufficient condition for high quality controls and effective development[1].

Police protection

A crucial suburban service that most often reflects the community's "life-style" is the level of police protection. A recent study conducted by James Q. Wilson revealed that cities and suburbs vary greatly in the behavior typical of the police force.[2] He categorized the police forces of eight cities into three broadly defined styles of behavior: watchman, legalistic, and service.

In the watchman style, the operating code of the police department is the maintenance of order. Violations of law are ignored until they inconvenience someone or threaten accepted community mores. Regulation of illegal conduct—whether it be gambling, speeding, or juvenile actions—is not of primary interest to the police. Actions of individuals are judged by the standards of morality the police impute to the offenders' social group. The watchman style normally calls for police officers to ignore private arguments or disputes, regardless of the technical or legal provisions, until public order is threatened. Therefore, arrests are relatively low in jurisdictions where the watchman philosophy prevails in the police department.

The legalistic style handles most illegal events in terms of implementation of the law rather than maintenance of order. One standard of behavior is prescribed for the community, regardless of the groups involved. Altercations between individuals, or other private matters, are

---

[1] For an extended discussion, see Francine Rabinovitz, *City Planners* (New York: Atherton, 1969).

[2] James Q. Wilson, *Varieties of Police Behavior* (Cambridge: Harvard University Press, 1968).

subject to police intervention. Arrests are made and persons are booked whenever the officer feels that he is able to make the arrest "stick." Departments operating under this philosophy issue more citations than other types of departments, particularly in incidents such as public drunkenness and traffic violations. These departments encourage victims to report complaints and may prosecute shoplifters even without the approval of the merchant.

Wilson indicates that most of the cities that now display the legalistic style were once blatantly corrupt or ineffective, and that a reform police chief changed the department by insisting that all laws be enforced as uniformly as possible. Practitioners of legalistic behavior believe that people should be judged equally and that law enforcement should not vary according to an individual's socioeconomic status.

The service style police department emphasizes both order maintenance and law enforcement, but is less likely to use formal sanctions such as arrests. Police intervene by issuing written warnings, but few arrests are made for relatively minor violations, particularly among juveniles. These departments often have specialized units designed to help citizens, such as the Nassau County, New York, "assistance vehicles," which provide services to motorists in difficulty. The police are quite sensitive to public opinion and appear as well-dressed public servants. Wilson notes that this style is often found in homogeneous, middle class communities in which there are expectations concerning public order, and which have no administrative demand for a legalistic style.

Three of the eight cities Wilson studied were suburban. For example, the Highland Park, Illinois, police department displayed a legalistic style. Brighton, a suburb of Rochester, New York, and Nassau County, New York, illustrate the service style of law enforcement. The other five cities were industrial, working class cities with a considerable number of ethnic groups and large black populations. Police forces in these cities displayed the watchman style. Suburban value orientations, particularly in smaller, more homogeneous and more affluent townships, may not easily support the watchman style of order maintenance. They are much more comfortable with professional style approaches and these are compatible with both the legalistic and service styles.

In considering the police delivery system for suburbs, two major elements appear. The geneal socioeconomic nature of the community influences the attitude toward a watchman style. Higher socioeconomic groups usually do not tolerate this style over a long period of time, whereas lower socioeconomic groups often will. The second element that influences the police delivery system is the policy of the police chief. A chief who favors reform will often adopt a legalistic style, while many chiefs prefer to adopt a service approach. This is especially true under stable political and social conditions in a middle income town.

In either case, Wilson found that the orientation of the police chief seems to be the guiding criterion.[3]

Amenity services

Many suburbs, as indicated in Chapter 4, emphasize certain traditional services they feel increase the suburb's "quality of life." In such amenity-oriented suburbs, most public services are maintained at a high level, particularly if the city has above average resources. Park and open space areas and a public library are particularly prized as symbols of the "good life," although some suburbs may be in a park or library district that covers a larger and less homogeneous area. In these cases, the level of these services may vary considerably within the district, but it is likely that the wealthier suburbs will have the best maintained parks and the larger libraries.

Suburban provision of amenity services cannot be measured very precisely. A caretaker city may reflect its life-style orientation by limiting all municipal services, while a growth oriented city may emphasize industrial parks. A suburb's attitude toward planning and zoning and its prevailing style of police behavior are important clues in determining how the community translates its social values into public services.

Routine services

Most of the services suburban governments provide are noncontroversial and are essential to the citizenry. These "housekeeping" services range from catching stray dogs to removing trash and snow or fighting fires. A large proportion of the city's budget is allocated for these services. However, they are not always provided directly by the city, but may be contracted out or provided by special districts.

The public works departments perform maintenance functions that generally include street maintenance and patching; snow removal; street sweeping; maintaining and cleaning storm drains, sewers, and catch basins; and painting and removing street markings and signs. These functions almost always are provided by the city itself. Sewage disposal systems almost always are provided by the community, but often special districts provide the treatment of sewage. Garbage collection and trash pickup also usually are performed by city employees, but sometimes contracts are let to private collectors. The planning and acquisition of large sites necessary for solid waste disposal rapidly is becoming a very serious regional problem. While collection generally is performed at the city or district level, disposal increasingly is handled on a regional basis.

Since proper sewage disposal requires the utilization of expensive

---

[3] Ibid., p. 259.

sites with very large economies of scale, sanitary districts are common and often cover a broad area. For example, Los Angeles County, with a population of 7 million, has only two sanitary districts. Variations among cities in the level of these maintenance services is largely, although not entirely, a function of municipal revenues. Those cities that have substantial revenues tend to spend more on all services. Another explanation for variations in service levels is related to the degree of professional standards.

Occasionally, high professional standards will improve the quality of services and the manner in which they are performed. This is usually the result of a strong city or county manager, department head, or bureau chief who is able, by the force of his personality and his professional standards, to command higher quality and more resources for his programs. Sometimes, the same result is reached through the intervention of strong civic or citizen groups, who influence the allocation of resources into an area of particular importance to them.

Another cause for variaton in service levels is an individual suburb's circumstances. For example, in certain northern areas, snow removal expenditures are heavy. Communities with many arterial streets will spend comparatively more for traffic signals, markings, and traffic control. Because of their concentration of wealth and assessed valuations, industrial suburbs usually spend more on fire protection.[4]

VARIATIONS IN SERVICE LEVELS

It is important to analyze the factors that account for gross variations in suburban services. One explanation relates to the resources of the suburb, and another to the size of its population. These greatly determine the ability to pay and the need for services. The financial capabilities of most suburbs are determined primarily by property tax assessments and sales tax receipts. As indicated in Chapter 5, these are affected by state as well as local policy.

Generally, the residents of suburbs demand high service levels. Part of this demand is due to standards set by professional organizations, such as the International City Management Association or the International Association of Chiefs of Police. For example, standards calling for 1.5 policemen per 100 residents may be adopted.[5] As they are financially able, suburbs often try to meet these standards.

---

[4] See Table 5–2 in Chapter 5 for the police and fire expenditures of industrial suburbs in the Milwaukee area.

[5] Institute for Training in Municipal Administration, *Municipal Police Administration*, 5th ed (Washington, D.C.: The International City Management Association, 1961,), pp. 48–50, 87, and International City Management Association, *Local Planning Administration* (Washington, D.C.: International City Managers Association, 1959), pp. 262–71, has details on professional standards.

Population size is the second major determinant of service levels. Generally, expenditure levels and number of employees are proportionately much greater in large suburbs, because of the need for large police forces and the reduced likelihood of having volunteer fire departments. Large suburbs are more likely to have separate departments for more specialized functions such as planning. This specialization increases the number of city employees. The cost of supervision increases very rapidly in relation to the number, specialization, and professionalization of employees. This is partly due to bureaucratization and increasing hierarchical controls over employees; but it is also due to the cost of social controls in larger, more complex and densely populated suburbs. The density means that fires are potentially more serious, there are proportionately more calls for the police, and existence of more underground utility lines necessitate more frequent excavation.

Large cities also tend to provide more total services within a departmental budget. A large fire department is more likely to provide fire inspection services to businesses on a regular basis. This is partly a function of professionalism, as chiefs are guided by the "best practices" of other cities, and partly a response to citizen demands. The net result of all these factors, however, is that growing cities have a corresponding increase in service levels or at least an increase in the number of employees and the amount of spending.

Figure 6–1 illustrates the relationship between size of government and the number of suburban employees. All 40 Illinois cities with over 25,000 residents (excluding Chicago) in 1960, are shown. The number of suburban employees generally is directly related to the size of the government. As suburbs increase in size, their working staffs increase rapidly. In the deviant cases of Arlington Heights and Des Plaines, the suburbs have grown very quickly and the expected number of employees for the size of the suburb has not yet been reached. If growth slackens, these suburbs should resemble their neighboring suburbs more closely within a few years.

Clearly, the costs and number of employees increase very rapidly as a suburb or county increases in size, while small units of government are able to maintain themselves on extremely limited budgets. Many small suburbs operate with only a handful of employees. The police chief, receptionist-secretary, and maintenance worker may be the only paid employees, with record-keeping done by an elected city clerk.

Small cities can maintain low service levels because private social controls often compensate for more impersonal bureaucratized services. Private social controls, through the family, the neighborhood, and larger groups usually serve as adequate substitutes for larger police forces and extensive correctional or juvenile programs. Historically, this has been the way that small villages enforced social mores. Many still oper-

FIGURE 6–1
Relationship between government size and number of employees

Number of employees

Population of cities (thousands)

Note: $r = .88$
Source: John Rehfuss, "Municipal Bureaucratization in 40 Illinois Cites," unpublished manuscript.

ate in this way. The smaller the village or suburb, the smaller the differences between private and public mores, so that social approbation substitutes for police enforcement. Also, smaller units can maintain themselves by relying on larger units of government for specialized and expensive services, a practice quite common in small to middle sized suburbs. For example, many suburbs use the central city for recreational and cultural purposes. Few suburbs maintain their own criminal laboratory services since the county sheriff, state police, or central city police perform these services for them. Most formal police training is done at the facilities of a larger jurisdiction.

The Lakewood Contract Plan, operating in Los Angeles County, is an excellent example of a large unit of government providing services to suburbs and towns. The County makes available a range of services from building inspection and traffic law enforcement to road painting and sign maintenance at a set price covering operating and overhead expenses. The community can contract with the county for the services it wants. Even when a contract plan such as Lakewood is not available to the suburbs, larger unit responsibility for specialized services makes it possible for the small unit to meet its needs with less overhead and capital investment.

CITIZEN SATISFACTION WITH MUNICIPAL SERVICES

It is impossible to speak of municipal services and local delivery systems without considering the impact of citizen satisfaction. A citizen's satisfaction with local politics affects his evaluation of local services and how he views their efficiency. At the same time, his satisfaction with the level and type of local services is manifested through his support or lack of support for politicians.

Whereas some conflict in the suburbs arises over the level of public services, conflicts over lifestyle issues and personalities are the major sources of controversy. The average suburbanite views local government issues as "nonpolitical" or "technical," generally assuming that "there is no Republican or Democratic way to pave a street." Streets must be paved, and it is assumed (correctly, in most cases) that local city employees and the elected civic leaders will determine the thickness of pavement and the regularity with which street markings are painted.

Occasionally, a breakdown in local services may become controversial. These issues usually are settled quickly, since they rarely involve lifestyles or values. Civic arguments generally occur over competing claims of candidates or local parties regarding the necessity for tax increases or zoning regulations.

Most people have little basis for an assessment of municipal services, since they have insufficient knowledge of service levels in other communities to make a competent evaluation. Many persons cannot identify the specific deficiencies they would like to see changed. One St. Louis area study showed that 20 percent of the persons surveyed could not identify a single desired local community change and that only 21 percent could identify 3 or more desired changes. The persons in this study were interested primarily in the factors that made their immediate area livable. They were less interested in broader issues such as open space, public transportation, water supply, and air pollution.[6]

Somewhat different results were found eight years later in a study of metropolitan Syracuse, New York. Here, suburbanites regarded adequate and unpolluted water supplies as relatively more important than did central city dwellers, who were more concerned with housing, welfare, and street maintenance (Table 6–2). Both groups, however, regarded education and law enforcement of paramount importance and did not differ greatly in their assessment of their relative importance. The suburbs of Syracuse abut polluted Lake Onondaga, which may

---

[6] John Bollens, *Exploring the Metropolitan Community* (Berkeley: University of California Press, 1961), pp. 186, 306–7.

TABLE 6–2
Citizens considering urban functions "most important" in the Syracuse, New York metropolitan area

Function	Percentage of respondents considering it "most important"		Excess of suburban support
	Syracuse	Suburbs	
Adequate water	32	48	+16
Water pollution	48	60	+12
Education	78	82	+ 4
Police protection	68	70	+ 2
Traffic tieups	26	24	– 2
Employment.	54	49	– 5
Park and recreation facilities.	28	20	– 8
Welfare.	45	35	–10
Street maintenance	46	32	–14
Housing	50	24	–26

Note: Respondents could indicate that more than one function was "most important."
Source: This table from "Exploring Urban Priorities: The Case of Syracuse," by H. George Frederickson is reprinted from *Urban Affairs Quarterly* Vol. 5, No. 1 (Sept. 1969) p. 34 by permission of the Publisher, Sage Publications, Inc.

partially explain suburban preferences. Central city interests, perhaps, mirror the problems of a decaying, older city.[7]

The difference between suburban attitudes toward public services is often as great as differences between suburbs and the central city. For instance, "life-style" issues differ greatly between suburbs, and these attitudes often seem to reflect the citizens' class differences. Suburbs populated by upper income families tended to favor spending money on esthetic amenities. Support for these amenities decreases as the social rank declines. Likewise, support for keeping the tax rate down is strongest in low ranking suburbs and declines as social rank increases, although a majority of all respondents in Table 6–2 desired to keep taxes down. Finally, high income suburbs are more interested in maintaining the "quality" of residents than lower income suburbs. However, when asked about "keeping undesirables out," lower income suburban residents in Table 6–2 strongly support the statement. This suggests that the city typologies of Chapter 4 delineate certain types of attitudes toward municipal services that are strongly associated with certain kinds of cities. The views of public officials and their decisions on local services and policies mirror these citizen views.

Satisfaction with police services may be higher in smaller, more

[7] Table from "Exploring Urban Priorities: The Case of Syracuse," by H. George Frederickson is reprinted from *Urban Affairs Quarterly* Vol. 5, No. 1, (Sept. 1969), p. 34 by permission of the Publisher, Sage Publications, Inc.

homogeneous communities. This is illustrated by a study comparing two small black suburbs on Chicago's South Side to similar neighborhoods in Chicago.[8] Suburban community residents rated their police at about the same level as did residents of black neighborhoods in Chicago on a range of indicators. However, they did feel that their police were far more likely to treat citizens equally and they also felt that they had more access. Actual resources devoted to police protection were considerably greater in Chicago, but performance indicators suggested that service levels were similar in nature in both types of neighborhoods. The authors attributed the high level of support for local police, as contrasted to the low financial expenditure, to a differing sense of community. Community feeling increases satisfaction with services not only because they are responsive to community needs, but also because they are controlled politically and socially. This study tends to support the view noted earlier, that a sense of access and control over local institutions contributes to satisfaction with public services.

Most suburban satisfaction with local services probably is related to the residents' conviction that they have access to local decisionmakers and that their friends and neighbors, not distant administrators or politicians, are administering the system in their behalf. Thus, service levels are considered "good" because they result from a process of which the suburbanite approves. There is little evidence to indicate definitely whether or not suburbanites actually do have access to local decisionmakers. But it is true that suburbanites *feel* that they have access, and that local officials *seem to behave* as though they do. These attitudes may result from the homogeneity of many suburbs that put "like minded" persons into office. Even so, the threat of citizen dissatisfaction is a powerful influence encouraging local officials to provide the services they think residents want. When residents feel that officials are responding to their expectations, they are satisfied with whatever level they are receiving.

SUBURBAN SERVICE DELIVERY SYSTEMS

The services discussed so far in this chapter are provided primarily by suburban municipalities. Suburban counties perform many of these same services for unincorporated areas, and their role will be discussed

---

[8] Elinor Ostrom and Gordon Whitaker, "Community Control and Governmental Responsiveness: The Case of Police in Black Neighborhoods," in David Rogers and Willis Hawley, eds., *Improving the Quality of Urban Management* (Beverly Hills, Calif.: Sage Publications, 1974), pp. 303–34. See also Elinor Ostrom and Roger B. Parks, "Suburban Police Departments: Too Many and Too Small?" in Louis H. Masotti and Jeffrey K. Hadden, eds., *The Urbanization of the Suburbs* (Beverly Hills, Calif.: Sage Publications, 1973), pp. 367–402; and Elinor Ostrom and Gordon Whitaker, "Does Local Community Control of Police Make a Difference? Some Preliminary Findings," *American Journal of Political Science*, February 1973, pp. 48–76.

in Chapter 7. These counties, as well as nonurban counties, also provide a variety of unique county services to central city *and* suburban residents. Still other governmental services are provided to suburban residents by towns, boroughs, school districts, and other special districts.

Counties

Since the county is formally a unit of state government, its services are an amalgam of state and local functions. The state-mandated functions include activities such as deed recording, public health services, criminal prosecution, and the court system. The local services include those provided by the sheriff, the highway engineer, and the office of juvenile services.

Few cities have their own criminal court system, so this service usually is provided by the county. Many suburbs have municipal courts that deal with misdemeanors such as traffic violations. However, the sheriff is the only law enforcement officer in unincorporated areas, serving as the backup for local police service in suburban incorporated areas. He rarely operates within the boundaries of the central city in an urban county. The sheriff also serves papers throughout the county on behalf of the county court system. In most counties, the sheriff is responsible for operating the county jail.

Public health and welfare are other countywide services. While separate public health and/or welfare departments exist in large cities, they are the exception rather than the rule in suburbs. In many cases, the public health function is handled exclusively by the county, due to the expense of maintaining it.

Public health functions include hospitals, maternal and pediatric services, sanitation inspections, and public health education. However, many jurisdictions, including smaller ones, have efficiently run municipal hospitals. Larger communities encounter greater financial difficulty in maintaining such facilities because of higher percentages of indigent patients and expensive specialized operations, such as intensive care units, quarantine sections, or emergency rooms. Maternal and child care services usually are provided by private physicians in most moderate to high income suburbs, whereas, in larger cities or counties, they are available through public clinics. In general, the functions of public health are relatively noncontroversial, professionalized, and do not affect lifestyles of a suburb. There is little incentive for a suburb to provide the service itself, particularly when additional costs are involved.

The county, operating as a state agency, usually administers welfare programs. Federal funds are provided for old age assistance, aid to the blind, dependent children, and the disabled. Few suburban governments operate welfare departments.

There are several other important countywide functions. One of the more significant ones is road building and maintenance. Since state and federal funds cannot support all road building and maintenance, some local agency has to build those roads that carry moderate to heavy traffic loads but do not qualify as state or interstate highways. The county is the logical unit to provide this service. In unincorporated areas, the county highway department acts as the city public works department. In states with townships or boroughs, this responsibility usually is shared.

Townships

Townships, which are smaller than counties in terms of land area, are an important part of the local governing system in certain states. In 1967 there were over 17,000 townships, located primarily in the eastern, midwestern, and great plains states. The township was originally a New England institution. It represented a preference for government "closer to the people," as opposed to the Southern tradition of stronger counties, stemming from a plantation economy that supported large landholdings and a more elitist tradition of governance. This contrast is illustrated in Illinois where the Constitution of 1848 called for local option on townships. Eighty-five of the state's 102 counties voted to create townships. Those counties that did not choose townships were in the southern portion of the state and had been settled by Southerners.[9]

States containing over 900 townships include: Illinois, Indiana, Kansas, Michigan, Minnesota, New York, Ohio, Pennsylvania, North and South Dakota, and Wisconsin. These 11 states have over 85 percent of all townships in the United States and use them to provide certain public services. The township usually has primary or secondary responsibility for town roads. In sparsely populated areas, township government is often the major provider of municipal services and supplies a rudimentary form of general purpose government.[10] In Illinois, townships are authorized to administer health and welfare services, aid to youth and the aged, and to foster civic, educational, and cultural activities. General welfare assistance is the primary social service. Townships located in metropolitan areas have been the most active in this function. In suburban DuPage County, for example, 5 of the 9 townships levied a tax for general assistance, raising over $193,000 in 1970. In Cook County, 27 of 30 townships outside Chicago raised from $5,000 to $360,000 each, for a total of over $3,000,000.

---

[9] L. D. Ahlswede, *Township Government Today* (Springfield, Ill.: Township Officials of Illinois, 1968), pp. 34–35.

[10] Thomas Hady and Clarence Hein, "Congressional Townships as Incorporated Municipalities," *Midwest Journal of Political Science*, November 1964, pp. 408–24.

Public school systems

The most significant suburban public service, in terms of expenditures, is education. Roscoe Martin found that, in the early 1960s, citizens in 34 metropolitan areas ranked schools first in service effectiveness, comparerd to fire, police, health and welfare services. The preference probably would have been even stronger if only suburban residents had been surveyed. Martin concluded:

> The findings . . . corroborate a fundamental tenet of the public school credo, for education is accepted as the basic function of local government by the people, by well-educated and reasonably skilled observers as well as by the common citizen.[11]

Each state has a state department of education headed by a commissioner or superintendent. Often, there is also county school officer or superintendent who provides consultative and technical services to local school districts and sometimes has the power to inspect and regulate them. The primary organizational unit, however, is the local school district. Almost every school district fiercely resists outside control. Residents often take greater pride in their local school system than in their city government. One priority, especially in suburbia, is to "keep the schools out of politics." Suburbanites who left the central city, often so that their children could attend better schools, prize their school system as the basic element of a new or improved life-style.

Wealthy suburban schools have better facilities and can recruit better teachers than central city slum areas. Suburbanites, particularly those in high income areas, generally plan to send their children to college. There is a tendency for curricula to overemphasize a "college track" program at the expense of vocational instruction. Foreign languages and advanced science labs frequently are provided in lieu of home economics and auto mechanic shops. Consequently, the high school student who has little ability or interest in college preparatory programs is penalized.[12]

Many suburban school districts seem to have the best of all possible worlds. They have greater ability than central cities to pay for education, since their tax bases are not as committed to traditional services. Further, there is a financial bias in most state equalization formulas that works in favor of suburban systems and against the central city school district. For example, in 1966–67 the central city school districts in the six New York State metropolitan areas each received at least $100 less per student in state aid than the districts in the rest of the counties. The extremes

---

[11] Roscoe Martin, *Government and the Suburban School* (Syracuse, N.Y.: Syracuse University Press, 1962), pp. 80–81.

[12] James Conant, *Slums and Suburbs* (New York: McGraw-Hill, 1961), pp. 105–9.

were found in the Syracuse area and in Albany. Syracuse received $356 and the suburban Onondaga County districts received $531, a difference of $195 per student. In Albany, central city aid was $307 per pupil compared to $493 for districts comprising the rest of the county, for a difference of $186.[13]

This discrepancy may be remedied by the *Serrano* v. *Priest* decision in California. The court ruled that the state must reallocate school funds to obtain precise equity among districts, so that the quality of a child's education would not vary with the wealth of his school district. It is not likely that this will diminish the favor with which suburbanites eye their school districts. It may alert them, however, to the fact that local control over education may be diminished by state and federal requirements.

Since fewer crucial decisions are being made locally, real local control is vanishing. Professionals control the local managerial positions, teachers come from state schools, school district bureaucracies resist change and absorb tax dollars, and curricula are controlled by the state. Frederick Wirt has argued that when newcomers stimulate controversies over curricula or finances and even take over the school board, little really changes. The new superintendent is usually another trained professional who is unlikely to return control to the "locals." According to Wirt, this trend is even stronger in suburbia due to increased professionalism, support for nonpartisan efficiency and, in general, a low level of political conflict.[14]

Since parents in higher status suburban schools tend to be professionals themselves, they are more supportive of professionalism in the schools. Minar found that support for the schools was higher in high status suburbs, and that social conflict over school status matters occurred more frequently in lower status communities. Higher status districts had lower voting turnouts, but were much more supportive of school policies and tended not to question professional values.[15] The higher the status of the district, then, the more likely that the residents will agree with professional values, reducing the degree of true local control.

Legitimizing professional norms may be the real function of the

[13] Committee for Economic Development, *Reshaping Government in Metropolitan Areas* (New York: Committee for Economic Development, 1970), p. 36.

[14] Excerpt from "Financial and Desegregation Reform in Suburbia," by Frederick Wirt is reprinted from *The Urbanization of the Suburbs*, UAAR, Vol. 7(c) 1973, p. 476 by permission of the Publisher, Sage Publications, Inc.

[15] David Minar, "The Community Basis of Conflict in School System Politics," *American Sociological Review*, Vol. 31 (1966), pp. 822–35. Also see Louis Masotti, *Education and Politics in Suburbia: The New Trier Experience* (Cleveland: Western Reserve University Press, 1967); and Laurence Iannaccone, *Poitics in Education* (New York: Center for Applied Research in Education, 1967).

elected school board. The board almost universally defers to these norms and often perceives itself as responsible for "educational quality" as defined by the superintendent, rather than for representing the voters who elected them. Several factors contribute to this tendency: the superintendent's self image, which demands his autonomy in decision-making; the relative absence of strong constituencies in the community; and the community's ignorance of the school district programs or policies. School board candidates often know very little about the important issues and have a rather vague concept of the board member's role. The superintendent usually socializes the new board members to the workings of the board. Outside criticism aligns the board with the superintendent so that a united front may be presented to charges by citizens or the media.[16] Thus, by accepting the superintendent's definition of the system, the board legitimizes the status quo.

Despite the emphasis on retention of the existing system and the "cooptation" of the new school board members, conflict over school policies occurs. It normally arises in the context of the following major decision areas: curriculum, facilities, organization of districts, personnel, or finance. Generally, curriculum decisions are made by professionals, although conflict can arise at times over content. Decisions on facilities, such as new school sites, often require a local vote. This is one area where citizen control has the greatest effect.

District organizaton decisions usually are made by state legislatures. Conflict arises when state legislators want to consolidate districts for financial or curriculum reasons when citizens prefer smaller units. Since 1942, the number of school districts in the United States has declined from slightly over one hundred thousand to 15,781 in 1972. Nebraska has the most school districts (1,374), and California, Illinois, and Texas each have over 1,000.[17]

Conflict over school policies can become exceedingly rancorous. A recent highly controversial issue is busing to achieve racial balance among districts or within a district. When the issue involves combining a suburban school district with the central school district to form one metropolitan area district, violence is not unusual. The most publicized disturbances were in Detroit, Michigan, and the Richmond-Henrico County, Virginia, area. There was even more violence in 1974–75, when black students were bussed into a white ethnic neighborhood in South Boston. In all of these cases, the decisions were made by the courts rather than the local citizens.

Another area of conflict revolves around the question of curriculum,

---

[16] See Norman Kerr, "The School Board as an Agency of Legitimation," *Sociology of Education,* Vol. 38 (1964), p. 58.

[17] *U.S. Bureau of the Census, 1972 Census of Governments, vol. 1, Governmental Organization* (Washington, D.C.: U.S. Governmental Printing Office, 1973), p. 4.

particularly that which may be regarded as subversive or destructive of the life-styles or values of groups within the district. In 1974, savage divisions occurred over allegedly "filthy, anti-God, and un-American" passages in textbooks used in the Kanawha County, West Virginia, school district, which includes Charleston, the state capital. Classes were suspended for several days by the superintendent because violent demonstrations by hundreds of angry parents, mostly coal mining families from the Kanawha River Valley in the rural southeastern part of the county, made school attendance unsafe for pupils and teachers.

Kanawha County and Boston represent extreme cases; open conflict is the exception rather than the rule. The general problem is how parents or board members can wrestle control from school district professionals. However, gaining control may be a meaningless victory. The school board may discover that the school system is dominated by the teacher's unions or that the need for funds is so critical that outside financial assistance has become essential. Robert Bendiner has stated that boards of education are no longer suitable instruments for dealing with these problems. He believes that the old question of the board's relationship to the superintendent is no longer relevant, and that boards have declined in status and effectiveness.[18]

Special districts[19]

Largely due to financial considerations, unincorporated areas and many small to medium sized cities rely heavily on special districts for the provision of basic services. Many cities cannot tax or bond themselves heavily for legal, financial, and/or political reasons. They must rely on an outside agency not subject to those limitations to provide additional services. Thus, an airport authority builds and finances an airport; a

---

[18] Robert Bendiner, *The Politics of Schools: A Crisis in Self-Government* (New York: Harper and Row, 1969), pp. 82, 154, 162. See also James Guthrie, "Public Report" (Berkeley: Institute of Governmental Studies of the University of California, June 1974), p. 4.

[19] The classic and still most comprehensive work on special districts is John Bollens, *Special Districts in the United States* (Berkeley: University of California Press, 1957), even though it is now two decades old. Another comprehensive study quite reformist in its tone is Advisory Commission on Intergovernmental Relations, *The Problem of Special Districts in American Government* (Washington, D.C.: Advisory Commission on Intergovernmental Relations, 1974). A good recent bibliography is by Anthony White, *Non-School Special Districts in the United States, A Selective Bibliography* (Monticello, Ill.: Council of Planning Librarians Exchange Bibliography, no. 435, 1974). There are two fairly good state surveys. One is on Kansas by William Cape, Leon Graves and Burton Michaels, *Government by Special District* (Lawrence: University of Kansas Government Research Center, 1969). The other is more selective, by David Tees, "A Fresh Look at Special Districts in Texas," in *Government Organization and Authority in Metroplitan Areas,* ed. by Texas Urban Commission (Arlington: Institute of Urban Studies University of Texas, 1971), pp. 37–82.

park district buys and operates park and recreational areas; and a sewage district operates a sewage treatment plant. In almost all cases, the tax base of these improvements still rests on the same property tax base; but a unit that can fund the services is made formally responsible.

Another common reason for reliance on special districts is the need to tailormake service areas. Sewage disposal and fire protection are needed by unincorporated areas as well as by cities. A special district can overlap boundaries to serve the necessary area. This is a very useful device when geographic considerations are important, such as the need for a sewage disposal district to follow the boundaries of a watershed area. Special districts provide a multitude of services and make possible service provision on a larger than local but smaller than county basis. In many cases, they cover parts of several counties, serving those areas that demand urban functions but which cannot or do not want to incorporate as a city. City residents often object to the portion of their county taxes that goes for unincorporated areas. This may make it politically necessary to use a special district with a specific tax base for a specific purpose.

Because of their flexibility, special districts are the fastest growing and most numerous unit of government in the United States. Without them, suburbs would find it much harder to provide services and many urban fringe areas would have to incorporate or be annexed to the city to receive crucial services. Conversely, cities would have to provide those functions, which would considerably increase their total expenditures.

The extensive use of special districts evokes strong feelings from their supporters and from students of the metropolitan and urban scene. Conveniently shaped service areas with taxing freedom can be useful, particularly when the difficulty of arranging comprehensive service delivery systems is considered. In addition, those individuals and groups who are associated with, or benefit from, special districts are their most vociferous supporters. They feel that any attempt to transfer their particular function to a larger unit will cause it to be "swallowed up" by politics. A good deal of citizen interest, time, and energy is channeled into special district activity, which, if incorporated into a larger unit, would probably be lost to more professional and impersonal agencies.

Criticisms of special districts fall into three general categories.[20] The most common criticism involves the way in which they contribute to the fragmentation of the metropolitan area. Service systems are cut up

---

[20] For examples of extremely critical evaluations, see Stanley Scott and John Corzine, *Special Districts in the San Francisco Bay Area: Some Problems and Issues* (Berkeley: University of California, Institute of Government Studies, 1963); Portland State Research Bureau, *Voter Participation in Special Districts* (Portland, Ore.: Mimeo, 1965); and Institute for Local Self-Government, *Special Districts or Special Dynasties? Democracy Denied* (Berkeley, Calif.: Institute for Local Self-Government, 1973).

into single purpose, noncooperating units when one or two multiple functions units might suffice. These fragmented units make little or no contribution to comprehensive metropolitan decisionmaking processes.

Economic drawbacks are another criticism. Most special districts are too small to achieve economies of scale, while they result in creation of more jurisdictions relying on the same property tax base. Although they are useful in some taxing arrangements, they can erode the credit rating of other jurisdictions.

Perhaps the most critical issue is the lack of citizen control. The voter turnout for the election of special district governing boards is well below that of general purpose units of government, often falling as low as 5 percent. These relatively poor turnouts are not surprising, since the average citizen could hardly be expected to keep track of five or ten special districts as well as the more visible units of government that compete for his attention. This "low visibility" of special districts often results in uncontested elections.

In spite of these criticisms, special districts can be more effective in delivering urban and suburban services than broader and more inclusive metropolitan governmental devices or districts. Special districts are growing rapidly and it is likely that they will continue to be a major part of the urban delivery system, because of their flexibility and the fiscal and jurisdictional inability of cities and counties to provide services on the same basis.

GOVERNMENTAL FRAGMENTATION IN THE URBAN AREA

The overlapping of special districts, school districts, townships, cities, and counties, coexisting with separate delivery systems in the metropolitan area, raises questions about the economy and effectiveness of the present system. A variety of more comprehensive systems have been proposed. These proposals include complete consolidation of the metropolitan region into one government, extensive annexation by the central city, establishment of large and powerful multi-purpose districts for regional functions, and delegation to counties of responsibility for urban functions outside the central city.

All of these proposals seek to reduce the excessive fragmentation of governing power that the present system encourages. Large units are considered more economically viable than small units, and more politically responsive than special districts. Presumably, they would improve the service delivery systems by rationalizing boundaries, evening out present service inequities, and equalizing finances. Further, to some reformers the thought of a larger decision-making system is more appealing from a philosophical and, perhaps, psychological point of view. The present system is excessively decentralized and has no capacity for making areawide decisions on major metropolitan problems such as mass transit or open housing. This inability to settle political issues at the local level results in no decisions or in state or federal intervention. Most reformers want a specific locus for the discussion of local urban problems, and no institution has emerged since the central city lost its preeminence.

This demand for a more centralized and rationalized governmental structure is not universal. In the first place, citizens generally have been distrustful of bigness in government. They have rejected almost all metropolitan government proposals. Further, the matter is too complex to be treated as a choice between centralization and decentralization. More of each is needed for different kinds of functions. In addition, there are social integration and economic arguments that *support* the current system and its inherent fragmentation.

Social integration

The social integration approach places primary emphasis on the metropolitan system as it affects the social, psychological, and political needs of groups and individuals. The following list includes the advantages of a decentralized system with many small units, based on a study of the Philadelphia metropolitan area:

1. It provides a source of social identification for individuals and groups, enabling them to relate themselves to the metropolitan system.
2. It curbs feelings of anomie, apathy, and isolation among citizens by reducing the scale of social experience.
3. It provides an institutional device for subpopulations to use in shielding themselves from those with a way of life of which they disapprove.
4. It provides institutional settings for the release of individual and group frustration and grievance through public catharsis.
5. It offers an opportunity for a larger number of elites to exercise power.
6. It expands available opportunities for individual participation as a means of contributing to public policymaking.
7. It assures that political demands will be heard by providing additional points of access, pressure, and control.
8. It permits minorities to avail themselves of government position and power and exert greater influence over policy.[21]

Many of these advantages have been noted earlier. Charles Adrian has placed special emphasis on the value of access to the suburban

---

[21] Thomas Dye, "Metropolitan Integration by Bargaining among Sub-Areas," *American Behavioral Scientist*, May 1962, p. 11.

dweller, and others have noted the advantages of a system that allows free choice of life-style and a grassroots approach to local politics. Self-sufficient suburbs are still an important part of political life in the United States. They could, indeed, act as a buffer against the increasing technocratization and bureaucratization of modern life. In addition they could screen the complexities of metropolitan life for their residents. A multitude of small units performing this important function, at little or no cost to broader social goals, might offset the negative aspects of fragmentation of the metropolitan area.

The urban marketplace

A second, more recent, argument for fragmentation argues that a decentralized system of many diverse local units will result in a better and more satisfactory set of public services. A related position is that such a system of "democratic administration" is close to the political theory of James Madison, who envisioned a system of competing interests checking one another.[22] According to both views, cities and other small units of government are individual actors on the governmental scene, playing out roles either as particularized purveyors of services (the economist's view), or as specialized sets of interests (the political scientist's view).

From an economic standpoint, a multitude of sellers of services would enable citizens to select and purchase the life-style they choose or can afford. The sum of the individual happiness of each citizen might be greater through this process of choice than that resulting from a system dominated by one economic monopoly—like a metropolitan government. This economic viewpoint is strengthened by the findings that economies of scale in providing public services diminish rapidly after a city reaches a population of 50,000.

---

[22] Charles Adrian, "Metropology: Folklore and Field Research," *Public Administration Review*, Summer 1961, pp. 148–57. See also Edward Banfield and Morton Grodzins, *Government and Housing in Metropolitan Areas* (New York: McGraw-Hill, 1958), p. 156; Charles Tiebout "A Pure Theory of Local Expenditures," *The Journal of Political Economy*, October 1965, pp. 416–24; Robert Wood, *Suburbia* (Houghton-Mifflin, 1958); and Robert L. Bish, *The Political Economy of Metropolitan Areas* (Chicago: Markham, 1971). A recent argument for this is by Vincent Ostrom, *The Intellectual Crisis in American Public Administration* (University, Ala.: University of Alabama Press, 1972). Perhaps, the classic argument for the multitude of jurisdictions in the metropolitan area is made by Charles Tiebout, "A Pure Theory." Certainly members of the Public Choice Society look at the metropolitan region in this fashion, and Ostrom adapts their arguments and outlooks to the political theory of Hamilton and Madison in his work cited above. Elinor Ostrom and Gordon Whitaker, "Community Control," follow this line of research in their study of differing police service levels and citizen perception of them between suburbs and central cities. They have extended their Chicago study to Indianapolis, with very similar findings: "Does Local Community Control of Police Make a Difference? Some Preliminary Findings," in the *American Journal of Political Science*, February 1973, pp. 48–77.

Vincent Ostrom, quoting extensively from *The Federalist Papers*, shows that Madison and Hamilton had developed a theory that is applicable to local government and that finds a place for small, fragmented, and overlapping units. Ostrom states that *The Federalist Papers* argued that authority allocated to government structures should be divided to require concurrent majorities among each party to any agreement, and that the legal and political competence of each unit should be limited *vis-à-vis* each other. The domain of a unit of government may be too small to take into account the common interests of interdependent units, but a higher unit of government can resolve the issue, since all governmental units have overlapping functional responsibilities. Finally, dispersion of authority among diverse decisionmaking units assures that rules of law will be enforced against governments officials.[23]

Thus, both fragmentation *and* overlapping responsibility are required for a "democratic administration." It should be clear, nevertheless, that this formula calls for coordination with metropolitan or state authorities. Also, Ostrom indicates that "balkanization" of local units can only be prevented if there is enough overlapping of responsibilities to assure that interdependencies of a metropolitan nature can be handled by competent authorities.[24]

Ostrom's theory, derived from *The Federalist Papers*, is a call for the simultaneous establishment of metropolitan delivery systems as well as independent local units of government. Even though local governments overlap, and some may be less economical than others, they are necessary to the social well being of the citizenry.

Without a mechanism for metropolitan service delivery, where appropriate, the marketplace and social integration models cannot operate effectively. The two-tier system, proposed by the Committee for Economic Development (CED), allows for the strengthening of *local* units through the establishment of strong metropolitan units.[25] However, most metropolitan areas are not taking the CED's advice. Since urban delivery systems in most areas continue to be fragmented and overlapping, the struggle to establish appropriate metropolitan service delivery systems will continue.

SUMMARY

This chapter has examined the ways in which local governments organize to provide services and the reasons for variations in service levels. We have noted that the most significant services characterizing a sub-

---

[23] Vincent Ostrom, *The Intellectual Crisis*, pp. 88–89.

[24] Ibid., pp. 119–21.

[25] Committee for Economic Development, *Reshaping Government in Metropolitan Areas* (New York: Committee for Economic Development 1970), pp. 19–20.

urb's "way of life" include planning, zoning and police protection. Zoning generally involves rigid ordinances that are modified by the process of negotiation. However, municipalities vary greatly in terms of the extent of professionalism employed in the zoning and planning process. As has been noted, no significant relationship has been proven as yet between the use of professional planners and improved urban development.

Styles of police protection also reflect varying community "life-styles." The watchmen, legalistic, and service types each apply different standards in providing protection and, to some extent, reflect different socioeconomic biases and expectations as well as the orientation of a particular police chief.

In contrast to "lifestyle" services are the essential and noncontroversial maintenance or "housekeeping" functions that municipal governments all must perform. These generally are provided directly by the city, but may be contracted out or provided by special districts. Variations in the levels of these services can be attributed to disparities in municipal revenues, variations in professional standards and circumstantial or geographic factors.

A closer assessment of the reasons for variations in service levels reveals that the key factors are the suburb's ability to pay, based upon the extent of its resources, and the need for services, determined by the size of its population. Expenditures, employment levels, the range of services provided and the degree of specialization are disproportionately greater in larger municipalities. Smaller units maintain low levels of services by relying on larger units for many specialized functions.

An analysis of citizen satisfaction with municipal services reveals that it probably is related to the resident's conviction that he has access to local decisionmakers and that officials are responding to his expectations.

A survey of the various governmental units that provide local services includes suburban and nonurban counties, townships, school districts and special districts. Since the county is formally a unit of state government, its services include both state and local functions, including public health, criminal prosecution, juvenile services, and road construction. Townships, located primarily in the East and the Midwest, are often a major provider of municipal services in sparsely populated areas. They often are the prime supplier of general welfare assistance in metropolitan areas.

The fiercely independent local school districts vary greatly in terms of the quality of service provided, suburban districts often being disproportionately advantaged in terms of state aid. But however independent residents wish them to be, school district operations more often are determined by fixed professional standards, inherent bureaucratic resistance to change, state control of curricula, and the general tendency for school board members to comply with the superintendent's values, usually reinforcing the status quo. However, disagreement does occur over highly controversial issues, as demonstrated by recent consolidation, busing, and curriculum conflicts.

Special districts for service provision result from limitations on municipal capacity to raise revenues and from the effort to rationalize the geographic scope of a particular service. Although increasingly popular, special districts have been criticized for fragmenting the metropolitan area and for undermining citizen control.

As the survey of municipal service providers indicates, fragmented patterns prevail in most metropolitan areas. Although reforms designed to centralize service delivery systems have been suggested, numerous advantages of a decentralized system also have been cited. Most notably, fragmented and overlapping systems afford the citizen greater access and control of the system and greater choice in determining his own life-style. Perhaps the ideal formula is one that preserves the "democratic" advantages of the decentralized pattern, while checking individualistic excesses by establishing strong regional authorities.

7

Suburban county government

URBAN SERVICES traditionally have been provided by cities rather than by counties. Until the suburban growth following World War II, counties were the principle administrative units of state government, while city governments provided the fundamental social, economic, and political services. Consequently, many urban citizens viewed the county either as a rural anachronism or as a superfluous level of government, and generally recognized the city rather than the county as their place of residence, even when they lived in the unincorporated suburbs.

When county boundaries were established in the 19th century, geographic considerations were paramount. For example, county boundaries in Iowa were designed so that the county seat would be located within a day's buggy ride of any point in the county. This approach resulted in a very symmetrical pattern of 99 counties in the state. However, the development of automobiles, highways, and telephones has made the original criteria for determining the size of the county obsolete. At the time of the 1970 Census, an average of 28,000 people lived in each Iowa county, which would seem to be hardly enough to provide a tax base for operating a county.

American counties acquired traditional governmental functions when states decided to delegate to them those services that are best administered at the local level. These generally included services such as welfare, juvenile care, roads, public health, court administration, supervision of elections, and maintenance of law and order. A review of the budgets of most of the counties in the United States indicates that these functions

144

are still performed. However, it is no longer possible to generalize about county governments. The functions of *urban* counties—those having a major central city—have changed drastically, and those urban counties that are predominantly suburban have changed even more. In this chapter, *suburban* counties will be defined as counties located in metropolitan areas and having no central city, or which have a central city constituting less than 50 percent of the population.

THE EMERGENCE OF SUBURBAN COUNTIES

Suburban population has grown dramatically since World War II. The 1970 Census documented that 315 counties have a population over 100,000 and 23 of these have populations in excess of one million. Only a handful of medium-sized cities can match the growth rates of the 50 large and rapidly growing counties listed in Table 7-1. Twenty-six of the 50 counties are strictly suburban counties with *no* major central city. In several of the other 24 counties, the central city is not really large enough to dominate the county, so they also might be considered predominantly suburban.

As counties have grown in population, their functions and their citizens' expectations also have changed. Most suburban city populations are too small to support efficient delivery of urban services and many lack the necessary tax base. For these reasons, counties increasingly are being requested to extend existing services and to perform new ones. Such requests are most frequent in suburban counties, especially those without a central city. In counties such as Jackson County (Kansas City), Missouri, and Shelby County (Memphis), Tennessee, where the central city contains a very high proportion of the total county population, the suburban jurisdictions still rely largely on the central city for numerous services that would otherwise have to be provided by the county. However, even these urban counties have increased their services.

The traditional city services that counties now provide include fire protection, writing building codes, providing code inspections, constructing sewer systems, and operating libraries. Suburban counties, like most city governments, recently have become involved in providing a rapidly expanding variety of new governmental functions. Examples include the construction and operation of rapid transit systems, airports, zoological parks, urban renewal projects, sports stadiums, expressways, colleges, universities, water distribution, and air pollution control systems. As population overflowed into the suburbs, the counties had to perform these functions. The increased densities and mounting concern for the environment and the quality of life have had drastic impact on suburban county government.

TABLE 7–1
Fifty fastest growing counties with 1970 populations over 250,000

County population	Percent increase 1960-70	Central city	Suburb of	1970
1. Clark	115.2	Las Vegas	–	273,288
2. Orange	101.8	none	Los Angeles	1,420,386
3. Ventura	89.0	none	Los Angeles	376,430
4. Broward	85.7	Ft. Lauderdale	–	620,100
5. Prince George's.	84.8	none	Washington, D.C.	660,567
6. Suffolk	68.7	none	New York City	1,124,950
7. Santa Clara	65.8	San Jose	–	1,064,714
8. Fairfax	65.5	none	Washington, D.C.	455,021
9. DeKalb	61.8	none	Atlanta	415,387
10. Jefferson (Parish). . . .	61.7	none	New Orleans	337,568
11. DuPage	56.9	none	Chicago	491,882
12. Santa Barbara	56.4	Santa Barbara	–	264,324
13. Macomb.	54.1	none	Detroit	625,309
14. Snohomish	54.0	none	Seattle	865,236
15. Montgomery	53.3	none	Washington, D.C.	522,809
16. Palm Beach	52.9	West Palm Beach	–	348,753
17. Riverside	49.9	Riverside	–	459,074
18. Morris.	46.6	none	New York City	383,454
19. Maricopa	45.8	Phoenix	–	967,522
20. Anne Arundel	44.0	none	Baltimore	297,539
21. Burlington	43.9	none	Philadelphia	323,132
22. Harris	40.1	Houston	–	1,741,912
23. Dallas	39.5	Dallas	–	1,327,321
24. Pinellas	39.4	St. Petersburg -Clearwater	–	522,329
25. Travis	39.3	Austin	–	295,516
26. Monmouth	37.4	none	New York City	459,379
27. Contra Costa	36.5	none	Oakland/San Francisco	558,389
28. San Bernardino.	35.8	San Bernardino	–	684,072
29. Dade	35.6	Miami	–	1,267,792
30. St. Louis	35.2	none	St. Louis	951,353
31. Middlesex.	34.6	none	New York City	583,813
32. Bucks	34.5	none	Philadelphia	415,056
33. Plymouth	34.2	none	Boston	333,314
34. Richmond	33.1	New York City	–	295,443
35. Tarrant	33.0	Ft. Worth	–	716,317
36. Pima.	32.4	Tucson	–	351,667
37. Chester	32.1	none	Philadelphia	278,311
38. Oakland.	31.5	none	Detroit	907,871
39. San Diego.	31.4	San Diego	–	1,357,854
40. Dane.	30.7	Madison	–	290,272
41. Orange	30.6	Orlando	–	344,311
42. Mecklenburg	30.3	Charlotte	–	354,656
43. Lake.	30.3	none	Chicago	382,638
44. Pierce	27.8	Tacoma	–	411,027
45. Baltimore.	26.1	Baltimore	–	621,077
46. Monterey	26.1	Salinas	–	247,450
47. Honolulu	25.7	Honolulu	–	629,176
48. Sacramento.	25.6	Sacramento	–	631,498
49. New Castle	25.5	Wilmington	–	385,856
50. San Mateo	25.2	none	San Francisco	556,234

Source: U.S. Bureau of the Census, Census of Population: 1970, vol. 1, *Characteristics of the Population*, U.S. Summary, part 1 (Washington, D.C., U.S. Government Printing Office, 1971), pp. 1-90, 1-111.

Another significant element in the evolution of suburban county roles and functions has been the key position counties have occupied in the American political party system. The Democratic and Republican parties are actually confederations of state political parties—not national, ideologically-based parties like those in Britain or France. In the 19th century, county party units controlled state politics, since they were the only units to span the entire state. But, in the first half of the 20th century, the city-based party organizations in the major industrial states became more powerful in their metropolitan area than the county organizations. City leaders gained control of both the city and county parties. However, this base of political power again is shifting due to urban growth. County leaders are becoming more important in most urban states. Even in some counties that contain a major central city, the county leader resides in one of the suburban jurisdictions.

Like the states, many counties had gerrymandered the seats on the local legislative board to maintain control over expanding urban areas. By the time the U.S. Supreme Court handed down its one man-one vote ruling to county governing bodies in 1968, the cities generally had passed their population peaks and suburban areas were experiencing a faster rate of growth.[1] The Supreme Court ruling resulted in an increase in the political significance of suburban counties as well as of the suburban portions of large urban counties.

Other factors, including technology, the population explosion, and urbanization also have had a drastic impact on suburban counties. Great pressures have been placed on suburban county governments because rural-dominated state legislatures have not been willing to recognize the inexorable spread of urbanization and also because many cities have attempted to use massive annexation movements as a tactic to maintain their tax base and governmental predominance. Most major central cities are now locked in by the annexations of suburban municipal governments. This situation has created a need for county governments to provide "city-type" services in the unincorporated suburban areas as well as to supplement the services provided by small suburban jurisdictions.

METROPOLITAN IMPACTS

Less apparent than the increased demand for direct urban services by suburban cities has been the impact upon urban leadership. In most metropolitan areas, the major city no longer is able to coordinate governmental services. Many of the small suburban governments were created as a means of avoiding annexation by the central city; these governments remain suspicious of the power of their neighboring large cities. But

---

[1] *Avery* v. *Midland County, Texas,* 88 S. Ct. 1114 (1968).

current service demands are greater than most of these individual suburban units can support. Not only have some state governments failed to help, they often have not even provided legislation that would permit the cities to collect more local taxes for programs requiring metropolitan coordination.[2]

Due to these straining demands, counties are under the same fiscal pressures as central and suburban cities, one factor that contributed to the approval of the federal revenue sharing program. Further, urban fiscal capacity is quite uneven. Most suburban governments have adequate resources, but some smaller suburbs have disproportionately low tax bases and are relatively as poor as many central cities. A leveling device is needed for the financing of urban services to provide more uniformity of tax responsibility and to promote greater management efficiency in the delivery of services.

There are only two sources powerful enough to provide such an organizational or fiscal umbrella—the state and the federal governments. The state governments could impose progressive taxes to help fund some new urban services. They also could utilize the managerial capabilities of their existing administrative units, the counties, either by decentralizing additional functions or by giving counties the full authority they need to meet their new operating responsibilities. Few states have been inclined to such action, even though their cities have been unable to handle the problems which now stretch beyond their borders.

Even cities that have successfully used annexations have learned that many of their problems require regional solutions. In many metropolitan areas, the counties are the natural governmental units to provide such regional solutions since they have the areawide jurisdiction necessary to deal with these problems.

One reason for the intransigence of state governments has been the judicial interpretation of state constitutional powers. Dillon's Rule, first enunciated in 1872, and consistently upheld in state court decisions, limited the powers of municipal corporations or cities.[3] Since counties are not even municipal corporations, the courts have been quite restrictive in determining the extent of county powers to perform urban services. The limitations have hindered suburban counties most since they do not have a central city to rely upon for major services, which their unincorporated areas and small suburban jurisdictions need.

The need for additional area-wide governmental coordination has been obvious for some time. In many respects, especially in the single

---

[2] Laszlo Ecker-Racz, *The Politics and Economics of State-Local Finance* (Englewood Cliffs, N.J.: Prentice Hall, Inc., 1970).

[3] J. F. Dillon, *Commentaries on the Law of Municipal Corporations*, vol. 1 (Boston, Little, Brown and Co.: 5th ed., 1911) pp. 448–50. The ramifications of this ruling will be examined in the following chapter.

county SMSA (127 of the 267 SMSAs), counties are moving to fill this gap in the American federal system.[4] Intergovernmental cooperation, shared powers, metropolitan planning, and functional consolidation are some new approaches being used to resolve urban problems. Urbanization has given the cities and counties a new opportunity to work out a meaningful partnership in the interest of their citizens, and many counties are responding. Further, individual counties, led by a new breed of county officials, are moving forward, even in some states which seem disinclined to play a key role in improving local government.

THE HOME RULE MOVEMENT

Creating metropolitan governments in one or more counties is a drastic measure. The generally unsuccessful attempts of such reform movements will be discussed in Chapter 11. The most characteristic governmental reforms consist of efforts to adapt the structures and functions of existing governments to the needs of 20th-century urban society. One means of accomplishing this is through the home rule charters, which some states permit. Like city charters, these charters are permanent grants of power. In effect, they designate counties as the units to provide city services in large urban areas. Even where home rule charters are not permitted by the state constitution and statutes, state governments may pass laws providing for county changes. Steps such as reorganization and upgrading of services in noncharter counties, facilitated by state legislation, are also helpful in reforming local government structure. Efforts to secure gradual adaptation are best identified as the "home rule" and "New County" movements.

Prof. Charles R. Adrian defines home rule as "the power granted to local units of government to frame, adopt, and amend charters for their government, and to exercise powers of local self-government, subject to the constitution and general laws of the state."[5] Home rule is one means of giving suburban county governments authority commensurate with their responsibilities—it gives them increased financial flexibility. Increased usage of the home rule concept in state-local relations also would free state legislatures from detailed local involvement, enabling them to concentrate their efforts on matters of genuine state-wide concern.

Gradually, the states are adopting more liberal local government controls. For example, 13 states—California, Florida, Hawaii, Maryland,

---

[4] U.S. Office of Management and Budget, *Standard Metropolitan Statistical Areas* (Washington, D.C.: U.S. Government Printing Office, 1967), as updated by periodic press releases.

[5] Charles R. Adrian, *State and Local Government* (New York: McGraw-Hill, 1960), pp. 122–24.

Montana, New Jersey, New York, Ohio, Oregon, Pennsylvania, South Dakota, Utah, and Washington—permit all counties to exercise home rule powers. Missouri and Texas permit the counties meeting a minimum population requirement to adopt home rule. New Mexico has established a criterion based on the assessed valuation of property; at this time, Los Alamos is the only county that qualifies. Illinois authorizes home rule only if an elected executive form of government exists.

Before establishing general authorizations, Florida, Hawaii, and New York granted specific home rule powers to special counties. These charters were not affected by the subsequent general grant of authority to counties. Finally, Indiana, Kentucky, Tennessee, and Louisana have granted special authority to specific counties, but have no general provisions permitting home rule for all counties or classes of counties. Similarly, counties in Georgia have been given home rule authority in terms of legislative power; except for the Columbus-Muscogee consolidated government, they may not change the structure of their government. Table 7–2 summarizes these state home rule authorizations.

Eight other states have some provisions relating to home rule for counties, but do not meet all of the Adrian criteria. Kansas and Minnesota have constitutional provisions authorizing home rule; but the state legislatures have not taken the necessary action to permit home rule. The Michigan legislation does not permit full home rule power but designates certain offices as elective and defines specific services and functions that counties may provide.

The incorporated boroughs of Alaska, as well as New Castle County in Delaware, operate under legal provisions that permit essentially the same powers the home rule statutes provide. However, they are not considered home rule counties because the respective state governments define the structure of government and even designate the powers of administrative departments.

Virginia has a unique city-county separation system. No cities are part of a county but they are empowered to exercise the powers of a county as well as of a city. This system also has encouraged numerous city-county consolidations, which are discussed in Chapter 11. However, the state controls too many specific aspects of local organization to qualify as a state that permits home rule. Virginia counties may adopt only five alternate forms of governmental structure.

In states that qualify, the county charters are written by local citizens and are voted upon by the county electors. Except in Hawaii, where the constitution permits only the governing board to establish a charter commission, voters in the county may initiate the charter procedure. In a number of states, the county governing board may also be the initiator. Texas, New York, and Ohio require that the charter receive majorities in both the incorporated and unincorporated areas of the

TABLE 7-2
State home rule provisions

Applicability	Year authorization passed
All counties	
California	1911
Florida	1971
Hawaii*	1963
Maryland	1915
Montana	1972
New Jersey	1972
New York†	1959
Ohio	1933
Oregon	1959
Pennsylvania	1972
South Dakota	1972
Utah	1972
Washington	1948
Counties in a certain classification	
Illinois‡	1970
Missouri	1945
New Mexico	1964
Texas	1933
Special counties	
Florida	
Jacksonville-Duval County	1967
Miami-Dade County	1956
Georgia	
Columbus-Muscogee	1970
Hawaii	
City and County of Honolulu	1959
Indiana	
Indianapolis-Marion County	1969
Kentucky	
Fayette-Lexington County	1972
Louisiana	
Baton Rouge-East Baton Rouge Parish	1946
Jefferson Parish	1956
New York	
Nassau County	1937
Suffolk County	1958
Westchester County	1937
Tennessee	
Nashville-Davidson County	1957

* This does not pertain to the City and County of Honolulu, which adopted a charter in 1959 under prior legislative authority.

† The three New York counties listed in the special counties category adopted charters under special legislative acts passed before the county charter law was enacted.

‡ The county needs an elected county executive form of government before it can become a home-rule county. This structural device is spelled out in the state constitution.

Source: Thomas P. Murphy, *Metropolitics and the Urban County* (Washington, D.C.: National Association of Counties and Washington National Press, 1970), p. 38.

county. California is the only state that requires that the county charter be approved by the state legislators as well as by the voters. This has not proven detrimental since all ten California counties that have submitted such charters have had them approved.[6]

Although home rule charters have been adopted more readily than proposals for metropolitan government, a number have been defeated. Further, many counties authorized to proceed with home rule movements have not done so. Consequently, home rule charter counties exist in only 14 of the 22 states listed in Table 7–2. In these states, there are 64 charter counties, of which 41 have been approved since 1960. New York and California contain 29 of the 64 charter counties. The year of greatest activity in terms of home rule legislation and constitutional change was 1974, when four New Jersey counties and another New York county adopted charters. This indicates that the movement is becoming more prevalent. It is no accident that over half of the home rule counties are clearly suburban counties.

The states that have authorized home rule but have not as yet had counties utilize it are Montana, Ohio, Pennsylvania, South Dakota, Texas, and Utah. However, some of these authorizations were passed as recently as 1972; as counties in these states take the necessary actions, the number of charter counties should continue to increase.

Although only California, Maryland, New York, and Texas require home rule charter counties to have a legislative body, all 50 charter counties in the country have provided for them. The expansion of county power to include legislative authority to pass laws and ordinances constitutes one of the most significant home rule powers. Most of the charters spell out the procedures to be used in passing legislation and amending the county charter.

The most striking structural change made by charter counties relates to the establishment of centralized executive authority. Only four of the charter counties have retained the traditional plural executive structure that incorporates both legislative and executive power. The majority of the charter counties established a county council and made some provisions for concentrating executive authority and leadership. In this way, the voters could hold one person directly accountable for actions taken on the county level. Even counties that chose to retain a relatively strong council, rather than to create an elected executive, provided for some centralization of executive authority, usually by creating the position of county manager. This chief administrative officer is empowered to develop the county budget for presentation to the county council, to direct the administrative departments of the county, and to appoint or to recommend the appointment and removal of department heads.

---

[6] National Association of Counties Research Foundation, *County Home Rule,* January 1968, pp. 9–11.

With the exception of those in California, most of the major urban and suburban counties established an elected executive position. This trend is particularly strong in New York, where 13 of 18 charter counties have an elected county executive. Two other counties have established a strong county council chairman position, analogous to an elected executive. Most of the elected county executives have authority to veto legislation passed by the council, subject to the council's power to override it.

A corollary to the establishment of either an elected or appointed central executive position, such as a county manager, is a general reduction of independently elected county officials. Counties adopting home rule charters generally have retained only those independently elected officials whose duties are at least partially judicial in nature, such as prosecuting attorneys and sheriffs.

These recent developments in county government demonstrate that the suburban county will have an increasingly significant role in the future of local government in metropolitan areas. Many major suburban counties now clearly are responsible for providing urban services throughout the county and are a major participant in metropolitan decisionmaking. The states that have supported these counties are contributing much to the vitality of the American federal system.

NEW COUNTY, U.S.A.

Home rule is not the only mechanism for county modernization. Other actions, such as state enabling legislation for reorganization, taxation, and new services, also can help suburban counties meet the demands of urbanization. Counties also can take some actions under existing legislation to improve their management.

Even a home rule charter will not insure county effectiveness unless good management techniques are developed. The functional shortcomings of counties are reflected in their organizational structure. Because of American experience with the British monarch and his royal governors, few counties originally were provided with a strong executive. In some states, their legislative authority is still unclear. The county governing body—board of supervisors, commission, county court, etc.—is a multiple member body of part-time officials whose experience is more likely to be political rather than administrative.

County administration generally has suffered from the absence of strong leadership and a lack of professionalism. This, in turn, has made it difficult to fix political responsibility for county government. Many of the original administrative functions assigned to the county—such as operating jails, patrolling highways, maintaining and constructing highways, providing welfare payments and juvenile care, assessing property, and recording deeds—were the responsibility of elected officials.

The county governing board had little power over such officials, who were subject only to the electorate. This type of structural arrangement encouraged logrolling (the trading of votes to secure favorable action on special interest projects) among elected officials, rather than responsible administration.

In 1969, the National Association of Counties (NACO), which has provided technical assistance to counties attempting to modernize their governments, organized a special campaign called "New County— U.S.A." Assisted by Ford Foundation grants, NACO systematically began to disseminate briefing material on reorganization and management improvement programs in various functional areas of county government. At the annual NACO conference, specific county improvements are acknowledged by a New County Achievement Award. As of 1974, 805 awards have been made for county programs dealing with such problems as delinquency, computer timesharing, library systems, jury reform, drug abuse, solid waste management, emergency ambulance service, and air pollution control. Many of these services have never been provided before by county governments.

In 1971, the Advisory Commission on Intergovernmental Relations (ACIR), in cooperation with NACO and the International City Management Association, surveyed the functions that city and county governments were performing.[7] The survey considered a total of 58 different functions. More than 50 percent of the 150 reporting urban counties performed 21 of those functions and more than 20 percent of the counties performed at least 45 functions. Table 7–3 lists the 45 major functions in order of frequency of performance. The additional 13 functional areas, in which a smaller percentage of the counties were involved, included the maintenance of cemeteries, auditoriums, fish and game, public housing, museums, power supply, parking facilities, irrigation systems, urban renewal, cultural affairs, and ports and harbors.

A relatively high percentage of metropolitan counties also performed major urban functions. In contrast, many nonmetropolitan counties were not involved with such programs as crippled children's aid, animal control, parks and recreation, public defense, planning, zoning, subdivision control, and veterans affairs. While this survey indicated the extensive involvement of urban counties in metropolitan functions, it also revealed some areawide functions where urban county involvement is essential but is still at a relatively low level. Specifically, only 19 percent of the urban counties were involved with public housing, 11 percent with parking, 9 percent with urban renewal, and 5 percent with mass transit. The percentage of counties performing these functions probably will increase as the density of urban counties increases.

---

[7] Advisory Commission on Intergovernmental Relations, *Profile of County Government,* January 1972, p. 22.

TABLE 7-3
Rank order of functions performed by 150 urban county governments

Function	Number	Percent of total
1. Jails and detention homes	145	97
2. Coroner's office	130	87
3. Courts	130	87
4. Tax assessment collection	125	83
5. Public health	120	80
6. Prosecution	120	80
7. Probation and parole service	119	79
8. Police protection	117	78
9. Roads and highways	117	78
10. General assistance public welfare	114	76
11. Planning	114	76
12. Agricultural extension services	112	75
13. Medical assistance	105	70
14. Mental health	104	60
15. Libraries	86	57
16. Veteran's affairs	86	57
17. Parks and recreation	83	55
18. Zoning	82	55
19. Crippled children	78	52
20. Public defender	77	51
21. Subdivision control	77	51
22. Animal control	75	51
23. Data processing	65	43
24. Code enforcement	63	42
25. Hospitals	61	41
26. Central purchasing	60	40
27. Soil conservation	59	39
28. Secondary schools	58	39
29. Special education programs	57	38
30. Mosquito abatement	56	37
31. Elementary schools	56	37
32. Solid waste disposal	55	37
33. Air pollution	55	37
34. Personnel services	52	35
35. Flood and drainage control	51	34
36. Sewers and sewage disposal	50	33
37. Fire protection	47	31
38. Water pollution	45	30
39. Junior colleges	40	27
40. Airports	36	24
41. Livestock inspection	34	23
42. Ambulance service	34	23
43. Industrial development	32	21
44. Refuse and garbage collection	31	21
45. Water supply	31	21

Source: Advisory Commission on Intergovernmental Relations, *Profile of County Government* (Washington, D.C.: U.S. Government Printing Office, 1972), p. 23.

A further significant indicator of the increasing county involvement in providing traditional municipal services is reflected in the transfer of governmental functions from cities to counties. In over 20 percent of the counties reporting, nine functions (police protection, health services, planning, libraries, jails, public welfare, roads and highways, sewers and sewage disposal, and refuse and garbage collection) had been transferred from subcounty areas to the county government. Further, there was no function that as many as 10 percent of the reporting counties transferred to a sub-county jurisdiction. Two areas involving significant transfers to subcounty governments were roads and highways (9 percent) and fire protection (7 percent). These data were drawn from a survey sample that included both urban and rural counties, but the expansion of county services would appear even more pronounced if only counties in urban areas were considered.

In addition to these transfers of functions, suburban counties also can perform services for their municipalities on the basis of a contract. All states permit local governments to contract among themselves for the performance of governmental services. Most states require that there be a favorable county-wide referendum before such a transfer of functions takes place. In other cases, a local ordinance must be passed or an agreement ratified by the county and the other units of local government involved.

The ACIR survey indicated that 29 percent of the responding counties provided one or more municipal services for the individual local governments within their boundary on a contractual basis. The same percentage of counties perform functions in cooperation with local governments in the county on a joint or consolidated basis. Finally, about 23 percent of the counties perform services on a joint basis with one or more other counties.

All services are not necessarily performed on a county-wide basis; that is, some of these functions are performed by the county only in the unincorporated areas. According to the ACIR survey, the functions most likely to be performed only in the unincorporated areas were planning, zoning, subdivision control, code enforcement, police and fire protection, and road maintenance. On the other hand, the services most likely to be provided exclusively in the incorporated areas are refuse and garbage collection, sewage disposal, water supply, police and fire protection, airports, and libraries.[8]

Urban counties are expanding their powers over land use at a very rapid rate. A survey of 45 large metropolitan counties indicated that a surprisingly high percentage—78 percent—had adopted a comprehensive land use plan. In addition, the counties were very active in controlling zoning ordinances and subdivision regulations for unincorporated

---

[8] Ibid., p. 29.

areas. The number of counties dealing in municipal zoning ordinances, subdivision regulations, and subdivision plats has increased in recent years but is still relatively low considering that the sample was restricted to the 45 largest metropolitan counties.[9]

As suggested in Chapter 6, the growth of special districts indicates the counties' inability to provide areawide services. Often this inability is financial and the special district is organized to circumvent the county's financial limitations. In 1972, there were 23,885 special districts, excluding school districts. This represented a 40 percent increase over the previous decade. Even this is misleading because the total number of school districts—the largest category in the total—declined during the decade.

The most common special districts in metropolitan counties were for education (60 percent), soil conservation (41 percent), fire protection (37 percent), sewage (36 percent), water supply (29 percent), libraries (27 percent), hospitals (26 percent), and parks and recreation (26 percent). Seventeen percent of the metropolitan counties reported special districts related to housing and renewal, 15 percent for air pollution, and 11 percent for solid waste disposal.[10] According to the ACIR survey, over 80 percent of the counties (rural and urban):

> are authorized to approve formation of eight types of special districts: drainage, irrigation, flood control, air pollution, solid waste, water supply, housing and urban renewal, and sewage. Fifty percent or more of all the responding counties were empowered to approve special district formation for all categories, except education. One third or more of the counties were empowered to approve the budgets of, and provide financial assistance to each of the listed special districts.[11]

As indicated in Chapter 6, special districts fragment governmental authority, but in many cases, the counties had no alternative mechanism available to provide the service and fund it. Many states restrict the amount that counties may tax their citizens. At the same time, these states usually permit the establishment of districts for specialized purposes, which districts, in turn, are permitted to levy a tax in addition to that imposed by the county. Consequently, even though the county may have the power to prevent their establishment, special districts may be the only option it has to fund the service. Some states also restrict counties from having a differentiated level of services throughout their territories. Thus, the only way to provide an urban service to a part of the county may be to create a special district. In some cases, counties are restricted from using their general revenues to perform

---

[9] Ibid., pp. 34–35.
[10] Ibid., p. 39.
[11] Ibid., p. 40.

new urban functions. In these instances, special districts are one of the few means of providing the services for the affected areas.

FORMS OF COUNTY GOVERNMENT ORGANIZATION

The forms of county government may be classified by identifying where the responsibility lies for administering county functions. There are a variety of forms, ranging from the simple to the complex, and from those highly accountable to the electorate to those relatively insulated. Administrative effectiveness depends as much on form as it does on leadership and professionalism.

Virtually all counties originally were established with a board of commissioners, supervisors, or judges prescribed by the state. This form of government provided for a large number of independently elected county officials for the various functional offices, such as treasurer, attorney, assessor, coroner, sheriff, and even highway engineer. Accordingly, there was no single responsible administrator in the typical county government. The board of commissioners generally had budgetary authority over the other elected officials and acted as the county legislature. Under this system, county executive functions were performed jointly by a handful of administrators hired by the board and by the other independently elected officials. This form of government may be characterized as the plural executive form and is similar to the commission form of city government.

If there is any central administrative force under the commission or plural executive form of government, it derives from the power and capability of the administrators working for the board of commissioners, especially those in the budgetary role. However, there is rarely even a central personnel officer for the county. Also, the independently elected officials, who have their own base of political power, are not very responsive to central administration. They hire and fire staff on the basis of political rather than professional criteria.

The county administrator plan

Many suburban counties with a board of commissioners or supervisors have adopted a county administrator form of government. In some cases, state statutes have authorized the change. Because the county legislative body serves only part-time, it often hires a chief administrative officer (CAO) to perform staff work and to coordinate the activities of other administrative and clerical personnel who are responsible to the board. The CAO usually is responsible for making budgetary decisions, as well as for submitting staff reports on county functions and recommendations for ordinances. The office also attempts to centralize purchasing power in the county, including purchases made by the independently elected officials.

Though this plan represents an effort to centralize executive responsibility for the county, the continued existence of independently elected officials with administrative functions presents a major challenge to the power of the chief administrator. Further, many counties that have an administrative assistant or a chief administrative officer still employ a chief legal officer who reports directly to the board. This tends to dilute the power of the administrative officer. The county administrator plan is most prevalent in California where, as of 1972, 17 counties had established chief administrative officer positions under general state legislation.

The county council-manager plan

The council-manager form of government is patterned after the city manager form of government. While somewhat similar to the county administrator plan, it provides for a much stronger central administrator. This type of change generally requires authorization by state statute and perhaps even a constitutional amendment. Formal adoption of the county manager plan usually involves some reduction in the number of independently elected officials, as well as some of the functions and powers of the central administrator.

The board of commissioners or the county council usually hires the county manager, stipulating certain powers similar to those a city manager derives from a city charter. For example, the county manager ordinarily has a variety of powers including: the hiring and firing of county employees; formulating and administering the annual budget; evaluating the performance and coordinating the operation of the various county departments; negotiating county contracts for council review and approval; coordinating the operation of the various county departments; and exercising some leadership in proposing county functional programs and intergovernmental relationships in the metropolitan area.

Functions formerly performed by independently elected officials, whose positions are abolished by the establishment of the county manager form of government, are assigned to newly created administrative departments that report to the county manager. For example, most counties that abolish the elected positions of treasurer, assessor, recorder, and county clerk, organize most of these functions into a department of finance.

In the council manager form of government, the county council retains the ultimate power over the manager; but the council rarely interferes with the powers granted to him by the legislation or charter creating the office. Essentially, a county council's actions are restricted to legislative roles, including, of course, the power to adopt the county budget and to set tax levies. In some counties, the council chairman is elected by the council from among its members; in other counties, the chairman may be directly elected by the voters and may even be called "mayor," as in the Miami-Dade County Council.

The county executive plan

The county executive plan, patterned after the big city mayor-council plan, is the most popular form of government organization in the suburban counties that desire a full-time political leader. Variations of the plan may include: a two or four year term; membership on the county council; the power to veto bills or ordinances; and the power to hire a deputy county executive or county administrator to provide professional administrative support. Due to these differences as well as to variations in political talent, some elected county executives have greater influence than others. Regardless of the exact allocation of powers, the county executive is elected directly by the people and is expected to serve full time. The position includes nearly all of the administrative responsibilities of a strong mayor. However, in a number of cases, the appointment of the county executive's administrative deputy is subject to council approval. St. Louis County in Missouri; Nassau and Westchester Counties in New York; and Baltimore, Montgomery, and Prince George's Counties in Maryland are examples of totally suburban counties using the elected county executive system.

Organizational overview

The current trend in suburban government is to move away from the plural executive or commission forms. In the largest suburban counties, where political leadership is paramount, the county executive form is being introduced; other major suburban counties are adopting the county administrator and county manager forms.

NACO's "New County—U.S.A." program to update and modernize county government is accelerating the transfer of ideas between counties, while providing some technical assistance to counties seeking modernization. The pressures for counties to perform still more functions are steadily increasing and are precipitating modernization.

SUBURBAN COUNTY LOBBYING: A CASE STUDY

One of the clearest effects of suburban growth after World War II has been the increasing national role and political power of urban counties. Population overflow from large cities such as New York, Chicago, Los Angeles, Philadelphia, and Washington, and the rapid population growth in areas such as California, Arizona, Texas, and Florida, have increased the responsibilities and opportunities of suburban counties. This change was relatively rapid so that, even today, many intellectuals and federal officials discussing the "urban crisis" are referring only to the fiscal and social problems faced by the nation's central cities. Few realize that suburban counties are subjected to the same pressures and are in just as serious a crisis.

There are several reasons for this insensitivity to county problems. First, the growth of county power and needs has been a relatively recent phenomenon. Second, until the 1960s, NACO, which represents county interests at the national level, was dominated by rural counties. Third, state control of county functions, processes, and finances delayed the development of federal concern with county problems.

A significant impetus for an increase in county power came from the one man-one vote decisions of the U.S. Supreme Court in the 1960s. *Baker* v. *Carr* reduced the power of rural counties in state governments.[12] Equally significant was the case of *Avery* v. *Midland County*, which required the reapportionment of county governmental bodies as well as state legislatures.[13] In this case, 95 percent of the county population lived in Midland City, but only one of the six commissioners was selected from that city. The other 5 represented rural districts with populations between 400 and 800 persons. As a result of the reapportionment, Midland City residents were elected to all six positions. However, the long-term effect of the decision was to preclude central city politicians who were controlling major urban counties, from denying proportionate representation to their burgeoning suburbs. In some cases, this eventually resulted in political control of the county by suburbanites.

According to Robert C. Wood, former Undersecretary and Secretary of the U.S. Department of Housing and Urban Development, "people have been talking and writing books about the counties rising and the cities declining for decades. Two things have been preventing the counties from reaching their destiny—a big identity problem, and their structure."[14] The new suburban counties are confronting these organizational problems directly. Their more efficient governmental units are changing the image of inept county government, which has been the basis of the identity problem. The reorganized home rule counties and the large Western counties are increasingly taking on new urban functions. The elected county executive has provided the leadership focus that mayors always have provided for cities. Finally, since NACO is giving counties a "ringside seat" at Washington, suburban counties are being covered by more federal programs.

---

[12] *Baker* v. *Carr*, 367 U.S. 186 (1962).

[13] *Avery* v. *Midland County, Texas*, 88 S. Ct. 1114 (1968).

[14] William Lilley III, "Washington Pressures/Friendly Administration, Growth of Suburbs Boost Counties' Influence," *National Journal Reports*," May 29, 1971, p. 1132.

One factor promoting these changes is the fact that counties rather than the cities are growing in population and contain greater numbers of voters. Most major cities have leveled off and even have declined in population. Those that are still growing are doing so at a slower rate than their suburban counties. County executives now preside over more metropolitan constituents than do big city mayors.

NACO's Executive Director, Bernard F. Hillenbrand, has said that the power and influence of mayors at the national level is declining because their constituencies are a smaller proportion of the voters, and contain more than a proportionate share of the nation's aged, poor, and minority citizens.[15] In contrast, the suburban counties and the suburban portions of counties with central cities are the centers of economic growth. They rapidly are providing the services needed by the young adults and the professionals who comprise a higher percentage of the suburban than the city population.

It is no coincidence that NACO and the Nixon administration were very friendly. The most powerful counties in the nation in terms of flexibility, responsibility, and authority have been in California, the home state of the ex-President. Ex-Vice President Agnew was an elected county executive of Baltimore County, one of the major totally suburban counties, before becoming governor of Maryland in 1966. Furthermore, C. D. Ward, NACO's chief counsel and lobbyist from 1960 to 1968, became one of the former vice president's top assistants. NACO also capitalized upon personal friendships of its elected county officials with key administration leaders, including John D. Ehrlichman of King County, Washington, former director of the President's Domestic Council. NACO has used a variety of tactics to shake its rural image and to force the national bureaucracies to pay more attention to county needs.

To accomplish this, NACO had to overcome its resource problems. For example, the National League of Cities (NLC) and the U.S. Conference of Mayors (USCOM) have more than 60 professionals on their central lobbying, research, and representation staff. NACO has a smaller staff, which includes only five professionals, but has used a series of legislative steering committees composed of elected county officials who exert a direct lobbying effort with Congress, as well as with federal bureaucrats. As the political power of counties has increased, this process has become more effective and more counties have joined NACO. In 1975, the NACO budget was $1.3 million and over 1,1100 counties belonged to the Association.[16]

---

[15] *Interviews* with Bernard Hillenbrand, November 28, 1972, and January 12, 1975.

[16] This is over one third of the counties in the United States. NACO recognizes 3,106 counties, ACIR 3,049 and the Census Bureau 3,045. The differences are due to disagreement over how to count the Alaska boroughs and the city-counties. For more details see Susan W. Torrence, *Grass Roots Government: The County in American Politics* (Washington-New York: Robert B. Luce, Inc., 1974), pp. 211–12.

Recent reorganization of county governmental structures has helped to strengthen NACO's lobbying efforts. In earlier years, the counties were dominated almost uniformly by county commissioners, who represented government by committee. Now 58 counties, including 33 with populations over 100,000, have elected county executives. These elected executives are becoming extremely significant politically. In many cases, they far outshine the mayor of their central city. Several city council members have even resigned to run for county office because the county is now in a more prestigious and powerful political position.

Another factor in NACO's legislative success has been Hillenbrand's position that it should not act as anti-urban force, but rather as a metropolitan association concerned with both central city *and* county problems. This has enabled NACO to team up with NLC, USCOM, and other public interest groups to try to secure necessary new federal legislation and funding for urban county services.

NACO's new influence has been felt most strongly on basic issues, such as water and sewer grants for county governments. Federal legislation for this program, water and sewer facilities grants was approved in 1965 and provided for matching grants of up to 50 percent of the cost of the new water and sewer facilities. By making this program for *new* facilities, the legislation favored the suburban and rural programs rather than those in the inner cities. This alone represented a suburban county triumph. The county lobby also succeeded in increasing the authorization for this program from $100 million to $1 billion in one year. They accomplished this in the face of the combined opposition of President Nixon, the Republican leadership, and the Democratic chairman of the House Appropriations Committee. While these leaders were not necessarily opposed to the county program, they tried to stop it on the basis of its cost. Nevertheless, NACO successfully overcame a presidential veto to secure the money.

NACO used effective lobbying strategy and good staff work to achieve its victory. It mobilized a variety of private lobbies with an interest in the water and sewer projects. They included the National Clay Pipe Institute, the Cast Iron Pipe Institute, the Concrete Pipe Association, the Consulting Engineers Council, and a variety of individual companies from the building industry. During that 1970 battle, NACO secured from the U.S. Department of Housing and Urban Development (HUD), the department responsible for the water and sewer programs, a breakdown of requests from county and city governments. The data revealed a backlog of $2.5 billion in applications.[17] This information came out at a time when HUD was telling Congress that there was only a $500 million backlog and that the presidential request was adequate for current needs. NACO arranged that data by congressional district and publi-

---

[17] Lilley, "Washington Pressures," pp. 1138–39.

cized it widely. This forced a number of members of Congress into the position of either supporting NACO or opposing the interests of their home districts.

More recent NACO successes have involved the fight for welfare reform and for revenue sharing. In 22 of the 50 states, counties rather than states or cities are responsible for the welfare functions. California, Michigan, Minnesota, New Jersey, New York, and Ohio are included among those states. NACO's goal has been to insure that welfare costs are federalized so that this tremendous burden eventually will be lifted from the county budgets. The fight for family assistance, the Family Assistance Program, represented the first major piece of legislation in NACO's 36-year history on which it was the lead lobby. Although the measure was shelved in the closing days of the 92d Congress, the success achieved to that point served to strengthen NACO's political power with the administration.

NACO also played a major role in the successful campaign for general revenue sharing in 1972. Counties often have been excluded from the categorical grant programs of the 1960s. Therefore, they had more to gain from a plan which gave lump sums to local governments on the basis of their population. In the case of cities, much of the money to be received in the general revenue-sharing program would merely replace categorical aid money already being received. NACO worked carefully on the legislation with the major public interest groups. One specific provision favorable to counties written into the draft at the time prohibited a population cutoff for jurisdictions participating in the tax sharing. This enabled every county in the U.S. to participate. Under prior bills, only one in four counties would have been eligible.

NACO displayed extremely assertive and imaginative lobbying on the revenue-sharing measure. Regional "jet-ins" were scheduled throughout the country. Major administration and NACO officials and all county officials were invited. In addition to building support for the revenue-sharing measure and demonstrating the political clout of the counties—thereby strengthening its hand in other administration negotiations—NACO used the jet-ins to fortify its relationship with county governments.

In the Nixon administration, federal officials no longer traveled about the country making speeches concerning the "problems at the federal, state, and city level." They were very careful to recognize "county" government as part of the federal system. The Republican party demonstrated this new awareness in 1972. The Republican platform was the first party platform in history to make specific reference to the problems of county government. The Democratic party delegates probably will correct their party's 1972 oversight by writing a similar provision into its 1976 national platform. Thereafter, both parties presumably will make specific platform reference to the problems of county government and their plans to help alleviate them. Clearly, the National Association of Counties has made counties a new force in national urban and suburban policymaking.

SUMMARY

A county is the basic geographic subdivision of a state, and county government significantly affects most Americans. More than 3,000 counties provide services for some 43 percent of the populace. The fastest growing counties are the major suburban counties.

Counties occupy a key position in the U.S. political party system. Not only do they act as the primary organizational unit of political party systems, but county leaders play an important role in government decisionmaking at the metropolitan level. Increased urbanization has given suburban counties greater influence in metropolitan areas. Meaningful relationships can be established between county and city officials because the suburban counties now have something to contribute.

In an attempt to deal with 20th-century pressures, many counties have adopted home rule charters. However, to establish home rule authority, a county must receive sanction from its state legislature. The states jealously guard the power they exercise over counties. The establishment of power in a centralized executive and the legislative authority to pass laws and ordinances constitute the most significant effects of home rule. This power is essential if suburban counties are to perform well.

County governments are playing an increasingly important role in terms of the delivery of services to their citizens. Through the auspices of the National Association of Counties, a special effort has been made to help counties better manage and coordinate their functional programs. NACO has played an increasingly assertive role in making counties an effective and influential partner in metropolitan decisionmaking. The suburban counties being called upon to supplement the services of their small municipalities, as well as to serve their unincorporated areas, are in the best position to profit from NACO's leadership.

Suburban county governments have felt the pressures on their structure and organization in proportion to their service responsibilities, which have prompted many structural changes. Three forms of county government are being used today. The *county administrator plan* attempts to centralize executive responsibility in the chief administrative officer. The *council-manager form* is similar to the city manager form used in large cities. The role of central administrator is given to the manager, while the council performs the legislative function. The most popular and rapidly spreading of the three plans is the *county executive plan,* analogous to the large city mayor-council plan. The executive is popularly elected and acts as a full-time administrator—usually backed up by a professional deputy county manager.

As urban counties have increased their responsibilities, they have felt a great need to lobby for political power. The National League of Cities and the U.S. Conference of Mayors coordinate their activities on research projects and lobby for legislation. NACO has collaborated effectively with them on legislation affecting all metropolitan area units of government. It also has taken the lead in securing federal support for the new responsibilities and service roles of counties in general, but especially of suburban counties.

8

States and suburbs

SUBURBAN CITIES and counties are creatures of the state. Their actions, programs, and financial activities all ultimately are dependent upon their relationship to the state. In this chapter we will examine: (1) the legal and political relationship between city and state; (2) the issue of local structural reform as it relates to the state; (3) the manner in which states become involved organizationally in urban affairs; (4) the nature of state/local fiscal relations; (5) the extent to which states directly provide urban services; (6) the way states determine minimum standards and provide technical assistance to localities; and (7) the intervention of the national government into key areas of state/local relations. To illustrate these many complex relationships, a case study of state/local law enforcement activities will be provided.

STATE AND LOCAL RELATIONSHIPS—AN OVERVIEW

Chapter 7 discussed the relationship of counties to their states. The municipalities within a state also are legally subordinate to the state. This position was firmly established in 1868 when the Iowa Supreme Court handed down a ruling eventually to be known as Dillon's Rule. Iowa Supreme Court Judge John Dillon wrote in that decision:

> Municipal corporations owe their origin to, and derive their powers and rights wholly from the legislature. It breathes into them the breath

of life, without which they cannot exist. As it creates, so may it destroy. If it may destroy, it may abridge and control.[1]

Looked at from the viewpoint of the suburban city, what this meant, in Dillon's words, was that:

> a municipal corporation possesses, and can exercise, the following powers, and no others: first, those granted in express words; second, those necessarily or fairly implied in, or incident to, the powers expressly granted; third, those essential to the declared objects and purposes of the corporation—not simply convenient but indispensible. Any fair, reasonable, substantial doubt concerning the existence of power is resolved by the courts against the corporation, and the power is denied.[2]

The decision subsequently was upheld by the U.S. Supreme Court. Although Dillon's Rule has been tested numerous times by municipalities seeking loopholes or limitations, it continues to be the ruling principle governing the legal status of cities in the vast majority, if not all, of the states.[3] Legally they are creatures of, and are totally dependent upon the state; they have no rights apart from, or above, those granted by state law.

According to Anwar Syed, author of *The Political Theory of American Local Government,* Dillon's Rule prevailed because state constitutions were then being interpreted rather liberally in regulating private interests and, in this case, against local government interests. Higher courts preferred not to restrict state legislatures in dealing with social and economic problems, because they felt that popular sovereignty meant a broad interpretation of state powers.[4]

However, these legal restrictions on municipalities violate the spirit of local government independence, prevalent since colonial days. Local self-government was extremely important to the early Americans. The desire for local independence was one of the prime causes of the American Revolution, and a strong bias for independent local governments still exists today. Supporters of local government argue that citizens know their local representatives, are politically alert, and are the most qualified to govern themselves due to their proximity to local problems. However, the original independence of local governments, found in the earliest Rhode Island towns, was checkmated by the centralizing tendencies of the state governments, legally established by Dillon's Rule.

---

[1] *City of Clinton* v. *Cedar Rapids and Missouri River Railroad Company,* 24 Iowa 455, 1868; quotation at p. 475, cited in Roscoe Martin, *The Cities and The Federal System* (New York: Atherton Press, 1965), pp. 29–30.

[2] J. F. Dillon, *Commentaries on the Law of Municipal Corporations,* vol. 1 (Boston: Little Brown & Company: 5th ed., 1911), pp. 448–50.

[3] See *Trenton* v. *New Jersey* (262 U.S. 182, 1923), for example. In the decision handed down, municipalities were referred to as departments of a state.

[4] Anwar Syed, *The Political Theory of American Local Government* (New York: Random House, 1966), pp. 68–72.

Several factors considerably mitigate the harshness of this doctrine. One is political reality. Through the weight of sheer numbers of people, cities have political influence. In Maryland, for instance, any Democratic candidate for governor must have the support of the Baltimore Democratic Party. In New York or Illinois, any candidate for statewide office first must make his peace with New York City or Chicago. In any election, where large numbers of voters are significant, the influence of the central cities and their suburban municipalities is great.

Further, localities can secure autonomy over local affairs if the state authorizes home rule for them. Home rule, regarded as a "guarantee of institutional autonomy that enables local government to sit in on the game," varies in nature and scope from state to state.[5] As described in Chapter 7, the most liberal form of home rule grants power to the city to revise its charter at will, but subject to general state law. Since 1875, the Missouri Constitution has contained a provision giving the cities wide latitude with respect to the adoption and amendment of their charters. Other states granting their cities a broad measure of home rule are California, Michigan, and Texas. However, state legislatures have been known to override home rule provisions. Illinois' 1970 Constitution contains a strong home-rule clause, but the state legislature overrode it in 1974 when a bill was considered to exempt real estate firms from local regulations.

The most pervasive limitation on Dillon's Rule is the network of relationships that the federal government has recently established with cities. A large influx of federal aid from specific grants-in-aid for a wide variety of programs—housing, airports, community action, and more recently, revenue sharing—have played a strong role in reducing the cities' dependence upon state subventions. This bypassing of the states by the federal government has served to increase the role of the federal government in urban affairs, prompting recommendations that the states "buy in" to federal grant-in-aid programs. Under such an approach, states would assume the nonfederal share of the costs, reducing the total amount of funds local units would have to provide in order to participate in a particular program. New York State followed this recommendation when it supported the Federal-Aid Airport Program primarily through a sale of state bonds.[6]

Another challenge to Dillons' Rule involves state actions that discriminate against city residents on the basis of race or creed. The State of Alabama modified the boundaries of Tuskegee in order to prevent black

---

[5] Daniel Elazar, *American Federalism: A View from the States* (New York: Thomas Y. Crowell, 1966), p. 167.

[6] Advisory Commission on Intergovernmental Relations, *State Involvement in Federal-Local Grant Programs, A Case Study of the "Buying-In Approach"* (Washington, D.C.: U.S. Government Printing Office, 1970), p. 3 and pp. 32–33.

votes from being counted on the grounds that the citizens now lived in the county. The U.S. Supreme Court ruled, however, that this method of maintaining white control was a violation of the 15th Amendment, which outlaws restrictions of the right to vote based on race or creed.[7] If other states institute such excessive measures, various groups or municipalities affected by them might utilize this precedent to check state actions.

How do the suburbs fit into this legal picture? First, they are limited to the same extent as other units of local government by application of Dillon's Rule. Suburbs, rather than central cities, are the modern day analogies to the small, self-reliant communities of the early 19th century. Though the suburbs are a part of an interdependent metropolitan network, many suburbanites still respect the integrity and closeness of their city governments. Robert Wood has indicated that the ordinary citizen is still enchanted with this image of the "republic in miniature." Citizens prefer small local units to "king-size" governments and ignore the blandishments of large scale, distant structures such as metropolitan governmental units.[8]

Suburbanites may think of their governments as "republics in miniature," but they are legally bound to the state. The suburbs are not a distinct category of governmental unit. Most states establish population requirements for jurisdictions to qualify as different types of municipalities with increasing flexibility for the larger units. Legally and politically, suburbs share the same constraints as other jurisdictions in their classification.

It is possible to speak of state-suburban relations only to the extent that suburbs have a unique point of view and set of interests. But as suggested in earlier chapters, suburbs rarely speak with a unified voice because they have diverse interests. Politically, suburbs are increasingly tied to statewide voting patterns. In most cases, suburbs tend to vote along party lines. For instance, in Pennsylvania, over 80 percent of Philadelphia's suburbs and 69 percent of Pittsburgh's suburbs followed the statewide electoral trends in the elections of 1954, 1966, and 1970. Eighty percent of all suburbs more than matched a statewide Democratic increase.[9]

THE STATES AND URBAN STRUCTURE

There are many ways in which states may gain greater control over formal urban development and governance within municipal boundaries.

[7] 364 U.S 339 (1960), p. 342.

[8] Robert Wood, *Suburbia* (Boston: Houghton-Mifflin, 1958), pp. 85–87.

[9] Joseph Zikmund, "Suburbs and States in National Politics," *The Urbanization of the Suburbs,* Louis H. Masotti and Jeffrey K. Hadden, eds. (Beverly Hills, California: Sage Publications, Inc. 1973), p. 268.

While these activities are almost exclusively structural, they do provide a basis for affecting urban behavior.

The state may create a special state-appointed study commission to focus on the adequacy of local government organization in large urban and metropolitan areas. These commissions or study groups often identify problems and recommend reforms. Connecticut and Texas, for example, established such groups in recent years. In 1967, the Connecticut Commission to Study the Necessity and Feasibility of Metropolitan Government reported that metropolitan government was not feasible. In response to this report, a State Department of Community Affairs was created. In the same year, the Texas Research League studied the state's 22 metropolitan areas and urged the state to provide financial support for the creation and operation of Council's of Governments. This recommendation has since been implemented.[10]

In recent years, some states have taken stronger steps to affect local activities by passing laws that make it easier for cities to annex territory. This clarifies the legal responsibility for providing governmental services to a given area, aids in orderly growth, and strengthens both city and county planning. While hardly a strong trend, this movement does indicate more effective state action toward controlling urban fringe development. This movement has considerable effect on suburbs since this fringe activity occurs along their borders.

Along with easing the annexation process, some states have slowly begun to make separate incorporations of new cities more difficult. The states of Ohio, Tennessee, California, and Florida have discouraged the creation of new suburban cities. In some cases, new incorporations in certain regions or within a minimum distance from existing cities are outlawed. In others, higher population minimums for incorporations have been set. Most reformers feel that this combination of more difficult incorporations with easier annexations by existing cities eventually will encourage larger, stronger, and more responsible municipal governments in metropolitan areas.

As explained in Chapter 7, states can help to make local government more viable by supporting county home rule and modernization. They also can initiate urban and regional restructuring. Though most states are reluctant to take such strong action, many students of intergovernmental relations believe it is necessary. However, some states may find that assuming responsibility for providing a local public service is less politically distasteful than initiating reorganization. In this way, the state becomes an active partner in urban administration. Massachusettts, for example, operates a number of metropolitan special districts in the Boston area.

---

[10] Daniel Grant "Urban Needs and State Response: Local Government Reorganization," in Alan Campbell, ed., *The States and The Urban Crisis* (Englewood Cliffs, New Jersey: Prentice-Hall, 1970), pp. 77–85.

Considering historical precedents, it is unlikely that many states will adopt all or most of the foregoing measures in the near future. Alan K. Campbell notes:

> On the whole, the states have not seen it as their function to encourage basic governmental reorganization at the local level. They have, in some instances, aided the establishment of advisory regional planning authorities and, on occasion, have permitted the establishment of metropolitan-wide functional districts. With one or two exceptions, however, these actions have never been taken in order to bring about a basic new governmental system at the local level.[11]

With a few exceptions, the states that have taken steps to impose some requirements on their local governments have not gone as far as the Canadian provinces.

The Municipality of Metropolitan Toronto is an interesting case because it was created by the province of Ontario without a local referendum. This Toronto action resulted from a controversial annexation hearing. After studying the merits of the case for annexation, Ontario created the Toronto federated government—which was not the outcome requested by either party to the case. The specific form of the Toronto government will be discussed in greater detail in Chapter 11. However, the principle of the province dictating the relationships of the various layers of local government and even reducing the borders of the central city is without precedent in the American system. Additional strong provincial action in metropolitan areas has been taken by the provinces of Saskatchewan, with regard to Winnepeg, and Quebec, with regard to Montreal.

The closest United States approximations to such aggressive action were the Minnesota decision to establish the Twin Cities Metropolitan Council and the Indiana decision to establish UNIGOV in metropolitan Indianapolis. The Twin Cities unit is not a metropolitan government in the sense that it has consumed the other governments already operating in the area. The state legislature previously came within a handful of votes to establishing such a metropolitan government. However, the legislature backed off from that action and instead assigned certain functional areas to the Twin Cities Metropolitan Council.

Unlike councils of governments in other metropolitan areas of the United States, the Metropolitan Council was given limited taxing authority by the state government. Also, the persons appointed to the governing body are not elected officials representing local governments in the area, but are direct appointees of the governor. They have the authority to

---

[11] Alan Campbell, "States at the Crossroads," *National Civic Review*, November 1966, p. 559.

levy a per capita tax to fund the payment of various services they provide. In addition, they have the authority to issue bonds with state backing to support their operations.

The kinds of functions included within the jurisdiction of the Twin Cities Metropolitan Council are preparing guidelines for regional development; disapproving plans inconsistent with these guidelines; issuing bonds for regional parks; constructing regional housing; and approving budgets and user charges for regional transit and water control facilities.[12]

While state legislators often have failed to act in progressive ways with regard to improving the ability of local governments to manage their affairs and reorganize their structures, the major United States local government reorganizations would not have been possible without cooperation from the state governments. For example, as explained in Chapter 11, the Florida legislature made possible the Miami-Dade County government as well as the Jacksonville-Duval government and the Tennessee legislature facilitated the establishment of the Nashville-Davidson County government.

In the case of the Indianapolis-Marion County UNIGOV plan, the Indiana legislature took action at the state level to require the structural changes. In Florida and Tennessee, the proposed reforms were subjected to lengthy and bitter campaigns to secure the support of local voters. No vote was taken by the local cities when UNIGOV was established. The action had far-reaching effects but was less radical than the Nashville and Jacksonville reorganizations. Further details are provided in Chapter 11.

The pattern of weak state responses to urban structural reform is primarily due to the nature of state governments. In many states the governor does not possess the powers he needs to be a real chief executive. Some governors do not even have the veto power. In some states, the legislature is the primary vehicle for local government reform and, within the legislature, there is a practice of *local* delegation courtesy. Matters affecting only one county are settled by that county delegation and ratified by the total legislature. In some cases, constitutional provisions set arbitrary limits on fiscal efforts, which are difficult to overcome, particularly as they affect the structure of local government. Although some states are expressing greater urban concern, the results of this trend may not be apparent for some time.

STATE DEPARTMENTS OF URBAN AFFAIRS

A rapidly growing phenomenon is the creation of State Departments of Urban Affairs. Their names and duties vary widely. Approximately

---

[12] "Metropolitan News," *National Civic Review,* July 1974, pp. 371–73.

20 of these departments have been formed since 1960. The Tennessee Municipal Technical Service, established in 1949, is one of the earliest and most developed. It is oriented largely toward university assistance to cities. This approach is similar to the Oregon Bureau of Municipal Research, housed at the University of Oregon.

The New Jersey Department of Community Affairs

One of the most ambitious Departments is the New Jersey Department of Community Affairs, created in 1967 as a cabinet level department. The Department had a budget in fiscal 1974 of about $56 million, and spent another 9 million dollars of federal grants.[13] The majority of this money was designated for local support, $11 million of which was allocated to local units under a Safe and Clean Neighborhoods Program for clean up and improvement activities and for foot patrol in target neighborhoods. These grants are awarded on a matching dollar-for-dollar basis. Part of this component is designed to reduce resident fear of crime, and largely goes to local police departments. The balance goes to improving the physical appearance of municipalities, including the rehabilitation of parks and playgrounds and the creation of miniparks. Urban aid allocations, totaling over $24 million, are distributed to cities on the basis of a formula that weighs poverty at 60 percent and tax burden at 40 percent.

In addition to these activities, there are a substantial number of other activities at lower budget levels. The Department provides urban renewal assistance to municipalities to help them meet the local share of federal matching requirements. It approves all debt proposals by cities, counties and school districts that exceed a set limit based on assessed valuation. It reviews all local budgets, budget amendments and revenue sharing expenditures. The Bureau of Local Management Services provides substantial technical advisory services to strengthen local management. In 1974, a total of nearly 400 management and technical assistance programs were conducted. The Division of State and Regional Planning is involved in state-wide planning, including a New Communities Planned Unit Program, which provided assistance to local units on planned unit housing developments, and other matters involving large new developments. The Department also administers the Model Cities program and, in 1974, granted about $2.5 million to local units for these projects.

Early in its life the Department was deeply involved in many contro-

---

[13] Also see *National Civic Review*, May 1973, pp. 269–70. Much of the following information is from the New Jersey Department of Community Affairs, *Seventh Annual Report 1974* (Trenton: New Jersey Department of Community Affairs, 1974), p. 53.

versial activities. It was created from a conglomeration of new and existing agencies such as the Housing and Urban Renewal Division, which
was new, and the Division of Local Finance, which had established
a solid existing reputation. The new Department encountered early opposition when it challenged existing agencies. A significant early action
was the Department's role in the conflict between black residents and
the police in Plainfield and Newark. The Department provided emergency services and set up communications between the residents and
the legal authority. The first director, Paul Ylvisaker, physically threw
himself in front of National Guard armored carriers to quiet a tense
situation in Plainfield. The Department remains as one of the best known
state agencies of its kind.[14]

The New York Urban Development Corporation (UDC)[15]

One of the most far-reaching attempts of a state to develop urban
renewal projects and to replace the private financing market for low
and middle income housing projects was the UDC. The UDC was created in 1968 by the New York legislature at the urging of then Governor
Nelson Rockefeller. New York elected to rely on a government nonprofit
corporation to intervene in the housing market, rather than rely on the
State Office of Planning Coordination, with much more limited powers.
The UDC had the power and the mandate to build housing in slum
areas where private financing was unavailable, to provide for redevelopment and urban renewal programs, and to finance new towns. The UDC
was to have built three major new communities. Radisson was a $500
million suburb near Syracuse, which ultimately attracted a regional
Schlitz Brewery as part of the economic base. Audobon was a $500
million new town near Buffalo on the campus of the State University.
Roosevelt Island was a $375 million, 5,000 apartment community on an
island in New York City's East River. By the time the UDC defaulted
on its short term notes in February 1975, it had begun or had completed
construction on 33,600 apartments in 50 communities. It had spent $1.1
billion and planned to spend another $900 million.

UDC's major difficulty lay in its heavy commitment to finance new
apartments under Section 236 of the Housing and Development Act
of 1968, which relied on rent subsidies. When the Nixon administration
placed a moratorium in all housing subsidies in 1973, about 90 percent
of all the loan commitments of the UDC were affected, including a

[14] John Kolesar, "The States and Urban Planning and Development" in Alan
Campbell, ed., *The States and the Urban Crisis* (Englewood Cliffs, N.J.: Prentice-
Hall, 1970), pp. 116–19.

[15] This account is from Steven Weisman, "Nelson Rockefeller's Pill: the UDC,"
Washington Monthly, June 1975, pp. 35–46.

large number which were based on "administrative assurances" from HUD. Banks had never supported the UDC, claiming that it made unrealistic commitments and that they could not get accurate information on repayment schedules. Their distrust was increased by UDC's practice of pooling all projects, weak and strong, and borrowing against the total.

In early 1975, newly elected Governor Carey allowed a $104 million bank loan to lapse, and the UDC collapsed. He had no choice, for only small revenues were available to support the 500 employees and 8,000 construction workers involved in various projects. Carey later proposed a new agency to complete the UDC construction program, but the ambitious program was dead. This attempt by a state to intervene in the housing market and to redevelop urban areas failed, and it will probably be a long time before another program as grandiose and innovative is attempted.

Illinois Department of Local Government Affairs (DLGA)

A final representative of the varied types of Departments of Urban Affairs is the Illinois Department of Local Government Affairs (DLGA). The Department has twice as large a budget (see Table 8–1) as the New Jersey Department, but $103 million of this total is a mandated distri-

TABLE 8–1

Illinois Department of Local Government Affairs
Budget appropriation
1974–1975
(in thousands)

Local government distribution (State revenue sharing with cities and counties).............		$114,000.0
Department operations		
General administration.............	$ 366.3	
Community and financial advisory services	1,286.7	
Housing and urban development	236.8	
Property tax appeal board...........	168.1	
Research and planning.............	143.2	
Total.....................		2,201.1
Other distributions or payments to local government		
Local planning assistance		2,738.3
State share of state's attorneys		1,592.6
States share of local assessors		207.5
Total.....................		$ 5,238.4
Grand Total...............		$121,439.5

Source: *Illinois Department of Local Government Affairs, 1975 Budget.* (Springfield: Governor Daniel Walker's Proposed Fiscal 1976 Illinois State Budget, Governor's Office, 1975), p. 100.

bution of $\frac{1}{12}$ of the state income tax collections to local units. The Department has no discretion over the allocations. Most of the other distributions are at least partially mandated. Half of the $4.5 million goes to regional planning agencies, which are partially funded by federal funds from the Department of Housing and Urban Development. The Department also pays for a portion of county district attorneys and local assessors.

There is relatively little money left for other departmental operations. They mostly involve technical assistance to local officials, such as financial and property tax assessment management. The housing and development expenditures are for work with local housing authorities. The Department also conducts an equalization procedure for property tax assessment in the state's 102 counties. Finally, the research and planning section works on long range projects such as substate districting, catalogs on state local assistance programs, and community criteria for flood plain management.

The Department is hopelessly underfunded and has relatively little impact on local government activities. Its financial and technical assistance program is understaffed and except in unusual cases, cannot provide much assistance to local units of government. The one area in which the Department has considerable influence is property tax assessment, for it sets "multiplier" rates on county tax levies. These rates are designed to equalize assessments over all counties and to prevent any one county from avoiding its tax liabilities or qualifying for state subventions with illegally low effort. This power, which may compel three- or fourfold assessment increases in rural counties, is very controversial. It reinforces the Department's reputation as a regulatory agency rather than as an agent of assistance to counties and municipalities. Thus a formal state-wide tax assessment appeals board, outside the agency, probably will be established. If this occurs, the Department will lose one half of its budget, outside of the mandated distributions, to the new appeals board.

Within the past year, the DLGA has been given some influence over distribution of Intergovernmental Personnel Act (IPA) federal grants that affect local government. This small amount (perhaps $200,000 annually) will enable it to begin some initiatives of its own. However, like many similar state agencies, cities and counties are not significantly affected by the Department's actions.

STATE–LOCAL FISCAL RELATIONSHIPS

There are a number of arrangements states can make with their local governments regarding the distribution of state tax receipts. At one extreme, the state can choose not to support any local functions. Theoretically, this refusal can extend to educational matters or to urban issues associated with cities and counties. At the other extreme is state remission of sufficient revenues for a substantial number of local functions. All 50 of the state/local systems fall between these extremes, though some states are far more generous to their localities than are others.

In 1972, the median per capita amount of state aid to all units of local government was about $142 per capita, ranging from $386 per capita in New York to $24 per capita in Hawaii. In all states but Hawaii, education was the most widely supported function. Since Hawaii has but one school district and virtual state operation, this may explain this seeming exception. The median levy of support for education was $98 per capita, about 70 percent of all intergovernmental expenditures. About half of the remainder was for highways and general support with the balance mostly for public welfare and miscellaneous items.[16] In 1972, total state aid to local governmental units totaled about 35 percent of all local general revenue. This figure has been increasing in recent years.

The state response to local financial problems generally has been limited to contributing to traditional functions. The total investment is actually very large and localities would encounter great difficulty in providing these basic services without state aid. Without aid to schools, welfare, and highways, local governments could not operate effectively.

Mayors look to the federal government to help them solve their problems primarily because state activity in urban programs unrelated to education, highways, and welfare has been minimal. For political and financial reasons, few states have been willing to support such city endeavors as housing, or environmental control, generally abandoning the field to the federal government. Few specialized programs receive substantial state aid, and only a few states have "bought into" local programs. The Advisory Commission on Intergovernmental Relations (ACIR) has suggested that "buying in" is the only major way in which states may become more involved in solving urban problems. The original idea, proposed by the ACIR in 1964, was for federal grants-in-aid to be channeled through states whenever possible, if the states would make significant contributions and provide appropriate technical assistance. Few states have offered the significant sums of money (20 percent to 50 percent of the local share) suggested by ACIR to become truly involved.[17]

Table 8–2 indicates that the 37 states that responded to a 1969 ACIR request for information had provided $229 million for "buying into" local programs. More states sponsored urban planning assistance and

<hr />

[16] U.S. Bureau of the Census, *Guide to the 1972 Census of Governments* (Washington, D.C.: U.S. Government Printing Office, 1975), pp. 239, 241.

[17] Advisory Commission on Intergovernmental Relations, *A State Response to Urban Problems: Recent Experience under the "Buying In" Approach* (Washington, D.C.: U.S. Government Printing Office, 1970), p. 5.

TABLE 8–2

State involvement in selected federally aided urban programs, 1969
(number of states participating)

Federal urban development program	Make financial contribution ("buy in")	Amount of state funds (000)	Require channeling of federal funds	Require review and comment on local applications	Approve local applications	Provide technical assistance
Urban renewal.	4	$ 17,099	1	5	2	5
Urban mass transportation.	4	16,961	1	4	2	2
Waste treatment facilities	11	45,628	20	26	27	19
Urban planning assistance	21	2,562	22	23	20	23
Model cities	4	1,130	3	16	7	13
Airport development	17	8,216	14	19	16	18
Air pollution control	8	2,324	10	17	12	14
Aid for educationally deprived children	3	89,709	27	26	29	26
Community action	8	9,039	4	28	19	26
Solid waste disposal	13	816	11	14	11	18
Juvenile delinquency Prevention and control.	12	237	14	16	12	16
Low rent public housing	2	35,617	3	7	4	5
Total.	24	229,338				

Source: Advisory Commission on Intergovernmental Relations, *A State Response to Urban Problems: Recent Experience under the "Buying In" Approach* (Washington, D.C.: U.S. Government Printing Office, 1970), p. 5.

airport development programs than any others. Waste water treatment programs and aid for educationally deprived children received the most money. Only 4 states spent as much as 10 percent of their total intergovernmental expenditures on "buying into" local programs. Nationally, only 1.1 percent of state intergovernmental expenditures were so used.

The ACIR argued that "buying in" is designed to coordinate state and local efforts, to relieve local tax burdens, to reduce state and local conflict, and to make positive state contributions to programs, while avoiding "rubber stamp" review. Unless states become more financially involved, they will lose a chance to influence these programs and to become urban partners. There is little evidence to date, however, indicating that states are genuinely interested in such a partnership.

Nevertheless, most students of state and local governments argue that still more state aid is required. In 1967, the Committee for Economic Development recommended that states assume greater responsibility for education and welfare, either by direct payments or grants-in-aid, in order to equalize local tax raising efforts and to improve the financial ability of local governments to meet needs.[18] Roy Bahl proposed that financial responsibility for education should be shifted almost exclusively to state government while public assistance, including Medicaid, should be supported exclusively by the federal government.[19]

Until recently, state tax systems as well as local tax systems were regressive. States used sales taxes heavily. If income taxes were levied, they rarely were progressive and were sometimes nearly proportional. The federal government provided the only tax system that was progressive. This now is changing, as more states are adopting income taxes with at least partially progressive rate structures. To balance local reliance on property taxes, states are being urged to broaden the coverage of sales taxes by including such items as rent, professional services, and food. Bahl suggested that states increase reliance on the personal income tax by introducing one where none exists, or by increasing the rate of progressivity of existing taxes.[20] The fact that this is a break from the traditional pattern of federal income, state sales, and local property tax responsibility has impeded change.

States have the power to increase and simplify local revenue patterns by providing for local sales or even income taxes, and by requiring that they be added to the state rate to ease administration and promote uniformity. Maryland is one of the states providing for the piggybacking of local income taxes on the state income tax. Baltimore and Maryland's 23 counties may levy local income taxes up to 50 percent of the state tax. As of 1975, 21 of the jurisdictions had done so and the other two counties levied about half of the total permitted. No local tax return is needed as the taxpayer simply calculates the state tax and then adds the local percentage. The tax is then paid to the state, which sends the localities their share.

TECHNICAL ASSISTANCE AND MINIMUM STANDARDS

An important state function that often is overlooked by state and local policy makers is the dual role of setting minimum standards and providing technical assistance. In theory, these are separate functions, but when localities have difficulty meeting legal standards, the state often is called upon to provide technical assistance.

For example, the state must set minimal standards of property tax across the state. Such disparities may have deleterious effects on pro-

---

[18] Committee for Economic Development, *A Fiscal Program for a Balanced Federalism* (New York: Committee for Economic Development, 1967), p. 31.

[19] Roy Bahl, "State Taxes, Expenditures and the Fiscal Plight of the Cities," in *The States and the Urban Crisis*, Alan Campbell, ed. (Englewood Cliffs, N.J.: Prentice-Hall, 1970), pp. 104–7.

[20] See, for example, James A. Maxwell, *Financing State and Local Governments*, 2nd ed. (Washington, D.C.: Brookings Institution, 1969), pp. 96–100, 130–32.

grams such as statewide aid for equalization of school districts. The state, through some review process, must compel counties to meet a statewide average, usually expressed as a percentage of true market value (for example 50 percent). The true market rates are usually checked to see whether individual counties meet the average. If not, the state may modify the assessments set by the local assessor. Often, these variations are caused by deliberate attempts to keep rates low, thus placing the county or class of property owner in a preferred position. There also may be a need for technical assistance when sheer ineptness causes substantial but unintended variation. In these cases, the state also must help local officials develop a measure of expertise through schooling or training sessions. Sometimes the state even may require that candidates for certain posts pass tests indicating a minimum competence.

Hence, the states usually are involved in setting minimum standards and providing technical assistance coverage. In some instances, the state merely may set standards without assuming the responsibility of providing technical aid. For example, the state may stipulate terms for city building codes, require a traffic survey before signals are installed, require that restaurants undergo health inspections and be graded on their cleanliness, or specify certain materials for street signs in new subdivisions. Though not all of these requirements demand a considerable degree of expertise, many do.

A crucial concern is whether the state actually will enforce standards or whether it will leave implementation of state rules to local units. If local jurisdictions are responsible, they may be lax in enforcement. The locality and the state are more likely to cooperate in assuring effective regulation if the state provides technical assistance or actually becomes involved in enforcement. In providing technical assistance, the state must "buy into" the function if there is to be significant accomplishment. Otherwise, local underenforcement may result.

Most enforcement, particularly in times of financial difficulties, results from complaints or is of a "crisis intervention" nature. Difficulties are detected after a critical stage is reached, such as the mismanagement of nursing homes or the overcrowding of prisons, which are common problems in almost every state. Sometimes minimum standards are not even set until this stage is reached, and the seriousness of certain problems is not perceived until it is too late. An example of the latter is the use of collective bargaining for better labor relations. Here the states' failure to set a code, or at least to demand some consistent local action, has resulted in confrontation, strikes, and unresolved grievances.

In some states, there is a substantial amount of administrative supervision over local actions. Some states directly control local functions, rather than establishing standards for local agencies to meet. For example, the budgets for the St. Louis and Kansas City, Missouri, police departments are set by a group of local commissioners appointed by the governor. The cities are required by law to include this figure in their total budgets.

Technical assistance, in the form of crisis intervention or direct administrative supervision of local functions, is not the only type of state involvement in local operations. There exists a broad spectrum of cooperative state and local actions. It is possible to support maximum local flexibility and discretion in areas as diverse and vital as police protection and employee relations, and yet to recognize that the state's interest in the area demands the setting and enforcing of minimum standards and the provision of technical assistance.

DIRECT STATE SERVICES

Suburbs, as well as all other local government units, are affected by services provided directly by state governments. Important, but often overlooked as a state service, are the state supported universities and colleges and, more recently, the ubiquitous community colleges. These educational institutions can alter the nature and socioeconomic level of the area, because of the large number of faculty, students, and administrative personnel associated with them. The social and cultural patterns of an area near a college or university often become more socially and politically pluralistic.

The state highway system also has a dramatic effect on suburban life. Most state highways are routed through cities and many run directly through the downtown shopping area. In such cases, street maintenance and cleaning, parking enforcement, and traffic control become very important. Negotiations with the state, or with the district or regional highway office, become a crucial part of suburban political life. Two of the political tasks, then, are bargaining and negotiating over service levels and regulating highway uses. Service and regulation are constant issues since local desires and traditions must be reconciled with state legal powers.

A major state direct service in urban areas is the corrections and parole system. The state hires two-thirds of all employees and makes two-thirds of all expenditures, but there is a local share. However, the maintenance of adult correctional institutions, covering a wide range of facilities and programs, as well as the supervision of parolees from these institutions, are almost entirely state functions.

At least 60 percent of all felons now are being paroled. State parole officers supervise the parolees and facilitate their adjustment to the community into which they are released.

The location of state correctional institutions often is an issue in suburban and other urban governments. Residents are afraid that dangerous criminals may escape, and also are reluctant to welcome into the community persons who have served long periods of incarceration.

The total correction system, of which adult correctional institutions are only a part, is a mixed system of state and local administration. The total correctional population is subject to community based probation and parole programs. Juvenile courts, probation, misdemeanor cases, and city jails are predominantly local responsibilities. Although states have the legal power and responsibility, they generally provide assistance or set service standards. The result is a mixture of state and local control over the corrections functions, with the state legally empowered to act but choosing to finance only adult institutions and probation.[21]

Aid to education, a special type of state intervention, commands a major portion of the total local tax burden. Since the social and political ramifications of education are so powerful, the state assumes an overriding interest in the quality of local schools. Indeed, the state is usually constitutionally responsible for education, even though it often is considered a purely local issue.

State attitudes toward financing school districts are particularly important to suburbs. Since their school districts are often a crucial aspect of their life-style, any adverse distribution is likely to challenge the very reason many persons became suburban residents in the first place. The *Serrano* v. *Priest* decision in California, requiring the state to insure that students living in school districts with low tax bases receive a quality education, is a direct challenge to this suburban value.

Redistribution of state funds for education now seems inevitable. The recent school financing cases suggest that statewide equalization may be completed within this decade in most states. There are three possible actions states may take in these cases: (1) redistribute (equalize) funds on a regional basis; (2) extend traditional equalization patterns, exerting a stronger effort for real equity among districts; or (3) assume educational costs and simultaneously redistribute funds based on some determined "need," such as educational deficiencies.[22] State action to compel redistribution will affect funding levels, and also will affect the mix of students attending each school. Larger districts probably will become less homogeneous. Busing will become more prevalent, and the trend towards fewer school districts will continue.

A study of 13 states indicated that if states assumed full funding of education, central cities would have increased taxes but no expenditure gains, rural areas would receive substantial expenditure increases

---

[21] Ibid., p. 113.

[22] Advisory Commission on Intergovernmental Relations, *State-Local Relations in the Criminal Justice System* (Washington, D.C.: U.S. Government Printing Office, 1971), pp. 119–37.

and minor tax increases, while suburban areas would have a varied tax impact and lowered expenditures. However, in four of these states, suburban areas as a whole would benefit.[23]

The state's role in urban and suburban education does not end with financing. The state sets professional requirements for teachers; controls curriculum; often prescribes, and sometimes buys, textbooks for all students; and can set or change the size of school districts. The state also plays a role in school racial integration, but this role largely has been superceded by federal courts. Since most states are not eager to involve themselves in this issue, it will continue to be in the federal domain.

THE STATES AND URBAN DEBT MANAGEMENT

The President's Task Force on Surburban Problems, created in 1967, proposed a significant change in state policies in order to help small suburban cities make better use of their funds and to aid them in borrowing new money. These cities generally get poorer financial advice than their larger counterparts, since they often cannot afford experienced legal and financial counsel. Influential bond rating houses do not rate their bonds favorably. This factor, added to the higher costs of small issues, forces suburbs and other small jurisdictions to pay disproportionately higher rates.[24] In response to these difficulties encountered by small suburban and urban jurisdictions, the Task Force recommended creation of an Urban Development Bank. This bank could provide longer term financing of municipal development projects; broaden the search for capital by removing the tax exempt status of municipal bonds, thus attracting new investors who are different from current investors interested in tax exempt bonds; lower the cost of borrowing by encouraging more competition and by having the United States return its tax revenues from municipal bonds to the bank; and hire a group of technicians to advise local development plans.[25]

While states are not empowered to change laws on the taxability of municipal issues, they can do much to help very small units. Accordingly, the Advisory Commission on Intergovernmental Relations included, in its outlines for state legislative action, a program of state assistance for local government debt management. The proposed legislation noted that "states have an inescapable interest and concern with the quality of debt management practices of their local governments.

[23] Excerpt from, "Financial and Desegregation Reform in Suburbia," by Frederick M. Wirt is reprinted from *The Urbanization of the Suburbs,* UAAR, Vol. 7(c) 1973, p. 476 by permission of the Publisher, Sage Publications, Inc.

[24] Joel Berke and John Callahan, *"Serrano* v. *Priest;* Milestone or Millstone for School Finance," *Journal of Public Law* (vol 21, no. 1, 1972), p. 66–67.

[25] Charles Haar, ed., *Report of the President's Task Force on Suburban Problems,* copyright 1974 by Ballinger Publishing Co. Reprinted with permission.

. . . The suggested act provides for state technical assistance and sets standards for official statements on local debt offerings by authorizing a designated state agency."[26]

The recommendations of the President's Task Force have not, and may never, become law. However, they do underscore the importance of state action in these important urban policy areas. Obviously, other issue areas also are interrelated with state and national policy. The state remains a silent partner in every urban endeavor, and often is deeply and directly involved in urban functions, even when the responsibility may appear to be purely local.

Judging from past experiences, it may be difficult to overcome local and state resistance to externally imposed "order and rationality." It may be more difficult to force these jurisdictions to accept a federally formulated solution than to get a Task Force to write a report prescribing it. However, it is clear that if any laws or policies evolve in response to the report, the states will be as deeply immersed in local affairs as the federal government.

LAW ENFORCEMENT—AN EXAMPLE OF THE STATE ROLE IN A LOCAL FUNCTION

Law enforcement is an important municipal service upon which the states have substantial impact. Local governments have the major fiscal and personnel responsibility for police, but the states play a key role in providing fiscal and technical services, as well as establishing laws that regulate various facets of police work.

The state's role in police work

The police function is a shared responsibility of state and local government. In very broad terms, local governments handle most types of police work, while state governments have more limited, specialized police duties. About 90 percent of all police personnel are employed at the local level. The size of a local force can range from New York City's 30,000-person force to Rangley, Maine's, one-person police department. Local forces generally are small and have remained a function controlled by the jurisdiction within which they operate. Area-wide consolidations of local police forces has been rare. Thus, fragmentation of the police function, with its advantages and disadvantages, is a prominent characteristic of United States police protection.

The state is the one structure capable of unifying these many local police forces. It has several distinct roles in this area. It regulates the election of law enforcement officers, and can impose restrictions on the

---

[26] Advisory Commission on Intergovernmental Relations, *1967 ACIR State Legislative Program* (Washington, D.C.: U.S. Government Printing Office, 1967), p. 341.

number of terms an elected official, such as a sheriff, can serve. In some states, sheriffs have collateral duties as tax collectors. Other elected law enforcement officials regulated by the state are constables, coroners, and medical examiners. States also can impose requirements concerning wages, hours, fringe benefits, and working conditions of the local police organizations. Some states also have stipulated that local police must meet mandatory employment qualifications before they receive permanent appointment. As of 1970, 25 states had enacted legislation providing minimum education and training requirements for local police officers.[27]

States also have criminal codes that detail the exercise of local police power. For instance, only a state may provide powers for extraterritorial arrest and pursuit, or write statutory provisions regarding the scope of police powers in the matter of arrest and search and seizure. Since 1970, new or substantially revised criminal codes have been implemented in 14 states.[28]

All states provide direct police services except Hawaii, which has no state police force. While these state police forces differ from state to state in size and scope of duty, usually they account for approximately 10–15 percent of the total police manpower within a state.[29] Table 8–3

TABLE 8–3
Characteristics of four state police systems

	Mississippi	New York	Wash-ington	California
Statewide crime		X		
State patrol		X	X	X
Unincorporated area patrol	X			X
Statewide investigation		X		
Investigation on request	X			
Statewide crime laboratory	X	X		X
Crime lab services to local police	X	X		X
Investigate complaints about local police		X		
Teletypewriter services		X		X
Percentage of time spent on				
Traffic	70	46	87	88
Criminal investigation	20	40	9	1

Source: Advisory Commission on Intergovernmental Relations, *State-Local Relations in the Criminal Justice System* (Washington, D.C.: U.S. Government Printing Office, 1971), Table 12, pp. 84–85.

[27] Advisory Commission on Intergovernmental Relations, *State-Local Relations in the Criminal Justice System* (Washington, D.C.: U.S. Government Printing Office, 1971), p. 83.

[28] Ibid., p. 265.

[29] Council of State Governments *The Book of the States 1974–75* (Lexington, Kentucky: Council of State Governments, 1974), p. 418.

illustrates the wide fluctuation in responsibilities of these police forces in four states. The state of Washington has a highway patrol, but does not conduct statewide investigation or maintain a crime laboratory. The Mississippi state police force performs no statewide investigations or highway patrol, but operates a crime laboratory. In contrast, the New York State Police Department performs all three of these functions, along with many others.

California with a highly professional force, spends the highest percentage of time in patrol activity and the least time in criminal investigation. Overall, there are a relatively small number of state police agencies that have a full range of police responsibilities. These state agencies are in Alaska, Delaware, New York, New Jersey, Michigan, Pennsylvania, and Vermont.[30]

Perhaps the most important state responsibility is in the area of technical and financial assistance provided to local departments through state police forces and investigation bureaus. This assistance ranges from investigation services, available to localities on request, to state-sponsored training programs. Thirty-three states have central crime laboratories that provide assistance to local agencies. Almost all states authorize their police forces and other state agencies to provide supportive communication services to localities on request. Sometimes this kind of assistance comes from a number of state agencies rather than from a centralized policy agency.

These technical services are absolutely necessary if today's law enforcement officers are to function effectively. Centralized training facilities, expensive laboratory equipment, and the skilled technicians to operate it, are all necessary. When provided by the state, unnecessary duplication of effort can be prevented. Further, if these services are not provided by the states, most jurisdictions would not be able to fill the gap.

State fiscal aid for local police operations is a relatively new phenomenon. Most states now provide some fiscal aid of one kind or another. One of these areas is the police pension system. The fiscal viability of these systems has been a recurring problem. They tend to be underfunded, to have too small a membership, and to be poorly managed. To alleviate these weaknesses, several states adopted state-administered limited coverage systems. Others, including Alaska and Hawaii, have centralized all police retirement systems into state retirement systems.

States are the principal agents in the establishment of interstate police agreements. One mechanism that is utilized is the interstate compact. Currently, a number of these agreements directly or indirectly relate to police work. Almost all states have ratified uniform laws on the extra-

---

[30] Advisory Commission on Intergovernmental Relations, *State-Local Relations in the Criminal Justice System*, p. 83.

dition of out of state witnesses and also on criminal extradition. Most states have approved the uniform law on interstate fresh pursuit allowing "hot pursuit" of criminals crossing state lines.[31] By 1973, a total of 17 states had ratified the Interstate Compact on the placement of children.[32] Other similar compacts involve the return of escaped juveniles and supervision of parolees from other states.[33]

There are other compacts between individual states. For instance, the New England State Police Compact provides for central criminal records and emergency assistance among the six state police forces of New England. The purpose of the Waterfront Commission Compact between New York and New Jersey is to improve the coordination of state efforts to check organized crime in the New York port area.

While these compacts are the most advantageous type of interstate agreements, there are other mechanisms for interstate cooperation. Administrative agreements are the most informal. They are not legally binding, but do serve as a convenient device for intermittent cooperation among states. These types of agreements exist where fixed legal procedures are not required. Another form of agreement is the passage of parallel laws by two or more states, instituting uniform procedures in a given field. These uniform laws reduce the differences in state legislation and provide cooperating states with a common basis of understanding as to a given statute.

Some states have authorized interlocal cooperation in police functions between interstate metropolitan areas. Kansas and Missouri, for instance, have supported metropolitan activities of the Kansas City area police departments. Maryland, Virginia, and the District of Columbia have authorized mutual aid agreements among local government police forces in the Washington, D.C., metropolitan area. But the interstate compact can provide for truly regional and lasting action in a given functional field.[34]

The California Highway Patrol—a case study

Supplementing the earlier discussion of state police departments, we are presenting a brief case study of the California Highway Patrol. This should give some idea of the operation of a state police force and the issues involved in police management at the state level. The California Highway Patrol (CHP) is typical, perhaps, of those state highway de-

---

[31] Ibid., p. 84.

[32] Ibid., p. 178.

[33] Council of State Governments, *Book of the States*, p. 269.

[34] Advisory Commission on Intergovernmental Relations, *State-Local Relations in the Criminal Justice System*, p. 66.

partments whose primary responsibility is to enforce traffic laws. The sheer traffic volume in California, of course, is staggering, but the range of duties is not unlike other states.

There are 20 million people in California, spread over an area third largest among the 50 states. Californians are very heavy car users, partly because the development of the state was through a complex and massive set of freeways aimed at maximizing automotive convenience. Except recently in the San Francisco area, there are no mass transit systems. Thus the state is held together by a vast highway and freeway system stretching from North and South, a distance of some 800 miles. Highway patrol offices at the extremes were further apart than Chicago and New York.[35]

The emphasis of the CHP on traffic enforcement to the exclusion of other duties, as shown in Table 8.3, is not surprising given the geographical dimensions and work volume of traffic enforcement. Another reason may be the generally highly regarded professionalism of police work in California cities and counties, which alleviates the necessity for intervention by a state agency.

However, the CHP still must find time to engage in a variety of activities that are incidental to its major traffic law enforcement mandate.[36] It investigates auto thefts. It also inspects school buses periodically. It weighs and inspects trucks suspected of being overweight or unsafe. There are other activities that are a routine part of the CHP's responsibilities. They include changing tires for helpless motorists, providing emergency transportation and traffic control at the scene of accidents, notifying farmers of broken down fences or livestock on the roads, escorting hazardous trucking loads, emergency transport of medical supplies to outlying communities, and traffic direction during times of high vehicular concentration such as conventions and fairs. Many of these activities require extensive cooperation with local law enforcement agencies.

Since the present CHP was created in 1929 and given formal departmental status in 1947, the practice has been to move officers between district offices rarely except at their own request. Thus, in many cases and to a substantial degree the individual officer became a "local" closely tied to influential local personalities and political organizations as well as to the local law enforcement agencies. This integrated the CHP with local leaders but also worked against professional development from time to time. Thus, there had grown up in the CHP a system geographically dispersed with field officers and staff partially linked to local com-

---

[35] This account is largely from Phillip Foss, "Reorganization and Reassignment in the California Highway Patrol," in Frederick C. Mosher, ed., *Governmental Reorganizations: Cases and Commentary* (Syracuse N.Y.: Inter-University Case Program, Inc., Syracuse University, 1967), pp. 185–212.

[36] Ibid., p. 189.

munity and political leaders. Paradoxically, the CHP also suffered from over centralization in the Commission's office. Complaints, for example, had to go through the office of the Commissioner, a time consuming process in a large state. This centralization is not usual in a paramilitary police organization particularly one with an "elite corps" tradition and virtually closed lateral entry, but it often made communication difficult.

In 1958 Governor Pat Brown, the first Democrat in 16 years, was elected at least partly on a campaign to reduce highway traffic accidents. Change was coming to the CHP, although the exact form had not been determined. The new Commissioner, Bradford Crittenden, had been a long friend of the new governor, although he was a Republican. His management views of "holding all the reins" of his agency was shared by the governor. It was but a short time before he initiated a substantial reorganization designed to decentralize decision-making and involve himself in the patrol activities. This intent is in a very broad sense typical of the attempts that many states are making to improve services by decentralizing authority to regions. The trick is to maintain overall state standards while granting autonomy and flexibility to local units. This was easier in the CHP because of the belief of the officers that they constitute an "elite corps." Crittenden had relatively little difficulty in accomplishing reorganization. He eliminated a Deputy Commissioner, a Commander of Field Operations and centralized supervisory responsibilities in his own office, aided by a slight rearrangement of his own staff. The decentralization to the field was accomplished by reassigning offices throughout the state. Complaints were to be settled within zones, as were all decisions regarding individual patrol Officers other than policy or civil service questions. Assignment of automotive and maintenance equipment became a zone function. Question of policing local emergency situations resulting from floods, fires, and storms were further delegated to patrol area captains.

Apparently there was little serious opposition to the reorganization. CHP members themselves were used to hierarchical authority and sensed the legitimacy of a new administration. Furthermore, Crittenden wooed the members by visiting each of the 90 patrol offices and talking to the men. With a background as a district attorney and on familiar terms with patrol members by his visits, Crittenden avoided potential internal disagreement. There was little difficulty with outside factors. The Governor, the Department of Finance, and the State Personnel Board accepted the details of the plan. The Legislative Analyst, who had been critical of earlier operations, also agreed with the plan. His acceptance may have been influential in heading off legislative opposition, since his position is most prestigeous, somewhat similar to the federal Comptroller General. Even more important in avoiding legislative comment was the fact that no additional funds or positions were requested, and thus legislators had less chance to intervene directly.

The reorganization was generally conceded to be a success with decentralization accomplished to a substantial degree. The Commissioner became head of the Patrol in reality as well as in name, which was the real underlying reason for the reorganization. It is not clear what long term effect on the CHP the Crittenden changes had, but the short term effects were satisfactory. Since potential leaders are "short timers" this may have been all one could expect.

Having examined a state police force, we now turn to an examination of the federal impact on state policy leadership and coordination efforts in the law enforcement system.

Impact of the federal government on the states' role

There always has been a strong need for mechanisms to help coordinate activities of the criminal justice system at the state, county, and local levels. The federal government first provided the impetus by providing matching funds in the Law Enforcement Assistance Act of 1968. Under the terms of the act, states have been required to establish State Planning Agencies as permanent decisionmaking and administrative bodies to receive block grant awards from the Law Enforcement Assistance Administration (LEAA). These agencies would also be responsible for disbursing subgrants to local governments. All 50 states have now established such agencies.

The Safe Streets Act of 1969 also encouraged states to initiate criminal justice planning on a metropolitan or regional basis. Nearly all states had established these regional bodies by 1970. Although the majority of these regional bodies are performing planning functions, many also are responsible for coordinating the efforts of localities within their jurisdictions. The federal government also has coaxed states and local jurisdictions to upgrade their police selection methods and their training capabilities.[37]

As the crime rate continues to rise in the 1970s, and as inflation cuts into local revenues, the states will be called upon to play an even greater role in the area of law enforcement. States continually are revising their criminal codes and many are reviewing their penal systems.

SUMMARY

In theory, the state exercises complete authority over the local units of government within its boundaries. This practice developed in the

---

[37] Advisory Commission on International Relations, *State–Local Relations in the Criminal Justice System.* Also see the President's Commission on Law Enforcement and Administration of Justice, *The Challenge of Crime in a Free Society* (Washington, D.C.: U.S. Government Printing Office, 1967), pp. 1–3 and passim.

late 19th century as a result of Dillon's rule, which held that cities were completely subservient to their states. However, many practical factors mitigate this harsh rule. Home rule can be granted to the local units by state legislative action or constitutional provision. Political reality, which prevents gross tampering with local units by the state, and the fine network of relationships between cities and the federal government, also largely weaken the absolute exercise of state power.

States have not used their powers very extensively or consistently. They could gain a great deal of control over metropolitan development by intervening to prescribe urban-suburban structure, as Canadian provinces have done. However, except in a few instances, the most notable being UNIGOV in Indiana and Twin Cities Metropolitan Council in Minnesota, they have not chosen to do so. This inaction largely can be attributed to the fact that state governments are not really organized to exercise leadership in any area. Governors often have weak powers. Legislatures defer to local delegations on matters dealing with that area, and constitutional provisions discourage innovation by states. Some states are beginning to act more aggressively by controlling the creation of small units of government and by making it easier for larger units to annex.

Another way in which the state could benefit local units is by creating activist Departments of Local Affairs, which could provide technical assistance and monitor local actions in fiscal and managerial areas. About 20 states have done so, but most departments are not as strong or committed as, for example, the New Jersey Department of Community Affairs. The recent collapse of the New York Urban Development Corporation may discourage states from becoming too activist in the housing area or, unfortunately, in using their Departments of Local Affairs to upgrade and support local governments.

Statistically, states are providing large sums of aid to local units. In 1972, the total was about 35 percent of total local expenditures, most of which was for education. However, most of the money is not focused on specific programs but can be used for general purposes within broad functional areas. The states have not "bought in" to specific urban programs or committed themselves to active involvement in program areas, preferring to restrict their activities to dispensing money. Critics, however, suggest that they neither dispense enough money nor concern themselves deeply with crucial program areas. Certainly, they have not followed the suggestion of the President's Commission on Suburban Problems, which advised them to become more activist in creating urban development banks to help small suburban cities use their borrowed money more effectively.

Finally, a case study of the policy function demonstrates how closely intertwined are state and local functions. While the state can set standards, the administration of the various elements is mixed, and the only direct services area in which the state predominates is in detention of prisoners and in adult probation. In some states, the state highway patrol assists in policing suburban areas. As the case study indicates, the highway patrol has a substantial role in the automotive centered state.

The state-local relationship remains ambiguous. While the state maintains the power to act in almost any area to prevent local actions, it generally does not do so. At the same time, some states also have failed to empower local governments to deal with their own problems. To date, few states have been willing to commit time, energy and resources to attack urban problems directly in a partnership with local units.

9

Federal impact on the suburbs

THIS CHAPTER focuses directly on the federal government's impact on urban and suburban governments. Federal dollars, both through grant-in-aid programs and direct spending, have paved the way for federal policy impact. Major questions surround the extensive use of grants-in-aid and direct federal programs in urban and suburban areas. Whose interests do they serve? How do they influence the effectiveness of city and county governments? What effect do they have on intergovernmental relations in the metropolitan system? In answering these questions, metropolitan planning and grant coordination are discussed at length in this chapter.

FEDERAL GRANTS-IN-AID

The federal government has its greatest impact on a given urban or suburban area through the grant-in-aid process. Basically, this process is a technique used by the federal government to allot money to state and/or local units of government to carry out some desired governmental program or national policy. There is a bewildering variety of programs, many with different formulas determining the federal share and the qualifications state and local units must meet for funding.

Types of grants-in-aid

There are basically only two kinds of federal grants-in-aid, although wide variations exist within each type. Bloc or unconditional grants were the first types used by the federal government. Bloc grants provide more flexibility to lower units of government. There are no substantial federal "strings" or controls over how and where state or local units spend these federal monies. Generally, bloc grants disburse funds by a predetermined formula and give recipients discretion over utilization of the money. Douglas Harmon defines a bloc grant as ". . . an unconditional grant from the federal government to state government which can be used for any proper purposes in broad functional areas."[1]

The other type of federal grant is labeled a categorical grant, also called project or conditional grant. This type of grant requires the recipient government to meet certain federal conditions. This could include providing matching amounts of money, submitting a proposal or work program describing how the money will be used, or proceding only after federal approval of plans and specifications. Categorical grants are linked to specific purposes, or categories, of functions or problems. Also, these grants are generally so area-specific that they do not involve a state plan and are directed to specific targets. Geographically, they may involve neighborhoods, cities, metropolitan areas, or states.

Philosophies of federal aid

Traditionally, most federal aid has gone to states; at best, cities have been able to convince Congress to place a "pass through" provision in the legislation. This is because the logic of federalism establishes the states as the basic unit government and also because it is easier to work through states than through thousands of local units. In 1969–70, prior to the initiation of the revenue sharing program, 87 percent of federal intergovernmental aid went directly to states, although some of it was passed on to local governments by the states.[2] Revenue sharing and more federal programs have changed this emphasis.

Chapter 5 outlined some of the intergovernmental aid that cities receive from the federal government, indicating that relatively little of the monies went to suburban jurisdictions. Federal aid, which once went exclusively to states, was linked more directly to central cities in the 1960s. Due to revenue sharing, more aid is provided to cities and counties. Since population is the most important factor in the revenue sharing formula, this funding is distributed rather evenly among all local units of general government. However, the formula includes some weighting

---

[1] Douglas Harman, "The Bloc Grant: Readings from a First Experiment," *Public Administration Review*, March–April 1970, p. 141.

[2] U.S. Bureau of the Census, *Federal, State, Local Fiscal Projections* (Washington, D.C.: U.S. Government Printing Office, 1971). This figure is changing rapidly due to revenue sharing and the development of "direct federalism," or federal grants directly to cities.

for need and tax effort—central cities, which have relatively higher tax efforts and poverty levels, receive slightly more than a proportionate share.

The federal government began granting aid to states as early as 1805, when five percent of the proceeds of public lands in states was applied to the construction of roads. In 1818, this 5 percent was given to the states with the stipulation that 3 percent must be used for the "encouragement of education."[3] These early grants, including the Morrill Acts of the early 1860s, which gave both land and money to establish colleges in every state, involved no matching fund stipulations or federal supervision. It was not until 1911 that Congress imposed supervision of performance and approval of state plans upon recipients. Since the 1930s, federal grants have expanded substantially, and by 1966 there were 96 separate programs that funneled over $11 billion to the states. Only ten of those programs were encted before 1930. Approximately two thirds of the total was allotted for welfare and highway construction.[4]

Direct federal aid to local government originated in the 1930s as a part of the effort to fight the depression. Such programs included the Federal Emergency Relief Administration and the Works Progress Administration. A major increase in the scope and total funding occurred in 1965 when the Elementary and Secondary Education Act authorized grants to school districts with large numbers of children from low income families. This program and succeeding ones bypassed the states and provided money directly to the local level. While earlier programs also had benefitted local governments directly, they were "passed-through" the states. In federal grant programs enacted since the 1960s, the states often have been ignored, partly because cities did not want to be tied to state goverments and party because the states had not shown an interest in the program or even created an agency through which federal funds could be channeled. This "by passing" pattern began as early as 1946 in the Airport Construction Grant Program.

The changing nature of intergovernmental relationships has been marked by shifts in emphasis in the grant-in-aid program.[5] Prior to 1960, federal assistance programs generally did not define a specific national goal. Instead, they attempted to help states or local governments achieve

---

[3] James Maxwell, *Financing State and Local Governments*, 2d ed. (Washington, D.C.: Brookings Institution, 1969), p. 52. This and the following section on federal aid to local government is largely from this source, pp. 52–60.

[4] Ibid., p. 53. Also see Advisory Commission on Intergovernmental Relations, *Fiscal Balance in the American Federal System*, vol. 1 (Washington, D.C.: U.S. Government Printing Office, 1967), pp. 137–40, for a complete list of the 95 programs. Note: these 95 programs include local programs as well as those which could be identified as purely state programs.

[5] This section is largely from James Sundquist and David Davis, *Making Federalism Work* (Washington, D.C.: Brookings Institution, 1969), chapter 1.

their own objectives. Federally funded state highway systems, for example, were approved largely to help the farmer move his crops to the market.

Policymaking remained at the state and local level for established functions. Federal review of programs was to assure that they were conducted legally, economically, and efficiently. Federal agencies confined their role to providing technical assistance. Federal payments were allocated among the states on a formula basis and usually states were asked to match the federal funds. In this way, the federal government induced the states to help pay for a program that they might not have adopted on their own.

"Cooperative federalism" became the popular description of the process.[6] The federal government cooperated with the states and local units by providing assistance to them in accomplishing their own objectives. National goals were perceived to be advanced by the achievement of state and local objectives.

A decision was made in the 1960s to define national goals toward which the country could strive. Many of the resulting federal programs were to be implemented or administered through states and localities. Since a national interest or true *national* objective requires close federal control over the program content, project grants were used. Often the federal government paid as much as 100 percent of the costs of these projects. Frequently, the federal agencies selected the state and local agencies with which they wanted to deal—or even bypassed the governmental system by encouraging the establishment of community groups to carry out the projects. This was part of the "creative federalism" approach of President Lyndon Johnson's administration.

The shift from almost total reliance on state governments to direct partnership with local governments and community groups was a result of the increased pressure for federal involvement in central city and suburban problems. Lobbyists for urban organizations argued successfully that the states were wasting the federal money on traditional and outmoded programs, that they were not responding to urban needs, and that state governments lacked the professional staff to do an effective job of allocating federal money to the local governments.

In the 1970s federal emphasis again changed. The passage of the Revenue Sharing Act signaled the attempt to restore the state and local units as the priority setters. Revenue Sharing decentralizes project decisionmaking to state and local units. The federal funds are provided for use on broadly defined problem areas. The dominant theme, therefore, differs from that prevailing during the period prior to 1960, when

---

[6] George Gordon, "Office of Management and Budget Circular A-95: Perspectives and Implications," *Publius*, Winter 1974, pp. 47–48. Also see Daniel Elazar, *The American Partnership* (Chicago: University of Chicago Press, 1962).

formula grants were made for rather specific programs. "Creative federalism" centralized policy initiatives at the national level, but relied upon the competence and motivation of local officials for program management. Richard Nixon's "New Federalism" tried to decentralize much of the policy determination as well as the implementation to the local level. Proponents of revenue sharing maintain that local and state officials are likely to work harder to implement their own priorities. Ideally, local and state units will select programs more acceptable or useful to the particular local area than any that could be chosen for them by administrators based in Washington.

The new bloc grant mechanism: The Safe Streets Act[7]

The new type of bloc grants have increased state and local discretion, but they have not eliminated the natural rivalries that exist between the cities and states. These rivalries are well demonstrated by the struggle over the Safe Streets Act of 1968 (formally the Omnibus Crime Control and Safe Streets Act of 1968), one of the first major program of a bloc grant nature to be legislated. It was a new granting concept and it was addressed to a major urban problem. To qualify, a state had to establish a criminal justice planning agency under the governor. Allotments were dependent upon Law Enforcement Assistance Administration (LEAA) approval of the comprehensive plan.

The governor's unit could then make allocations to state and local law enforcement agencies, which would have substantial discretion to determine priorities. The Act required that 40 percent of the planning funds and 75 percent of the action funds go to local governments or combinations of local units.

At the time that the program was enacted, it was expected that the federal government would monitor it very closely. When the Democratic Congress passed the Act, it was clear that Attorney General Ramsey Clark, on behalf of President Johnson, favored strict interpretation of the federal mandate.

The LEAA, in the U.S. Department of Justice, carefully examined state plans, insisting that they comply with the national policy. However, when the Nixon administration inherited the embryonic plan, a much more modest federal role emerged. Very few programmatic controls and no detailed guidelines have been imposed; the states have been permitted "to determine the manner in which bloc grants are disbursed among different parts of the criminal justice system."[8]

---

[7] Information is from Edward Clynch and William Shaffer, "Policy Responsiveness in the American States with Respect to LEAA Bloc Grants," a paper presented to the 1975 Annual Meeting of the Midwest Political Science Association, Chicago, May 1975; Douglas Harman, "The Bloc Grant," and Edward Epstein, "The Krogh File—The Profile of Law and Order," *The Public Interest,* Spring 1975.

[8] Clynch and Shaffer, "Policy Responsiveness," p. 5.

To understand the bloc grant and the state and local interests involved in the Safe Streets Act, it is necessary to assess the political cross pressures which led to the establishment of the program. City representatives had a vested interest in proposing a categorical instead of a bloc grant program. When the bloc grant program was adopted, cities wanted to prove that it did not work and did not direct sufficient monies to the cities. States, of course, took the opposite position. Enactment of the law did not stop the political struggle, for the LEAA still had the choice of carefully evaluating comprehensive plans or of allowing states largely to determine their own plans.

Pressures on the LEAA came from such organizations as the U.S. Conference of Mayors, the National League of Cities, the National Association of Counties, the National Governor's Conference, the Urban Coalition, and Urban America, Inc.[9] The National League of Cities argued that local funds were being wasted in rural areas, while "crime in the streets" was being neglected. The United States Conference of Mayors, a big city organization, attacked the bloc grant concept, perhaps because central cities traditionally have secured more federal money through categorical grants and because they would receive more emphasis in a categorical program since their crime rates were higher. Other agencies, such as Urban America and the Urban Coalition, examined state planning and concluded that "pofessionals," with limited minority representation, were determining programs which were biased in favor of traditional, noninnovative practices with regard to police, corrections, and court reform.

The National Governors Council was finally victorious—the program created was based on a bloc grant approach. However, the big cities won at least a minor victory early in the program when LEAA agreed to use some of the discretionary money available to LEAA to fund directly the 11 largest cities. Congress, meanwhile, has shown no inclination to adopt a categorical funding approach.

While cities are generally more sympathetic toward categorical grants, their attitudes vary substantially by size. For exmple, a 1969 survey indicated that only 13 percent of the cities with populations under 100,000 felt that the state was seldom helpful and sympathetic, but 35 percent of the cities over 500,000 felt this way.[10] This atitude probably is a result of the previous lack of state interest in urban problems, and the struggles with the state over the allocation formulas and their application for previous categorical grants.

An urban bloc grant, such as the Safe Streets Act, also forces states to administer federal programs directly for and with cities. Suburbs and smaller cities have not had as much experience with state and fed-

---

[9] This section is from Harman, "The Bloc Grant," pp. 143–44.

[10] Ibid., p. 147.

eral grant relationships, so they have reacted less negatively to the new bloc grants. Further, as indicated in Chapter 2, legislators sometimes support rural interests as opposed to those of big cities. The federal government inevitably mediates this fiscal dispute between state and local interests by its decisions on each grant program. With the advent of unconditional grants of revenue sharing guaranteeing two thirds of the money to localities, the states have seen their position weakened.

Issues involved in grants-in-aid

Grant-in-aid programs raise a number of issues. One problem is the continuation of grant programs even when the original purpose for the grant has been fulfilled. Interests grow up around the distribution system, which make it politically difficult for change to occur. Generally, it is easier to begin a new grant program for a new need rather than to delete an old program. The result is that two or more grant programs exist in many functional areas. Often, a disorderly pastiche of outmoded and sometimes even contradictory grant programs exists.

Another effect of grant programs has been the distortion of state and local budgets. Legislatures at both levels often are persuaded to allocate funds merely to match or qualify for federal funds, bypassing more crucial programs for which grants were not available.

Matching requirements of federal grants frequently absorb larger portions of state and local tax revenue in the poorer states. Since poorer states have lower total revenue, matching provisions make up a larger proportion of their total expenditures. One survey indicated that relatively wealthy states, such as California and New York, spent less than six percent of their revenues to match federal grants, while poorer states, such as Mississippi and South Carolina, spent from 11 to 18 percent.[11]

Federal grants also redistribute income among states, a very important by-product of the entire grant-in-aid process. Urban oriented programs, which direct larger sums of monies to central cities, often represent a nationwide transfer from wealthier areas, particularly suburbs, to poorer and needier areas. Some grant programs include explicit recognition of per capita income by reducing the matching requirements for poorer states. However, many other factors are involved, such as need and the ability of the state to match the grant. Thus, there is little overall correlation between per capita income and federal grants per capita.[12] The most recent form of grant-in-aid, revenue sharing, explicitly takes into account the recipient government's per capita income and its tax effort in an attempt to establish some qualitative factors in its formula.

---

[11] James Maxwell, *Financing State and Local Governments*, p. 59.
[12] Ibid., p. 62.

Suburban government participation

There is a bewildering variety of grant-in-aid programs available to state and local government. Many of them are responses to the problems of large central cities and reflect the political influence of large city mayors during the 1960s, when most of the programs were adopted. However, many also benefit suburbs and noncentral city areas. As suburban governments become larger and more sophisticated, as suburban counties gain a seat at the national bargaining table, and as suburbs become better organized politically, more provisions favorable to their interests will be passed by Congress.

Table 9–1 indicates some of the programs that have been of significance to suburbs and independent cities as well as to central cities. Federal aid to highways, particularly since 1956, has facilitated the construction of highways, which are heavily used by suburban commuters.

TABLE 9–1
Major federal grant-in-aid programs affecting suburban areas

	Year established	*Current federal department responsible*
Federal aid to highways	1916	Transportation
Low rent public housing/.	1937	Housing and Urban Development
Urban planning	1954	(HUD)
Airport planning and development.	1946	Transportation
Urban renewal.	1949	HUD
Open space land preservation	1961	HUD
Law enforcement assistance	1965	Justice
Basic sewer and water facilities	1965	HUD
Elementary and secondary educational activities.	1965	Education
Demonstration cities and metropolitan development.	1966	HUD
Law enforcement assistance	1968	Justice
Intergovernmental Cooperation Act	1968	Office of Management and Budget
General revenue sharing	1970	Treasury
Comprehensive employment and training.	1973	Labor
Emergency medical services	1973	Health, Education and Welfare (HEW)
Housing and community development.	1974	HUD
Emergency jobs	1974	Labor
National mass transportation	1974	Transportation
National health planning act of 1975	1975	HEW

Source: Advisory Commission on Intergovernmental Relations, *Fiscal Balance in the American Federal System*, vol. 1 (Washington, D.C.: U.S. Government Printing Office, 1967), pp. 140–44, 165–68, and U.S. *Congressional Record*, 1967–75.

Many suburban downtowns have been rebuilt by urban renewal funds, although a majority of the sums have gone to central cities. The Elementary and Secondary Education Act of 1965 officially was intended to supply educationally deprived children with compensatory education. The intent of Congress, expressed in recent amendments, has been to convert the formula into a general aid to education, with over 95 percent of all counties across the country qualifying.[13] Many suburban and rural areas have used airport planning and development monies as well as open space land preservation funds. The Safe Streets Act of 1968 funnels considerable money through the states into suburban police, court, and corrections areas. Urban planning funds (Section 701) have enabled many suburbs to prepare master plans, while many local, noncentral city sewage treatment plants have been built with federal grants. Many public housing units, particularly for the elderly, have been constructed in the suburbs.

Metropolitan grant coordination[14]

The multitude of grant programs has proven to be a curse to federal planners who want the federal government to act upon the basis of a rational plan with a set of urban priorities. They are exasperated by the large sums of money flowing to various local units with no central purpose or coordination at the federal level. For example, both the Agriculture Department and the Housing and Urban Development Department were authorized to make grants for water and sewer facilities in 1965, in rural areas and urban areas, respectively. In addition, the Interior Department was granting funds for waste treatment works construction. Much duplication results from the nature of the congressional committee system, which encourages committees to maintain alliances with various federal agencies and clientele groups. Due to this lack of coordination, federal agencies tend to work at cross purposes. Further, the lack of coordination encourages "grantsmanship" at the local level, as central cities, suburbs, and counties shop for the best deal for their project.

Coordination of grant programs in urban areas has been a federal goal for many years, although it never has been implemented effectively.

---

[13] Floyd Stoner, "Implementation of Federal Education Policy: Defining the Situation in Cities and Small Towns," a paper presented to the Midwest Political Science Association, Chicago, May 1, 1975.

[14] This section relies on Advisory Commission on Intergovernment Relations, "Regional Decision Making: New Strategies for Sub-state Districts," *Substate Regionalism and the Federal System*, vol 1 (Washington, D.C.: U.S. Government Printing Office, 1973), Chapter 5; Joseph F. Zimmerman, "The Metropolitan Area Problem," *The Annals of the American Academy of Political and Social Science* November 1974, pp. 133–46; and George Gordon "Office of Management and Budget Circular A-95: Perspectives and Implications," *Publius*, Winter 1974, pp. 45–68.

For the past 20 years, the federal government has attempted to coordinate its efforts in metropolitan areas by developing coordinating mechanisms that require local review of requests for federal grants to insure that they represent regional needs. The Housing Act of 1954 required that communities applying for urban renewal funds develop a workable plan that included land use and public facilities. According to Section 701 of the Act, comprehensive regional planning was to be exercised to coordinate all local and state planning activity. Section 701 became the mechanisms for future federal programs requiring area-wide planning as a condition for federal grants. It also provided funding for planning activity. Several subsequent acts expanded area-wide planning to include numerous other functional areas, such as transportation and open space planning, as well as other eligible recipients of the planning funds.

Finally, Congress concluded that effective metropolitan planning was thwarted by the fact that planning commissions were not under the control of local elected officials, and so were often out of touch with political reality. The Housing and Urban Development Act of 1965 therefore opened up funds to associates or organizations of public officials who represented the political jurisdictions in the metropolitan area. These funds were to enable them to conduct studies and prepare regional plans. A year later, Section 204 of the Demonstration Cities and Metropolitan Development Act of 1966 required that all local government grant and loan applications be reviewed by an organization responsible for area-wide planning. This organization was to be made up of elected officials from local units in the region. The Intergovernmental Cooperation Act of 1968 broadened the scope of the 1966 Act. Immediately thereafter, many councils of governments (COGs) and regional planning commissions were formed.

It became clear that the federal government intended to force local and regional agencies to consider their programs in an area-wide context before they could receive federal funds. Section 204 initiated the metropolitan planning efforts authorized under the earlier 701 programs. Circular A-95 was issued by the federal Office of Management and Budget (OMB) as an attempt to coordinate federal efforts under Sections 204 and 701 and to ensure some systematic pattern of intergovernmental cooperation. Circular A-95 establishes a review process which forces lateral coordination among federal agencies and state and local units. It is designed to encourage the application of functional expertise to decisions at all levels, but to do so under the control of elected governmental officials. Programs traditionally developed by professional specialists, such as highway engineers or social workers, have resulted in specialized policies at the expense of broader programs. Circular A-95 is aimed specifically at weakening the control of professional specialists in favor of generalist-oriented planners, whose responsibility is to the entire metropolitan area. It broadens the range of potential grant coverage to about 150 separate programs, including nonmetropolitan and state programs.

A-95 reviews include three types of planning and development clearinghouses. One is a metropolitan clearing board, such as the COGs and regional planning agencies in metropolitan areas. The second type are the regional clearing houses for nonmetropolitan areas, generally established by the governors. The third type is a state clearinghouse designated by the governor; it is usually the state comprehensive planning agency. These clearinghouses receive and review applications, identify other agencies that should be notified, and send their views, along with those of other agencies, to the federal funding agency.

For a number of reasons, the clearinghouse procedures have not been effective in advancing goals set up for them. Comments by concerned agencies have rarely prompted substantive changes in the application and in only a small percentage of the cases were any adverse comments transmitted with the application. This reluctance seems to be due to the absence of clearcut areawide plans or policies that could guide reviewers and also due to the reluctance of staffs to critically evaluate proposals of neighboring governments. However, much informal revision takes place before the application is reviewed formally and this early identification of program defects may be the greatest payoff in the review system. Also, clearinghouses seem to have increased federal government coordination as well as public information on regional projects. Such benefits were cited in a 1971 study conducted by the Council of State Governments and the International City Management Association.[15]

The Advisory Commission on Intergovernmental Relations (ACIR) maintains that clearinghouses have reviewed large numbers of proposals in a speedy manner, and have provided useful information to federal and local agencies. Clearinghouses have coordinated local efforts in related functional areas, particularly in smaller, nonmetropolitan areas. However, they have not provided critical analyses of proposals since there is no penalty for perfunctory or weak reviews. Consequently, many local officials consider them merely another layer of red tape.

Joseph Zimmerman indicates that, by the mid 1960s, Congress no longer relied completely on local and state agencies when granting aid for environmental matters. Congress partially preempted state and local action on water and air quality. The 1965 Water Quality Act required states to adopt water quality standards and empowered the administrator of the Environmental Protection Agency (EPA) to set and enforce them if the states failed to do so. In 1967, Congress also preempted the states by setting minimum federal automobile exhaust emission standards. The

---

[15] Advisory Commission on Intergovernmental Relations, "Regional Decision Making," pp. 148–49.

Clean Air Amendments of 1970 stipulated that 1975 model automobiles must reduce certain 1970 level emissions by 90 percent, although in 1973 the deadline was extended several years.[16]

Even without preempting state action, the federal government has a major impact on intergovernmental relations. A number of analysts, including George Gordon and Daniel Elazar, fear that the A-95 Review Process may change the nature of federalism. Gordon suggests that the present decentralized system of "mild chaos" may be redefined so that local units are coopted by centralized decision making powers at the federal level which leave only the mechanics of implementation decentralized.[17] Revenue sharing has weakened the A-95 review process to a small extent by reducing the amount of categorical monies available for "coordination." The ineffective procedures conducted by these clearinghouses confirm that the federal system will continue to remain decentralized. If the federal role is to be increased at the expense of the state and local role, it probably will be through preemption of state action on the basis of jurisdiction over interstate commerce. Actions on civil rights and air and water pollution have demonstrated the utility of this approach, if the federal level is willing to maintain or expand it.

DIRECT FEDERAL SPENDING

Grants-in-aid are only one part of the two-pronged federal impact on urban areas. Direct federal spending also affects urban governance. While state and local spending for urban services exceeds that of the federal government, the federal government now dominates natural resources, air transportation, and housing and urban renewal spending. The total impact of federal direct spending in these areas is increased when grants-in-aid also are considered.

Other areas such as welfare are funded primarily by the federal government in the form of intergovernmental aid. Table 9–2 indicates the effect of federal expenditures in crucial areas, and the effect of intergovernmental aid.

The federal government dominates the natural resource and air transportation area, primarily with direct expenditures. Expenditures for natural resources are not of major concern to urban areas, although many of them are directed toward metropolitan areas. Examples include the Agriculture Department's watershed protection and flood prevention program in the Soil Conservation Service and the Interior Department's land and water conservation program. Air transportation involves the

---

[16] Zimmerman, "Metropolitan Area Problem," pp. 142–45.

[17] George Gordon, "Office of Management," pp. 65–68.

TABLE 9–2
Direct and intergovernmental expenditure responsibility by level of
government and type of function: 1970–71

Function	Percentage of direct federal expenditure	Percentage federal government pays through grants to state and local governments	Percentage of total governmental expenditure made by federal government
Natural resources	78	4	82
Housing and urban renewal	43	36	79
Air transportation	67	2	69
Welfare	11	48	59
Health and hospital	24	23	30
Highways	2	6	29
Total expenditures	28	13	41

Source: U.S. Bureau of the Census, *Governmental Finances in 1970–71* (Washington: Government Printing Office, 1972), Table 6. Quoted in Advisory Commission on Intergovernmental Relations, "The Challenge of Local Government Reorganization," *Substate Regionalism and the Federal System*, vol. III (Washington, D.C.: U.S. Government Printing Office, 1974), p. 5.

Department of Transportation's airport planning and development program. Through this program, the federal government develops most new airports, and supports the upgrading of existing ones.

The federal government also is involved heavily in direct spending for housing and urban renewal programs, but almost doubles its share of the total program through grants-in-aid. In this program, the balance of all spending is mostly local, with some states simply not participating. The classic case is welfare, where only 11 percent of total program funds involve direct federal spending, but an additional 48 percent involves federal grants-in-aid for a total of 59 percent. Most of the remaining 41 percent is paid for by the states.[18] Welfare is not really a local function, even though considerable discretion in applying the rules is granted to local units. Finally, 29 percent of highway spending is federal, with 27 percent of it through intergovernmental aid, paid mostly to the states. Although highways are often considered a local function, this is true only of local roads. In 46 of the 50 states in 1967, the state was the dominant service provider, if only direct expenditures are considered.[19] The federal level also outspends local units of government

---

[18] U.S. Bureau of the Census, *Governmental Functions in 1970–71* (Washington, D.C.: U.S. Government Printing Office, 1972) Table 7. Quoted in Advisory Commission on Intergovernmental Relations, "The Challenge of Local Government Reorganization," *Substate Regionalism and the Federal System* (Washington, D.C.: U.S. Government Printing Office, 1974), p. 5.

[19] Ibid., p. 6.

for highways. In addition to funding roads, the federal government also set standards in urban areas. Mandatory standards, such as lane widths, roadway markings, and control of access, have an enormous impact on state and local highway engineers.

Table 9–2 indicates that the federal share of direct expenditures of the functions listed is 28 percent and grants-in-aid are 13 percent, a total of 41 percent. Further, this aid is concentrated in certain areas such as welfare, highways, and housing and urban renewal, where the federal level has used the power of the purse to capture substantial, sometimes dominant, influence over policy and programs.

Direct federal spending also may have a substantial effect on the social, economic, and political life of the area that receives it. An example of this effect was the effort to consolidate the Public Health Service (PHS) in Rockville, Maryland, in the late 1960s. The Public Health Service, whose units were scattered through the Washington, D.C., area, was to be consolidated in a headquarters building near an existing unit in Rockville, where about half of the PHS employees already worked. The Maryland site was in an exclusive residential area with the highest median income in the state and very few minority residents. However, 32 percent of the PHS employees were receiving less than $8,000 per year, far below the income level necessary to afford a home near the site. Problems were compounded by the fact that there was no adequate public transportation available.

A court case was brought by one of the PHS employee unions against the agency to enjoin the move, alleging that PHS was fleeing the central city and leaving the clients it was supposed to serve. It also noted that the PHS was not following its own policies, which required evaluation of the availability of nondiscriminatory housing in site selections. Some suburban opposition also surfaced at a hearing before the U.S. Commission of Civil Rights. A Montgomery County councilwoman noted that the move would complicate transportation and traffic conditions. A Rockville city official noted that the city had not been consulted. Finally, the Suburban Maryland Fair Housing Board advised against the relocation because of the scarcity of low and middle income housing.

Despite opposition from within and without, the PHS proceded with the relocation. However, federal policies were changed as a result of the unexpected opposition. First, the General Services Administration, the "broker" for federal agencies purchasing land, revised its regulations to require consideration of the availability of low and middle income housing and transportation accessibility.

The Department of Health, Education and Welfare (HEW), parent agency of the PHS, announced the establishment of the "Job Guarantee Plan." This plan would guarantee any civil service employee who was below a certain salary level who did not want to move to Rockville another equivalent job in the Washington Metropolitan area. Eventually, about 10 percent of the employees applied for the program.

Finally, President Nixon issued Executive Order 11512, which required that federal space allocations exert positive economic and social influences on the development of the area in which the facility is located. While the impact is yet unclear, the order should remind federal agencies that their installations have a substantial effect on the immediate suburban area.[20]

COORDINATING THE FEDERAL AGENCIES

Successful funding of programs, at whatever level, does not insure that the intended aid recipients will receive the funds, will know how to use them, or will respond effectively. They may not understand the law, they may not qualify for payments, or they may not be reached by the local or regional agencies created for the service. The program may be diverted by sheer incompetence, the venality of officials, or ignorance and apathy on the part of recipients. It is a long way from legislation to effective response by bureaucrats and even further to favorable impact of government programs upon citizens.

The Great Society programs of the 1960s attempted to coordinate urban policy. It is widely believed that programs, such as the War on Poverty and Model Cities, failed due to lack of coordination. Federal policies could not be implemented at the community level because different programs, different levels of government, and different interests could not be integrated. The Great Society programs all involved different interests, clientele, agencies and legislative authorizations. The programs also had to be coordinated with traditional federal and state programs in urban areas, such as those of the Department of Defense, which determined where most of the federal school aid to federally impacted areas would be distributed, or to the state employment service, which was generally unresponsive to local needs.

Ideally, coordination should take place at the planning stage of legislation, so that conflicts and inconsistencies can be detected before the program is initiated.[21] Whether or not this occurs, coordination in the operation phase is essential to check duplication and overlapping, alleviate conflict, sequence activities over time, and refer clients to the appropriate agency efficiently. The A-95 review process was created to improve metropolitan coordination among local governments.

As the number of Great Society programs proliferated, an elaborate

---

[20] Neil Lawer, "The Relocation of the Public Health Service," *Public Administration Review*, January–February, 1972, pp. 43–49.

[21] Much of the discussion of coordination is taken from James Sundquist and David Davis, *op. cit.* (Chapter 1).

coordinating system was created in Washington. In functional areas, the Office of Economic Opportunity coordinated anti-poverty programs; the Department of Labor, manpower programs; the Secretary of Health, Welfare and Education, programs in those areas. In geographic areas, the Secretary of Housing and Urban Development was responsible for urban development programs and the Secretary of Agriculture for co-ordinated rural development programs. However, the Appalachian Regional Commission and five other regional commissions coordinated development in their areas, with the Secretary of Commerce responsible for regional development in general and for coordinating the coordinative efforts of regional commissions. All of these agencies and many more were operating programs at the local level and providing intergovernmental funding to suburban and central city jurisdictions, but this process rarely was effective because the federal coordination was rarely good enough. There were similar problems at the state and local levels.

The basic problem, however, was not bureaucratic rigidity and defensiveness, but the lack of an overall urban program at the federal level. There were a number of programs and a multitude of local units, all with different interests and priorities. Urban problems—including unemployment, delinquency, and drug usage—do not add up to one single issue that can be handled effectively by one federal program. Each project or grant-in-aid program deals with only part of the urban mosaic. Coordination was difficult, then, because there was no overall objective toward which different programs could be directed.

The difficulty of achieving even minimal levels of coordination among federal, state, and local agencies in a metropolitan area is immense. One study revealed that 38 federal agencies are involved in administering programs in Oakland, California, all of which have some impact on urban problems in that city.[22] There was no consensus among the federal administrators about the major problems in Oakland and what should be done about them. In most cases, the administrators defined Oakland problems in terms of their own specific program. The Labor Department saw unemployment; the Public Health Service saw health problems, and Housing and Urban Development officials perceived the need for development and low income housing.[23]

An overall set of priorities was needed as well as some central authority to serve as program manager. But there was no overall set of priorities

---

[22] Oakland Task Force, San Francisco Federal Executive Board, *An Analysis of Federal Decision-Making and Impact: The Federal Government in Oakland* (New York: Praeger, 1971). Originally published by Economic Development Agency, Department of Commerce, p. 52. These 38 agencies were only those responding to requests, so there might have been considerably more.

[23] Ibid., pp. 111–13.

and no powerful coordinator. The presence of a variety of interest groups in a pluralistic political system contributes to the difficulty of establishing such a system. As Norton Long noted some years ago:

> The difficulty of coordinating government agencies lies not only in the fact that bureaucratic organizations are institutions having survival interests which may conflict with their rational adaptation to overall purpose, but even more in their having roots in society. . . . Coordination of government agencies involves far more than changing the behavior and offices of officials in Washington and the field. It involves the publics that are implicated in their normal functioning. . . .[24]

The Oakland case

When programs are confined to one area and involve relatively few interagency complications, it is the job of the federal manager to deliver the program. This is difficult enough in a highly focused program with clear goals. However, since most federal programs involve grants-in-aid as well as direct federal activity, the federal manager cannot have complete control over all the actors involved. He must work with contractors and other federal agencies, negotiate with state and local governments, chart his way through the shoals of regional headquarters paperwork, and resolve conflict in his own agency. The Oakland case is a classic illustration of a federal effort to implement a major social change in a metropolitan area.

In 1966, the new head of the Economic Development Administration (EDA), Eugene Foley, decided that Oakland would be the subject of a massive effort to concentrate the resources of one agency on economic development and unemployment. At the same time, EDA hoped to demonstrate how the provision of public works and building loans can provide incentives for employees to hire minorities.[25] The following public works proposals were to receive EDA money:

Airport hangers and support facilities (Port of Oakland, leased by World Airways)	$10,650,000
Marine terminal and access roads (Port of Oakland)	10,125,000
Industrial park (Port of Oakland)	2,100,000
Access road to coliseum area (City of Oakland)	414,000
Total	$23,289,000

---

[24] Norton Long, "Power and Administration," *Public Administration Review*, Autumn 1949, pp. 261–62.

[25] This section is from Jeffrey Pressman and Aaron Wildavsky, *Implementation* (Berkeley: University of California Press, 1973) particularly Chapters 1–3. For a formal model, see Donald Van Meter and Carl Van Horn, "The Policy Implementation Process, A Conceptual Framework," *Administration and Society*, February 1975, pp. 445–88. Also see Amory Bradford, *Oakland's Not For Burning* (New York: McKay, 1968).

These grants and loans were to create 2,200 jobs, many or most for minority persons. Additional business loans would create 800 new jobs, totaling 3,000 in all.

Oakland was chosen because EDA's predecessor agency had extensive contacts with Oakland, its unemployment rate was twice the 1966 national rate, and it was considered a likely scene for a major urban riot. Also, since Oakland had a Republican mayor, EDA believed it could resist any political demands the city might try to make through the Johnson administration, if disagreements developed. EDA's $23 million commitment in loans and grants for one city was unprecedented. Finally, Foley wanted to move the rurally-oriented EDA into the urban scene and he felt that if sufficient resources could be committed to a middle sized city like Oakland (population 365,000) dramatic results could be achieved.

To assure that new jobs would go to unemployed inner city residents, EDA required employers who wanted loans to submit employment plans committing them to recruiting Oakland hard-core unemployed. These plans would be reviewed by a board of labor, management, and the poor before going to EDA for final approval, and monthly reports also would be required. EDA could hold up financial aid if the employer failed to comply.

The new program was greeted with considerable fanfare, both locally and nationally. It appeared that progress would be made and that the deadlock between the Oakland establishment and the black community would be broken. In fact, no major riots occurred in Oakland in 1967 and 1968. However, the program accomplished very little in its first years, and by 1969, three years after announcement of the forthcoming financial aid, only the industrial park and the access road were complete. These projects only produced a total of 30 jobs, and it was not determined how many went to unemployed minorities from Oakland. Considerable disappointment was expressed both by black leaders and by businessmen. By December 1970, only about 1,000 jobs had been created, one third of the projected total, and, of these, only 350 went to minorities. Hopes were dashed during the implementation process because of a number of unforeseen circumstances.

The program was adversely affected by changes in personnel. Foley resigned as director of EDA in October 1966, and Mayor John Houlihan of Oakland was convicted of embezzlement (not connected with the program). While these changes in personnel had some effect on the project, most of the difficulties in implementing the Oakland Project were due to more basic factors.

There were difficulties with the two largest elements of the public works program, the aircraft hangar and the marine terminal, each of which was to involve a $10 million committment. Sixty percent of the commitment would be from grants and 40 percent from the loans. The marine terminal was beset with difficulties. Disposal of project fill in the San Francisco Bay was a continuing problem because the contract for dredging and fill was not let until 1969, three years late. The Corps of Engineers would not issue a permit until the Bay Area Rapid Transit District withdrew its objections that the dredging operations were too close to its dikes. The Port of Oakland had difficulties with officials of the Alameda Naval Air Station, who feared that a construction crane at the end of the new marine terminal and the masts of ships would deter flight safety and operations. The Navy also delayed action because it felt the end of the new marine terminal would change water current patterns in the entrance channel to the Naval Supply Center. The U.S. General Accounting Office questioned the 60–40 ratio of grants to loans in the aid package from EDA to the Port of Oakland, since the traditional package was about 56–44.

These problems proved to be surmountable, but time consuming. Financial arrangements with the Port of Oakland itself proved more difficult. The Port required advanced funding, due to stipulations in the city charter, but the EDA general policy was not to advance grant loans for interim development. The Port also revised the EDA financed project by moving it to a different location to avoid the dredging problems and problems with its prospective tenant, Matson lines, which would not guarantee minority employment. Its new location was not submitted until April 1967 and construction finally was begun in 1969.

But the terminal was relatively successful compared to the ineffective aircraft hangar project. This project suffered substantial delays while leases were negotiated between World Airways and the Port. An initial architectural plan was not completed until April 1968, two years after the authorization date between EDA and the Port. When the construction plan finally was submitted, the cost had increased 45 percent due to increases in building construction costs, demands for fire protection, some office improvements, and increased airport paving and fencing. The Port requested about half of the increase in an additional grant and proposed to finance the other half by local revenue bonds. EDA's options were to fund the overrun, with no assurance that costs would not increase again; deny the overrun, probably stalemating the entire project; or cancel the project completely.

Complicating the picture was the failure of the World Airways training program, authorized under the federal Manpower Development and Training Act (MDTA). A complex program requiring approvals at the local, state, and federal levels, it had been approved initially in 1966, but languished in two state agencies for nearly a year. Meanwhile, it became apparent that World Airways' compliance record with the employment requirement was questionable, since the number of minority employees actually dropped while total employment increased. When it finally reached Washington, the three Departments involved—HEW, EDA, and Labor—were unable to reach agreement. Consequently, World Airways withdrew the proposal in 1968, dismantling a key part of the entire project.

EDA finally refused to accept the cost overrun unless it could approve all employment plans prior to approval. The Port would not agree, hoping to gain concessions from the new Nixon administration. The cost also had increased by another million dollars since 1968. But, the Port retained another architect who developed a much less expensive plan approximating the cost of the original authorization. Construction contracts were awarded in 1971—about five years after the program was initiated to relieve current unemployment problems.

Why couldn't the Oakland project be implemented more quickly? It had top level support, resources, and, unlike many other federal initiatives, it generally had local support. Part of the delay was due to the complexity of negotiating intergovernmental clearances. As noted, the Navy, the Bay Area Rapid Transit Authority, the Army Corps of Engineers, the City of Oakland, the Port of Oakland, the U.S. General Accounting Office, and several state and federal agencies related to the MTDA employment grant had to be dealt with. The interests of private employers, such as Matson and World Airways, also had to be considered. With the exception of the MDTA proposal, problems were worked out over time, but the vitality of the project was dissipated.

Many of the problems lay with EDA and the Federal government. There were many changes in top level leadership, including a change in administration from Johnson to Nixon. There were three different EDA administrators and four regional EDA representatives in five years. Their rapid turnover hurt the project. The process of appropriating and committing funds was rapid in the Oakland Project. This is rare because most bottlenecks generally occur in this phase of a program. In Oakland, purely "technical" problems prevented implementation of the grand scheme for over five years. By that time, much of the original plan was in shambles.

SUMMARY

The federal government is a major intergovernmental factor in the metropolitan area. Its greatest influence is in areas such as welfare, natural resources, transportation, and housing and urban renewal. In some cases, the grant-in-aid process accounts for the federal influence, while in others, such as natural resources, direct spending is the predominate influence.

Bloc grants were the first type of grants used by the federal government. Until the early 1960s federal grants-in-aid went to the states on bloc grant formula basis. In the mid-1960s of the Great Society, however, they increasingly have been designated for the cities on a categorical basis for programs with national goals. However, legislation such as the Safe Streets Act of 1968 and revenue sharing signaled a movement back to more local discretion bloc grants.

Federal grants are used to redistribute income between states as well as to encourage desired spending by states and local units. The major grants that have benefitted suburban areas are comprehensive planning aid to highways, law enforcement assistance, public housing, manpower and emergency employment, urban renewal, and airport planning.

The sheer number of grant-in-aid programs has fostered considerable confusion, provoking continuing attempts to coordinate disparate programs. For 20 years, Congress has been attempting to coordinate varied programs, the most recent attempt being through regional clearinghouses in metropolitan areas. Generally these attempts have not been successful.

In some cases, it is impossible to implement federal programs even when they are restricted to one agency and are relatively noncontroversial, due to circumstances at the local level that thwart the federal program. Such was the case in Oakland, where the Economic Development Administration program to provide construction jobs for minorities was suspended far short of its goals. This case study demonstrates many of the complexities of federal action in a metropolitan area.

10

The end of suburban isolation

SUBURBAN PROBLEMS and politics are important to any understanding of the urban system. This book was written largely because they have been seriously overlooked in the past. However, suburban problems and politics are only a part of the larger system; it is important to avoid the misconception that they can be treated in isolation. As indicated in Chapter 3, it is not even clear that suburbia is a definable subsystem of the metropolitan system. The problems, lifestyles, opinions and political interests of suburbanites are increasingly harder to distinguish from those of the central city or even rural populations.

If there actually ever was a period of suburban isolation, it clearly has ended. Suburbia currently is burdened by the same problems that face all other parts of the urban system. Crime is increasing in the suburbs as well as in the ghetto. Housing the poor is a serious central city problem, but the suburban poor also face the problem of inadequate housing. While many central cities are concerned with downtown renewal, suburbs are grappling with poor land use planning. In short, there simply is no single set of problems that require only suburban solutions.

FOUR CRITIQUES OF LIFE IN THE METROPOLIS

In this chapter, the issues of crime and housing will be reviewed to demonstrate how suburbs are affected by the same problems besetting

215

the central city. But before addressing these specific functional problems, we shall examine the metropolitan setting through the eyes of those who have criticized the present system of urban governance. All of their criticisms focus upon the predominance of decentralized suburban decisionmaking, which becomes increasingly anachronistic to the extent that the same problems coexist in all parts in the urban area. Governmental fragmentation, inadequate areawide services, a deteriorating quality of life and the absence of strong leadership have all been identified as weaknesses or consequences of the present system of metropolitan government.[1]

Fragmented government

Many critics view suburbia as a badly fragmented governmental system. There were about 17,000 municipalities in 1972, of which over 5,100 were suburbs. When the unincorporated suburbs are included, there are over 18,000 suburbs.[2] Some critics have claimed that these suburbs are too numerous and too small to be effective.

Other observers believe that the number of suburban governments creates fewer problems than do their jigsaw boundaries. Unincorporated islands are surrounded by several cities, finger annexations cut off other suburbs from commercial areas, and the heart of one neighborhood may be part of an adjacent city. This situation fosters service disparities, confusion, and cries for metropolitan reform. It is difficult for citizens to vote intelligently on candidates for four or five special district boards, the county, and whichever other units exist. Reformers in the state of Washington have maintained that

> local government in Washington was designed for a simpler day when people were fewer and the line between city and county was clear. It has grown by patchwork additions of cities and special purpose districts, and is now a crazy quilt of overlapping jurisdictions, costly in higher taxes to the homeowner and businessman alike.[3]

The most frequently cited example of this view is the report of the Committee for Economic Development, entitled *Modernizing Local Government.* This prestigious business organization proposed to reduce the number of local units of government by 80 percent, partly through the disincorporation of small cities, and the consolidation of nonmetropolitan

---

[1] John Rehfuss, "Metropolitan Government: Four Views," *Urban Affairs Quarterly,* June 1968, pp. 91–111.

[2] Reprinted by permission of Yale University Press from *Opening Up the Suburbs* by Anthony Downs. Copyright (c) 1973 by Yale University.

[3] Citizens Advisory Committee to the Joint Legislative Committee on Urban Area Government, *City and Suburb-Community or Chaos* (Seattle: Joint Committee on Urban Area Government, 1962), pp. 4–6.

counties.[4] Clearly, the committee thought that the existence of large numbers of small units is intrinsically bad and should be eliminated by structural reorganization.

All reformers sincerely want stronger and more responsible government, even if it is centralized and more distant from the citizen. However, criticisms that focus upon the number of local governments all tacitly imply that the number of governments is, in fact, a major part of the problem.

This view probably has less support now than it had a few years ago. The failure of major local government reorganization efforts indicates that local residents and office holders will resist change despite the fragmentation argument. Nevertheless, the profusion of suburban governments and their confused boundaries is a weakness of local home rule in the eyes of many influential persons, especially those in the businesss community, who are more concerned with economy than with political process. Eventually, suburban governments, as well as all small units, will have to justify their existence as separate units. If they do not, they will lose basic local powers over functions traditionally considered local responsibilities.

Lack of areawide services

Another common criticism of suburban government focuses on the lack of areawide services. There are two kinds of areawide services. The first involves traditional urban or urban fringe services such as police, fire, health, and recreation. As these service demands grow in volume and complexity, they usually can be met by interlocal arrangements. Such arrangements usually impose only a minimum level of inconvenience upon the citizen, even though trees may not be trimmed regularly and traffic laws may not be enforced to the resident's complete satisfaction. These deficiencies are not nearly as serious as the developing regional needs for mass transportation systems, air and water pollution controls, provision for clean water, and adequate sewage disposal. These are the needs that have sparked metropolitan reorganization through the creation of large regional governmental mechanisms such as the Port of New York Authority, the Bay Area Rapid Transit District, the Metropolitan Chicago Sanitary District, the St. Louis Bi-State Development Authority, and the Seattle Metropolitan Sewerage District. These regional structures tend to satisfy the areawide service needs and, on the surface, do not seem to threaten the powers of the local suburban governments. But closer scrutiny reveals that they form a larger and more significant governmental entity over which the suburbs have very

---

[4] Committee for Economic Development, *Modernizing Local Government* (New York: Committee for Economic Development, 1966), p. 17.

little control. In Chicago, for example, the Metropolitan Sanitary District has overridden local zoning ordinances in constructing sewage treatment plants. Suburbs will have to come to grips with these new units of government where they exist, for they strip more functions away from traditional local control. They further fragment the area by functional categories, making the urban governmental landscape more complex for all units, especially suburbs, which have relatively little access to their governing boards. It must be remembered though, that metropolitan districts were created because the suburbs and the central city could not or did not want to face these huge regional problems.

Quality of life

Many social critics and intellectuals are deeply concerned with the livability of cities rather than with their governments and the services they provide. Their most common complaint is that the urban scene is gray and ugly and that the typical landscape is polluted with neon signs. They not only find the central city disgraceful, but claim that the suburbs are now busy making the same mistakes. Their classic example is the newly developed commercial area, already littered with beer cans and candy wrappers, crowded with signs for hot dogs, service stations, and crowned with ugly overhead transmission wires. According to one conservation publication:

> The character and quality of such urban sprawl is readily recognized: neon-bright cities along main-traveled roads; housing tracts in profusion; clogged roads and billboarded alleys; a chaotic mixture of supermarkets, used car lots, and pizza parlors; the asphalt plain of parking spaces; instead of parks, gray-looking fields waiting to be subdivided. These are the qualities of our new urban areas of our slurbs—our sloppy, sleazy, slovenly semi-cities.[5]

Concern for the quality of urban life is an important consideration in attempting to create an urban society, and one that suburbs can not afford to ignore. Increasingly, the general public, as well as social critics, journalists, and intellectuals, are expressing concern for the quality of urban life. Many of these critics, applying the standard of European-type city life, regard suburban growth as a sign of cultural decadence in the United States. Dismay at the state of urban life is not a recent attitude of the intellectual. Thomas Jefferson complained that "the mobs of great cities add just so much to the support of pure government as sores do to the strength of the human body," and Thoreau's sylvan longing for Walden Pond finds its modern day spokesman in Lewis Mumford. Their criticisms, aimed at cities in general, are criti-

---

[5] California Tomorrow, *California, Going, Going* . . . (Sacramento: California Tomorrow, 1962), p. 10.

cisms of suburban life as well as of central cities. While today's suburban dweller is unlikely to give them much attention, intellectual advocates of America's pastoral myth often have had substantial impact.

Lack of governmental process

A fourth major criticism of suburban life is that the vast metropolitan area lacks any mechanism for making areawide decisions. The question is not "how do we do this," but "how do we decide what to do?" Few regional governmental units are in a position to set regional priorities, and usually no other mechanisms are available. The only exceptions are the advisory function of councils of government and regional planning agencies, or such specialized regional authorities as the metropolitan transportation districts. However, the councils have wide scope but extremely weak powers, while regional agencies may have substantial functional power but little scope. Neither is able to set priorities for the metropolis or to settle major issues affecting the suburbs. The suburban polity has little influence upon the regional decisionmaking process, although many of its residents expect some leadership from their city. Many metropolitan residents desire some basis for making areawide choices between transportation or open space, or between schools and flood control. They want to create a decisionmaking body that can at least discuss these basic alternatives. The present choices rarely are made centrally, between competing alternatives. Usually they are the sum of hundreds of choices made by many units, most of which are suburbs. But thousands of small changes do not add up to a regional choice. Consequently, decisions concerning local roads are easily made, but controversy surrounds the construction of expressways, and neighborhood parks are provided instead of a regional open space system.

These four views expose the numerous critical ills of urban America. Ugliness and sprawl injure the quality of urban life. The fragmented nature of suburban areas prevents change and often breeds pettiness and narrow-mindedness. Areawide needs are not met directly, but by narrow, functional, regional arrangements which further fragment the governmental process.

The growth of suburban governments is a symptom rather than a cause of these problems. Suburbs are part of an interdependent whole and must directly address urban problems. In the balance of this chapter, two major issues affecting suburbs, crime and segregation in housing, will be considered.

CRIME IN THE SUBURBS

For most suburbanites, criminal activity in their community triggers all the fears generally associated with urban living. Suburbanites are deeply threatened by crime and the dislocation of community life that it implies. Although suburbs no longer are self-contained, organic communities, many residents still believe that they should be. They often over react to the random assaults of robbery, violent crimes and theft by purchasing expensive burglar proofing or by carrying handguns.

These attitudes vary from person to person and from suburb to suburb. But one fact that does not vary is that the crime rate is increasing faster in suburbia than anywhere else. Violent crime in suburbs is up slightly more than property crime and, as a whole, the crime rate has increased 30 percent from 1967. Table 10–1 lists the national crime rates

TABLE 10–1
Crime rate by area, 1973
(rate per 100,000 inhabitants)

	Area			
Crime index offenses	Total U.S.	Cities over 250,000	Sub-urban	Rural
Total.	4,116.4	6,582.8	3,562.6	1,471.8
Violent.	414.3	1,003.4	248.5	147.4
Property	3,702.1	5,579.5	3,314.1	1,324.4
Murder	9.3	20.7	5.1	7.5
Forcible rape	24.3	51.4	17.8	12.0
Robbery	182.4	571.5	76.1	17.7
Aggravated assault.	198.4	359.9	149.5	110.2
Burglary	1,210.8	1,949.3	1,054.4	564.0
Larceny-theft	2,051.2	2,651.8	1,952.4	677.6
Auto theft	440.1	978.4	307.4	82.8

Source: Federal Bureau of Investigation, *1973 Uniform Crime Reports* (Washington, D.C.: U.S. Government Printing Office, 1974), p. 2.

for 1973. The amount of crime is staggering, and this represents only crimes reported to police officials. Since many citizens are reluctant to report crime, it is estimated that the true rate is considerably higher.

The first four listed categories comprise the violent crime index, while burglary, larceny-theft and auto theft are included in the property crime total. There were over 8.6 million crimes during 1973, occurring at a rate of 4,116 per 100,000 individuals.

Nationally, crime rose about 5.7 percent over 1972. As Table 10–1 indicates, the rate for large cities was nearly double that of suburban areas and more than four times that of rural areas. The difference is particularly striking in the numbers of violent crimes; a large city is many times more likely to be the scene of violence. In general, suburban areas are relatively close to the national crime average, about midway between rural and large city areas. More murders, however, are likely to occur in rural than in suburban areas.

This tells only part of the story, however, since suburban crime is increasing very rapidly. Table 10–2 lists crime rates for three selected

ABLE 10–2
rime rates in 1973 and increases over 1972 for selected crimes*

	Total crime index	Murder		Aggravated assault		Burglary	
		Rate	Per-cent increase over 1972	Rate	Per-cent increase over 1972	Rate	Per-cent increase over 1972
burban cities	391.5	8.9	3.9	19.3	139	13.0	1017	10.4
nsuburban (outside MSA) cities	375.6	8.2	6.0	13.8	169	7.8	940	12.6
ntral cities over 50,000	658.3	1.1	20.7	7.7	360	1.1	1949	3.7
Total, all agencies	438.9	4.9	9.7	9.2	241	6.8	1457	7.3

* Crimes per 100,000 population.
Source: Federal Bureau of Investigation, *1973 Uniform Crime Reports* (Washington, D.C.: U.S. vernment Printing Office, 1974), Tables 6, 7, 10, 11, pp. 98–100 and 104–6.

crimes and the increases over 1972. Murder was up 19 percent over the 1972 total in suburbs. About a quarter of the murders involve family members, and almost one third occur in conjunction with an illegal activity, such as robbery or gangland crimes. Aggravated assault, involving attacks against one person by another, was up 13 percent in suburbs. Burglaries, up over 10 percent in suburbs, involve unlawful entry of a structure to commit a theft or a felony. About 78 percent of these burglaries involve forcible entry, and daytime burglaries are increasing. The interesting fact that the number of burglaries, rapes, and larcenies is increasing faster in nonsuburban cities than in suburban areas demonstrates the national parameters of the increase in crime.

Table 10–1 indicates that the crime rate in independent cities is nearly as high as in suburbs. Suburban crime rates seem to vary little with city size. The larger suburban cities (25,000 to 50,000) have a crime index of about 4,256, only 7 percent higher than the entire suburban average.

Suburban arrest rates were up about 11 percent from 1972.[6] The

[6] All figures are from the Federal Bureau of Investigation, *1973 Uniform Crime Reports* (Washington, D.C.: U.S. Government Printing Office, 1974), Table 6–7, 15, and 41, p. 99–100, 127, 145.

crimes included in the FBI crime index increased slightly more rapidly for persons under 18. Arrests for narcotic drug law violations and for driving under the influence of alcohol in suburbia seem to be approaching the levels of central cities that have populations over 250,000. Narcotic arrests are now 288 per 100,000, about 70 percent of the central city figure. Arrests for diving while intoxicated are now 344 per 100,000, about 67 percent of the central city figure.

There are a number of reasons for the rapid increase in suburban crime, the sum of which suggest that the increase was inevitable. First, transportation patterns and linkages make suburban crime targets both inviting and accessible. Since freeways and beltways link all parts of the metropolitan area, criminals can leave the scene of a crime and be on the other side of the metropolitan area in a relatively short time. By crossing into a different jurisdiction, the criminal can greatly complicate police work.

Commercial developments, such as department stores, shopping centers and branch banks, have been crime targets for many years. In addition, industrial growth and associated support industries are now well outside the central city. Trade and industry have spread over the metropolitan area, encouraging a rate of burglaries and larcenies nearly as high in suburbs as in central cities. Finally, large numbers of suburban homes are left vacant, especially in the summer, when residents take vacations and weekend trips.

The sheer number and variety of persons living in suburbs is another factor stimulating criminal activity. More people currently live in suburbs than in central cities, and there is as much poverty in some suburbs as in the core area. Since poverty is a major cause of crime, it probably has contributed significantly to the increased suburban rate.

Suburban crime also may be increasing because suburban areas have relatively few policemen available to suppress or detect it. An Advisory Commission on Intergovernmental Relations (ACIR) study reported that in all metropolitan areas in 1967, 26 percent of all cities had less than 10 policemen on the force.[7] Even in 1975, the FBI Crime Reports indicate that many suburban cities have only one or two police officers. When only one patrol car at most can be summoned, criminals have relatively little fear of being caught or interrupted. To the extent that patrol deters crime, the lack of patrolmen further exposes suburban communities.

For these and perhaps other even less understood reasons, crime rates will continue to climb in suburban areas. As they do, suburbs will find that their "crime problem" is similar to that of the central city. Obviously, there is a growing need for closer coordination among the numerous police forces operating in any metropolitan area.

---

[7] Advisory Commission on Intergovernmental Relations, *State-Local Relations in the Criminal Justice System* (Washington, D.C.: 1971), p. 305.

HOUSING AND SEGREGATION IN SUBURBIA

Housing and racial integration are the most stubborn problems facing the suburbs in the 1970s. One example of the potential issues and conflicts was the case of Mt. Laurel Township, New Jersey, where the State Supreme Court ruled that the town's zoning policies were effectively excluding minorities.

Perhaps it is inevitable that this battle will be fought in the suburbs, for here the contending values are rooted most deeply. The Constitutional imperative that all persons, regardless of race or creed, have a right to seek employment, housing and other opportunities wherever they can be found is threatened by segregated housing and a segregated employment market. Yet, this segregated housing market is created largely by the web of legal and political connections in suburbia, where millions of individuals have formed little governments and communities designed to share life with only like-minded people. The abstract rights of all people to be treated as individuals, rather than as economic or racial units, clearly conflicts with the efforts of residents who want to choose their neighbors and control their own destinies.

This subject provokes strong feelings because the issue of personal freedom is at stake. Most social scientists and intellectuals are deeply committed to social integration and they easily can defend their case by the broad provisions of the federal Constitution. This view shapes most of the literature and the actions of the federal government, or at least of the federal courts, in their measures to force racial integration. In fact, this view is not limited to intellectuals or federal bureaucrats. A recent study in 15 American cities indicated that 40 percent of whites favored laws to prevent discrimination against blacks in buying or renting houses or apartments, while 51 percent either opposed such laws or felt that whites have the right to keep blacks out.[8]

Suburbanites appear to be ambivalent about racial integration, approving it in principle but not necessarily in specific situations. Many suburbanites near the central city fear mixed neighborhoods because they suspect that the community will not remain integrated—that it inevitably will become all black and that middle class norms will not prevail. The scenario is common place—whites leave, rapidly causing many inner ring suburbs to become largely black. This process enables a few blacks to find homes in the suburbs, but they usually are purchased at a rate considerably higher than the market price, largely due to the restricted housing supply for blacks in the metropolitan areas.

Open housing in suburban areas has profound implications for a host of urban policy questions. Some dispersal of housing is necessitated

[8] Angus Campbell and Howard Shedman, *Racial Attitudes in 15 American Cities* (Ann Arbor, Michigan: Survey Research Center, 1968), pp. 32.

by the decentralization of industry to suburban locations. It soon may be necessary for large employers to provide housing for their employees at a reasonable distance from the plant, if it is not already available. Suburbs then may have to choose between having industry combined *with* low cost housing, or to have neither. However, since nearby housing does not have to be within the same jurisdiction, or even the same county, some sort of metropolitan housing and fiscal equalization may be in order.

Integrated housing is one means of achieving integration in neighborhood schools. The ramifications of this issue are all too visible now, since court decisions have required extensive busing to assure quality education in Boston, Detroit, and elsewhere. However, these court actions do not require housing integration. If there were general racial integration in the United States, it would not be necessary to provide extensive busing. Many suburbanites fear a racial mixture in their schools because they feel that the quality of education will decline. This situation is unlikely since middle class domination of a school maintains educational norms even with a fairly large minority of lower income persons. But, however invalid, these fears are a factor in suburban receptiveness to minorities, and further indicate the web of issues that surround racial integration.

Many of the expensive transportation systems around central cities were created because of the distance between jobs and housing. Many black domestics and blue collar workers commute to suburban jobs, while suburban residents commute to their downtown offices. This is hard on low income persons whose earnings must be committed to transportation. The lack of public transportation at a reasonable rate is partly due to the low population densities caused by suburban growth. It forces low income people to live in central cities where public transportation is available.

Local control is at stake since the federal government may begin to invalidate local zoning ordinances and fiscal zoning patterns that were created to zone out low income persons. The pattern was set in the Civil Rights Act of 1964, when Congress decreed that past records of voting discrimination by some southern states and a few northern counties justified federal examination of all voting actions. Thus, even annexations of land that might influence local elections may be reviewed at Washington, and requirements for district rather than at-large elections may become a condition of federal approval. In view of these kinds of requirements, as well as court rulings on the sacredness of school district boundaries, it is possible that similar limits will be placed on local zoning powers and decisions regarding housing for low income persons.

Federal impact on suburban development

By and large, suburban areas have a substantial majority of the better housing stock in America that consists mostly of single family detached homes. Table 10–3 indicates that most multifamily homes are found in

TABLE 10–3
Housing stock, 1970 census

Type of unit	Percent of total	Percent in suburbs	Percent in central cities
Single family, detached.	66	73	45
Mobile homes or trailer.	3	3	1
Single family, attached	3	2	6
Multifamily, 2 to 4 units	13	10	21
Multifamily, over 5 units.	15	12	28
	100	100	100

Source: Bureau of Census, *1970 Census of Housing: Supplementary Report of Detailed Housing Characteristics for the United States Regions, Divisions and States: 1970,* Series HC (SI) 6, 1972 (Washington, D.C.: U.S. Government Printing Office, 1972), p. 1–287.

central cities, where about 49 percent of housing is multiple dwelling, compared to only 22 percent in the suburbs. Only about 12 percent of all Federal Housing Administration (FHA) multiple dwelling units are located in the suburbs.[9]

The present housing stock in suburbs and central cities has been affected substantially by federal policies dating from the New Deal. The single family detached homes in suburbs are substantially a creation of the FHA. FHA programs expanded mortgage credit by reducing risks to lenders, inducing them to make credit available. Their loans were guaranteed by the FHA and financed by charges on borrowers. The program greatly facilitated the migration of middle income families into suburban areas, particularly after World War II and enabled young middle class families to leave central cities for the suburbs. Since 1935, about seven million new homes and apartments have been built with FHA mortgages, mostly in the suburbs.[10]

Unfortunately, FHA and private lenders have refused to invest in central cities or even to lend to "economically unsound" groups such as blacks, divorcees, or other low income persons living there. The FHA

[9] Charles Haar and Demetrius Iatridis, *Housing The Poor in Suburbia,* copyright 1974 by Ballinger Publishing Co. Reprinted with permission.

[10] Much of this section is based on Alan Shank and Ralph Conant, *Urban Perspectives: Politics and Policies* (Boston: Holbrook, 1975), p. 344.

officially adopted segregationist policies and refused to insure projects that did not comply with them because it believed that integration destroyed property values. Its own "Underwriting Manual" required that FHA officials try to prevent fiscal risk by preventing "inharmonious racial groups." FHA policies intentionally discriminated against central cities and blacks, drying up most mortgage sources for them.[11] These practices were not officially halted until a 1948 Supreme Court ruling.

Public and subsidized housing has not been remarkably successful. The Public Works Administration replaced some 10,000 substandard structures with about 21,000 low income units. That paved the way for the 1937 Housing Act, which established the Federal Housing Administration, the forerunner of the present Department of Housing and Urban development. The federal government was to provide up to 90 percent of the development costs for local housing agencies. However, only about 170,000 units were constructed by 1948. The 1949 Act authorized more units, but these new goals had not been met. By the 1970s, 60 percent of the 3 million families in public housing were minority, and many of the rest were economically and socially disadvantaged whites.

Occasionally, the public housing program has been revised by subsidy programs based on different schemes. The 1961 Housing Act provided for "below market interest rates" (BMIR) to assist families displaced from urban renewal projects, but whose incomes were too high for public housing and too low for private housing. In part, the program was not successful because many of the sponsors were nonprofit corporations that lacked the expertise to administer projects. Also, since the program was an option of local governments, suburbs easily could reject it if they did not want "problem families."

BMIR became part of a direct subsidy program in 1965. The federal government began to pay direct subsidies to the landlord, covering the difference between 25 percent of an eligible tenant's income and the fair market rental value of the housing. As their incomes rose, those tenants qualifying for supplemental support would begin to pay more. However, Congress restricted the application of rent supplements and did not appropriate substantial sums for the program. In addition, rank and file FHA officials were unsympathetic because they were not at ease with their new clientele, who were philanthropic organizations or churches rather than mortgage bankers.[12]

The 1968 Housing Act, which pledged a 10-year national goal of 6 million new and rehabilitated subsidized housing units, included 2

---

[11] Gary Orfield, "Federal Policy, Local Power, and Metropolitan Segregation," a paper presented to the 1974 Conference of the American Political Science Association, Chicago.

[12] Shank and Conant, *Urban Prospectives,* pp. 360–61.

innovations. Section 236 of the Act was to replace BMIR and rent supplements with FHA mortgage financing to nonprofit housing sponsors. Unfortunately, maximum rent subsidies were established, which restricted benefits to families in the $4,000 to $6,500 income group. Section 235 subsidized, for the first time, home ownership in an effort to improve the image of housing aid. The program called for down payments as low as $200, with long mortgage terms up to 40 years, and with subsidized interest rates as low as 1 percent. FHA would reimburse lending institutions for the difference between these rates and the current market. However, there have been substantial irregularities associated with Section 235, including illegal speculation, collusion with FHA appraisers, and excessive mortgages on houses that soon fell apart due to cheap construction or renovation. Then FHA had to repossess them at substantial losses. In 1973, the Nixon administration placed a freeze on all new Section 235 and 236 commitments.

Under FHA, a total of 7 million new homes and apartments have been subsidized by mortgages. Almost all of the latter are located in the suburbs, while almost all of the apparently 1.7 million units listed of subsidized housing are located in the central city. The Farmers Home Administration programs are an exception to this pattern. Without these mostly rural housing starts, the total funded by HUD and its predecessors would be 20 percent lower. After seeing these figures, it is easy to appreciate the pro-suburban bias of federal, state, and local housing policies. Unfortunately, it is difficult to devise policies that will bring low and moderate income housing into the suburbs.[13]

Suburban resistance to low income housing

From 1960 to 1970, nonwhite population in the suburbs of the largest metropolitan areas increased from 4.2 to 4.5 percent, or about 750,000, representing the largest total in history.[14] However, this is still a relatively small percentage, especially because black suburbanites were not scattered but were concentrated in predominantly black residential corridors, often in older, inner ring, suburban communities. One study of 24 suburbs in which the black population more than doubled during the decade indicated that the black middle class group mainly penetrated selected suburbs. The new suburbanites surpassed their central city brethren in income, education, and job status.[15]

Suburban opposition to low income residents and to minority groups

---

[13] Ibid., p. 364.

[14] United States Commission on Civil Rights, *Above Property Rights* (Washington, D.C.: U.S. Governmental Printing Office, 1972), p. 7.

[15] Harold Connolly, "Black Movement into the Suburbs: Suburbs Doubling Their Black Populations during 1960s," *Urban Affairs Quarterly*, September 1973, pp. 91–111.

has been fierce. Suburbs have implemented zoning ordinances that rule
out small lots or houses with less than a certain number of square feet,
and have relied upon realtors, builders, and financiers to keep out undesirables. Some arrangements have been challenged successfully in court,
while others still seem to be in effect. Ironically, now that some of
the barriers to housing the poor in suburban areas are being effectively
challenged, the economics of the housing market may prevent further
dispersion of minority or low income persons. The costs of new housing
and of transportation may operate as an economic barrier to continued
suburban growth, and thus to significant dispersion. Whatever the future,
the past has been marked by suburban opposition; many suburban areas
still do not welcome low income neighbors.

It is widely believed that this opposition can be attributed largely
to racial prejudice. That was the position taken by the National Commission on Urban Problems in its report *Building the American City:*

> The suburban ring has a majority of the residents of the metropolitan
> area. It also has less than its proportionate share of the poor and only
> five percent of American nonwhites. . . . The suburbs, however, contain
> nearly half the white metropolitan poor—a figure which suggests that
> the suburbs discriminate more on the basis of race than on the basis
> of economic status.[16]

This is a critical issue, since objections based on race are not easily
overcome. If suburban units are mistakenly linking class and race, an
educational program may demonstrate that suburban minorities exhibit
typical middle class potential. This is not to argue that discrimination
based on class is justified, but only to note that there are substantial
numbers of poor whites in the suburb, while there are relatively few
poor blacks. A major question facing suburbs in the decades to come
is whether they can open their doors without discrimination based on
color. There is some hope, and perhaps some evidence, that objections
of suburbanites are based primarily on the fear of economic losses in
their neighborhood.

In his book *Opening up the Suburbs,* Anthony Downs argues that
"in the long run, I expect economic class discrimination to be more
persistent in American neighborhoods than racial discrimination, even
though the latter has been stronger until now."[17] He notes that the
profound difference between racial discrimination and economic class
discrimination is that poverty has a functional relationship to behavior
patterns that are relevant to the quality of neighborhood life. But race
and color do not.

---

[16] National Commission on Urban Problems, *Building the American City* (Washington, D.C.: U.S. Government Printing Office, 1968), p. 52.

[17] Downs, *Opening Up the Suburbs,* p. 101.

A report on the attitudes of typical suburban residents in Dayton, Ohio, is contained in Table 10–4. Opposition to low and moderate income households concerned property values, stability, and maintenance of the housing stock. Although only 2 percent of respondents mentioned

TABLE 10–4
Reasons for considering a low and moderate income neighborhood as an undesirable neighborhood
(percent responding)

	Very important or important	Unimportant
Property values would drop	84	9
Neighborhood would become less stable	83	9
Housing maintenance and conditions would deteriorate	82	9
These people would be a bad influence on my family because they don't believe the same things we do	38	54
Race	2	0

Source: Adapted from Nina Jaffa Gruen and Claude Gruen, *Low and Moderate Income Housing in the Suburbs* (New York: Praeger, 1972), p. 26. Note: Only the items most and least frequently mentioned were charted above. Among other reasons, which were not as salient as those mentioned above, was a decrease in law and order, although 73 percent of the respondents felt this was "very important or important."

race, it would be unwise to read these answers as suggesting receptivity to minority persons. To the extent that race and class are linked in people's minds, their objections would be triggered by minority groups moving into their neighborhoods. Further, some of the responses may be euphemisms, masking dislike of minorities in general. However, the fact remains that most objections in this study seemed to be rooted in economic and social factors rather than in the interpersonal relationships between individuals.

But whether they are primarily economic or a mixture of racial antagonism and economic fears, these objections certainly are potent. They have led to a range of actions, from those which are clearly discriminatory to those which merely involve a heavyhanded exercise of zoning powers.

One of the most blatant cases involved the newly incorporated Black Jack, Missouri, a town of 3,900 residents, almost all of whom were white. Prior to incorporation in 1970, the area had been zoned for apartments. A proposal by a church-sponsored, nonprofit developer to build federally sponsored low and moderate income housing was outlawed immediately upon incorporation because the new city council adopted one-acre, single family zoning. This case resulted in the first legal challenge by the federal government to the use of municipal zoning power to exclude subsidized housing. There was considerable evidence that racial discrimination was a major factor in the new city's action, although Black Jack officials claim that opposition was due to the project's unsound financial basis. The government's position was upheld on appeal, and the ordinance was struck down.[18]

In Arlington Heights, an upper income suburb of Chicago, the Roman Catholic Archdiocese sold a church site to the Metropolitan Housing Corporation, a nonprofit housing sponsor. Neighboring homeowners, who had considered a parochial school a good buffer against undesirable residential development, were outraged. When the Corporation attempted to rezone part of the site for townhouses, some of which would be for low and moderate income families, there was substantial objection from the neighborhood homeowners. They complained that the intrusion of multifamily houses would lower their property values. When the application was denied by the zoning board and the city council, the Corporation went to court charging racial discrimination. This case, which is still pending, is significant because there is no overt evidence that racial discrimination caused the resident's opposition. If these local zoning ordinances are overturned, the ruling would establish an important precedent.

One interesting development occurred in Stoughton, Massachusetts, a blue collar suburb of Boston, where 104 units of moderate housing, funded under Section 236 of the 1968 Housing Act, were built despite earlier council rejection. The decision to approve them apparently was the result of a tradeoff between HUD, which approved a $1.5 million water distribution system, and the Board of Selectmen (City Council).[19] In this case, a federal incentive, in the form of a badly needed water system, made the project acceptable when good will alone might have failed.

New challenges to suburban barriers

Several programs for housing the poor and minorities in suburban parts of the United States have surfaced in recent years. One receiving widespread attention is the Dayton, Ohio, metropolitan "fair share" pro-

---

[18] The United States brought action against the town of Black Jack under the Civil Rights Act of 1968, alleging that the city zoning act denied persons housing on the basis of race. The initial District Court decision ruled that racial discrimination was not a significant factor in the city's zoning law, noting that both poor blacks and whites were excluded. This seemed, on its face, to sanction economic but not racial discrimination. However, on appeal, the District Court of Appeals reversed this decision, holding that since the ordinance was shown to have a racially discriminatory effect, it could be upheld only on the showing of compelling government interest, which was not shown. *United States* v. *City of Black Jack, Missouri*, 508 F2D 1179 (December 27, 1974).

[19] This account of Stoughton is from Haar and Iatridis, *Housing the Poor*, pp. 239–81.

gram. This was adopted in 1970 by the Miami Valley Regional Planning Commission, which recommended that 14,000 additional units of low and moderate income housing, in including public housing, be constructed in the five county metropolitan area. Distribution was based on population factors, including the number of welfare recipients and aged residents, the quality of existing housing, and the availability of sewers, water transportation, schools, and jobs. The plan was adopted by a planning agency. Although there were no formal sanctions over member municipalities, the plan was successful; in the first three years, over 1,400 units of federally subsidized housing were built. Among these, 850 were in suburban locations. Another 3,950 have been granted or applied for, 3,700 of which are located in the suburbs. Although many suburban residents opposed the plan, their representatives raised no objections to it. Some of the more rural counties, however, are considering withdrawing from the program.[20]

Another plan that has been suggested involves a "unitary housing marketing system." This plan assumes that inner city residents who must commute to jobs in the suburbs would prefer to live near their jobs but cannot find inexpensive nearby suburban homes and apartments.

Inner city buyers cannot rely on local brokers, even minority brokers, for information, because a multiple listing agency has no economic interest in providing information outside the agency area. The unitary marketing system would require that all rental vacancies in a metropolitan area be listed in a state designated clearinghouse; that computerized data retrieval systems keep the listings current; that the system be available in all areas, particularly in the most segregated areas; and that some monitoring procedure, such as periodic site visits to rental offices, be utilized. Organizational options for the clearinghouse include a new state agency, a publicly owned corporation, a state contract with a nonprofit agency, or a state contract with a commercial apartment locator service. The recent Illinois Governors' Commission on Mortgage Practices has recommended what is in effect a unitary market.[21]

The social implications of such a centralized agency are enormous, particularly in large metropolitan areas such as Chicago. Even if the information processing technology and the information dissemination elements worked successfully, the job of monitoring such a system would be very difficult. However, the proposal is a clear alternative to the present decentralized system of housing arrangements in the metropolis.

Anthony Downs has developed one of the most comprehensive proposals for moving more of the poor and moderate income residents of the central city into the suburbs. According to Downs, America's urban

---

[20] United States Commission on Civil Rights, *Equal Opportunity in Suburbia* (Washington, D.C.: U.S. Government Printing Office, 1974), pp. 57–9.

[21] Lawrence Rosser and Beth White, "An Answer to Housing Discrimination: The Need for a Unitary Marketing System," *Civil Rights Digest*, Winter 1975, pp. 10–20.

system, outside of the South, exhibits a pattern of development peculiar to this country.

Urban growth in other cultures results in a mixing of wealthy and poor income persons, because there are few prohibitions against low quality housing in areas with new growth. In the United States, however the "trickle down" system prevents low quality housing.[22]

New and more expensive housing is used first by higher income families and then, after aging, it is passed on to succeeding generations of lower income owners, until, finally, the lowest income families own only the poorest housing in the oldest and most dilapidated areas. The trickling down process only works to the advantage of upper or middle income families because United States housing policies decree that all households should live in a decent housing unit, whether or not they can afford it. "Decent" is defined by middle and upper class living standards. Thus, it is illegal to create living units at a quality low enough for the poor to afford.

This trickle down process is accelerated by the construction of new housing, generally occurring in suburban areas, which enables many families, including ghetto residents, to move to better homes. If no wave of new immigrants enters the cities, the oldest housing will be abandoned, while the areas with the next worst housing will decay in time. However, in a tight housing market, the poor are trapped in the worst housing and no significant upgrading is possible, since the best housing is appropriated by higher income groups. Hence, declining birth rates and environmental attacks on new suburban housing also contribute to housing problems. Downs seeks a "loose market," with specific programs to prevent the decay described above.[23] His strategy for dispersed economic integration basically involves four phases:

First, creating a favorable general climate by maintaining a loose housing market and developing support for housing subsidies.

Second, providing specific motivations for [low and moderate income] LMI families to move and for suburbs to accomodate them, and encouraging the housing industry to build a variety of housing for LMI families.

Third, preserving middle class domination, partly by limiting the percentage of LMI families in each area.

Finally, improving inner city areas at the same time, by maintaining incomes and creating jobs rather than by constructing additional capital facilities.[24]

---

[22] Downs, *Opening Up the Suburbs*, p. 1–5.
[23] Ibid., chapter 1, pp. 115–18.
[24] Ibid., chapter 4, pp. 26–45.

He argues that opening up the suburbs in this manner would produce the following major benefits:

LMI families would have better access to middle class schools.

The nation would be more likely to reach its goal of improved housing for LMI families.

The fiscal and social costs associated with metropolitan poverty would be more equitably distributed.

Future confrontations between the haves and havenots in metropolitan areas (as in the urban riots of the 1960s) would be less likely.

Ghetto areas could be improved without displacing urban decay into adjacent areas.[25]

Downs' program provides both sanctions and rewards to suburban policymakers. The sanctions include creating "development targets" for LMI families in all large developments; attacking exclusionary zoning and local approvals for subsidized housing; regionalizing public housing authorities and programs to the metropolitan level; and requiring the acceptance of LMI families as a prerequisite for locating publicly financed facilities in a community.

The rewards include subsidizing suburban public transportation systems; shifting all welfare costs to the federal government; equalizing school financing costs and providing bonuses to school districts with LMI families; providing special community service funding to areas accepting LMI families; and providing property value insurance for homeowners near LMI housing.[26]

There would, of course, be substantial opposition to opening up the suburbs, even if most of the opponents agreed abstractly with the above list of benefits. The primary opposition would be due to economic fears. Suburbanites oppose the increased local taxes for supporting low income persons and the increased federal taxes for housing subsidies necessary to relocate LMI families. They fear that property values will fall and that crime rates will increase, although Downs convincingly argues that crime is not likely to increase in neighborhoods with a dominant middle class ethos. The suburban fear that school quality will decline is also unlikely, because middle class dominance of neighborhoods will remain, and thus will perpetuate current educational trends. Finally, many suburbanites still desire to maintain social distance from the underprivileged and to live with those of similar social status.

There are two major central city objections to the strategy developed in *Opening Up the Suburbs.* One is the fear that those who leave the

---

[25] Ibid., chapter 7, pp. 68–83.
[26] Ibid., pp. 134–35.

central city will be LMI leaders, who are more upwardly mobile and who maintain stability in their neighborhoods. In effect, the lowest class and those with the most severe problems will remain in the central city. Second, many black leaders see central cities as a base for exerting power, since they soon will have an absolute majority in many of them. Suburbanization dilutes this power base.[27] Downs does not underestimate the power of these objections. In fact, he is pessimistic about the chances for the policy changes he recommends.

Downs suggests that suburban areas are undergoing a period of change and increased pressure for adaptation to national housing goals. Suburbs have been criticized for a variety of faults, some alleged and some real. The charge of discrimination against minorities and the poor is probably the most serious, although it is usually too generalized. The right of local communities to plan and zone their own area is under serious attack. Downs' proposals would give some economic benefits to many suburbs, while destroying this most crucial power and function. This proposal is too wide ranging to be fully accepted by Congress, primarily because it threatens to undermine the right of municipalities to control their own planning and zoning powers. However, suburban freedom to exercise these powers without reference to broader societal issues is rapidly eroding.

SUMMARY

Suburbia no longer is immune from national and regional problems and no longer can escape the necessity of dealing directly with them. Criticism of urban life increasingly refers to suburban life as well. Deepseated urban problems are found in suburban areas even if they have not been recognized fully. As we have indicated, crime is increasing faster than in the central city and one of the most intractable problems is housing. In the United States, housing is dominated by a "trickle down" system which places artificial limits on the housing market. This inflates costs for low and middle income persons at the end of the process. Until recently, the trickle down process has been reinforced by FHA actions encouraging exclusionary zoning.

This process, which has been institutionalized in upper income suburbs, works to exclude low and middle income persons, particularly minorities. The fact that suburban housing is considered one of the last bastions of isolation from central city problems, the poor and minorities, has had a pivotal effect on education, employment, and land use policies. The struggle for open housing in the suburbs is fierce. It has resulted in court cases in which the federal government has chal-

---

[27] Ibid., pp. 161–63.

lenged local zoning laws on behalf of fair housing proponents. Proposals for solving this problem range from the voluntary "fair share" program in Dayton, Ohio, to Anthony Downs' far reaching plan described in *Opening Up the Suburbs*. Whatever solutions are proposed, however, it is clear that the four avatars of urban crisis—alienation, crime, poverty, and prejudice—have descended upon suburbia.

11

Metropolitan governmental adaptation and the lessons of reform

FOR GENERATIONS, the "textbook" solution to problems in metropolitan areas has been to institute metropolitan government. Theorists, critics, and reformers have maintained that order can be imposed, fragmentation eliminated and adequate services provided if existing units of government, including suburbs, are consolidated. This solution has appeared to be comprehensive and absolute. Should political forces resist the plan, reform still can be implemented through partial consolidation or even through two-tier governments, retaining most local units. However, consolidation in some form has been widely acknowledged as the most effective approach.

The only flaw in this "textbook" solution is its basic assumption that metropolitan problems are essentially problems of metropolitan government. If this were true, then problems could be solved merely by reorganizing government. Unfortunately, problems like crime and housing segregation are not so easily solved. These and other problems exist and will continue to plague urban areas with or without governmental reorganization.

However, even though it is too simplistic a solution for all metropolitan problems, reorganization may have many positive impacts. Consolidated government may improve program coordination throughout the area and provide services more evenly. A more rational division of services between urban and rural areas can be devised. Capital spending can be planned for the entire region, and certain regional functions such as sewage disposal can be provided. Finally, the new government may encourage the development of a regional consciousness among its residents.

These more modest accomplishments do not comprise an urban millenium. However, they promote governmental effectiveness and cooperative attacks on deep seated urban problems. This is no small achievement and certainly one that is worth pursuing. This chapter will describe how it has been pursued, in one form or another, throughout the past two centuries and still continues to be of interest today.

State legislatures were responsible for the first series of city-county consolidations including the merger of the city of New Orleans with the Parish of Orleans in 1805; the consolidation of the city of Boston with Suffolk County in 1882; the merger of the city and county of Philadelphia in 1854; the merger of New York City and New York County in 1874; and the consolidation of New York and Brooklyn and the counties of Queens and Richmond in 1898. The merger of the city and county of Honolulu was accomplished by the territorial legislature in 1907.

During the early years of the 20th century, municipal reformers wrested the power to make decisions concerning local government structure from the state legislatures. However, during this period, successful city-county consolidation was thwarted by the institution of reforms, which required constitutional amendments and/or referenda before local government could be restructured. Since 1907, over 21 city-county merger proposals have been rejected by voters. Numerous other efforts have failed to survive the necessary constitutional amendment process or to succeed in securing a revision of state statutes.[1]

The second series of successful city-county consolidations is related to the growth of the suburbs that has occurred since World War II. The "famine" in the consolidation movement ended in 1947 when the citizens of the city of Baton Rouge and the parish of East Baton Rouge, Louisiana, voted to consolidate most of their governmental functions and to establish one governing body for the entire area. Since 1947, 15 consolidated governments have been created, 13 by local referendum and 2 by state legislative action. The areas that successfully secured mergers through the mechanism of citizen referenda include:

Baton Rouge-East Baton Rouge Parish, Louisiana	1947
Hampton-Elizabeth City County, Virginia	1952
Nashville-Davidson County, Tennessee	1962
Virginia Beach-Princess Anne County, Virginia	1962
South Norfolk-Norfolk County, Virginia	1962
Jacksonville-Duval County, Florida	1967
Juneau-Greater Juneau Borough, Alaska	1969
Carson City-Ormsby County, Nevada	1969
Columbus-Muscogee County, Georgia	1970
Sitka-Greater Sitka Borough, Alaska	1971
Suffolk-Nansemond County, Virginia	1972
Lexington-Fayette County, Kentucky	1972
Savannah-Chatham County, Georgia	1973

[1] Charlene Caile, "Bringing the City and County Together," *The American County*, February 1972, p. 9.

In 1969, the Indiana General Assembly consolidated the governments of the city of Indianapolis and Marion County without any provision for a local referendum. According to the National Association of Counties (NACO), 36 areas currently are considering consolidation, indicating increased interest in the process in recent years.[2]

Several structural forms of government can emerge from city-county consolidation, the most comprehensive of which is the merger of two or more units of government into one. Through this process, one government becomes responsible for exercising all or most governmental powers for the area formerly included under the consolidation, thus replacing one or more existing governments. The new government that results from this merger is a metropolitan government—an areawide government with full municipal powers and functions. This type of geographic consolidation is exemplified by the merger of Nashville and Davidson County, Jacksonville and Duval County, and Indianapolis and Marion County.

Another structural form of city-county consolidation is the merger of specific functions into one areawide unit, while the existing governmental units within the consolidated area remain largely unchanged. Although there are differences between the two, the Baton Rouge and Miami-Dade governments illustrate a type of functional, or partial, city-county consolidation. Such functional consolidations differ from metropolitan governments since their scope of operation is considerably more limited. The primary city in the metropolitan area is still a functioning government, even though it has transferred some of its services to the county level.

A third form of city-county consolidation creates a federated system of government by establishing a new metropolitan corporation with areawide powers, while maintaining government local municipalities. This two-tier approach to metropolitan government has no American model, but is illustrated by the Toronto metropolitan government of Ontario, Canada. The Toronto approach has been very attractive to U.S. reformers and is the basis of many proposed metropolitan reorganizations. It differs from a functional consolidation in that it involves creating a new jurisdiction rather than merely transferring functions to a revised county government. This two-tier format may call for eliminating some of the city's boundaries and for replacing the city's decentralized communities or boroughs. It resembles a metropolitan government since its powers throughout the metropolitan area are supreme and often cover the full range of municipal services. It differs from a metropolitan government in that it delegates the responsibility for providing those functions to submetropolitan districts. In the following sections, examples of each of these types of consolidation will be described.

---

[2] Ibid.

FUNCTIONAL (PARTIAL) CONSOLIDATION

Baton Rouge

The first major city-county consolidation of the post-World War II growth period occurred in Baton Rouge, Louisiana, where business interests campaigned for local government reorganization. In contrast to a number of similar consolidations, the role of the state in this merger was limited to legislative authorization for a referendum on a constitutional amendment. In 1946, the amendment was approved by a margin of almost four to one.[3]

A commission succeeded in drafting a charter. In 1947, with only one third of the electorate participating, it was approved by a margin of just over 300 votes out of the 14,000 cast.[4] The plan probably would not have been approved had there been a requirement for separate majorities inside and outside the city. City voters supported the plan by about four to one, but the rural voters strongly opposed it.

Implemented in January 1949, the plan was not a complete consolidation. Both the city and parish governments maintained their identities, as did two small municipalities. An interlocking directorate was used to combine the city and parish. The city had seven councilmen; at that time, the parish council consisted of the city council and two (now three) persons elected from the rural area. Unified control over administration was provided by a mayor-president, elected from the entire parish, who presided over both councils but had no vote. He was charged with the appointment of police and fire chiefs, while the parish council appointed major administrative officers in finance, personnel, and public works. City and parish shared certain departmental costs, such as operating the finance department. Consequently, although the government was interwoven, two identifiable and separate governmental structures remained.

The parish was divided into urban, industrial, and rural service areas and the boundaries of the city of Baton Rouge were extended so that the city would encompass the urbanized area. This increased the city's territory from 6 square miles to about 30 square miles and tripled its population.[5]

Throughout the consolidated area, taxing zones also were created. Since they paid both city and parish taxes, residents of the urban area

---

[3] Thomas A. Reed, "Progress in Metropolitan Integration," *Public Administration Review*, Winter 1949, p. 8, and John C. Bollens and Henry J. Schmandt, *The Metropolis: Its People, Politics and Economic Life*, 2d ed. (New York: Harper & Row, 1970), p. 299.

[4] Bollens and Schmandt, *The Metropolis*, p. 299.

[5] Ibid., p. 300.

were provided with the widest range of services. These included urban services such as garbage and refuse collection and disposal, sewers, police and fire protection, traffic regulation, street lighting, and inspection services. Uniform parish taxes levied in the rural and industrial zones financed the public works department, which provided bridges, highways, streets, sidewalks, and airports on a parishwide basis. In the industrial areas, any necessary city-type services were provided by the industries at their own expense. Unless it established special taxing districts, the rural area could not receive city-type services, except for the services of the sheriff's department. Further incorporations were precluded; but contiguous developing portions of the rural area could be annexed to the urban area with the consent of the city council and a majority of owners of the property in question.

By establishing tax and service differentials based on varying need, the new government achieved a degree of flexibility that previously had been lacking. The consolidation eventually resulted in a superior level of service in the incorporated fringe areas and a marked improvement in the city services.[6] Comprehensive zoning, building codes, housing ordinances, and subdivision regulations were adopted throughout the parish. Public services, such as street maintenance, drainage, and waste disposal, were expanded. But the partial consolidation also had some shortcomings. The two law enforcement agencies remained separate, but had overlapping jurisdictions. Several other offices also remained outside of local control. In general, however, the reorganization seems to have worked well.

Miami-Dade County

The unique conditions of a resort area shaped the need for governmental consolidation to provide areawide services in the Greater Miami area. Foremost among these was the population boom in one of the fastest growing areas of the United States. In addition to its million permanent residents, Dade County hosted over 5 million tourists a year.[7] Unfortunately, the provision of government services never kept pace with the population growth and the seasonal influx of tourists. Services were developed on an *ad hoc* basis from year to year, with little or no regard for orderly planning.

The origin of formal consolidation movements in the Greater Miami

[6] Arthur W. Bromage, "Regionalism and the Allocation of Powers," *The Municipality,* August 1970, p. 176; and Bollens and Schmandt, *The Metropolis.*

[7] U.S. Bureau of the Census, U.S. Census of the Population: 1960," vol. I., *Characteristics of the Population,* part II, Florida (Washington, D.C.: U.S. Government Printing Office, 1963), p. 11. Also, see Florida Department of Commerce, *Florida Tourist Study* (Tallahassee: Florida Department of Commerce, 1971).

area can be traced to the early 1940s. Functional consolidation began in 1943 when various municipal health functions were consolidated into the Dade County Department of Public Health. In 1945, all of the ten Dade County school districts were consolidated into one countywide system; and in 1945 a Dade County Port Authority was established and given jurisdiction over ports and airport facilities. Four years later, the city of Miami relinquished its hospitals to the jurisdiction of the county.

There had been several attempts to achieve geographic consolidation of governmental units prior to 1957, when the County Home Rule Charter was adopted. A study was conducted to determine the need for reorganization after the unsuccessful consolidation attempt in 1953. A constitutional home rule amendment for Dade County was passed in the Florida state legislature and ratified by the electorate in November 1956. The measure passed by more than two to one in Dade County, although unincorporated areas voted against the proposal. Fortunately, dual majorities were not required.[8]

The new charter provided for a two-tier form of metropolitan government, which incorporated, to a limited degree, the principle of federation. The existing municipalities, Miami and 27 suburban cities, were retained to perform purely local functions, while metropolitan functions were allocated to Dade County. The Metro government was designated the only local government for the unincorporated areas and was given the power to prevent new incorporations.

The Metro government gained jurisdiction over all countywide functions except state courts and public schools. These included powers to provide and/or regulate roads and traffic, transportation and transit systems, utilities, zoning, building codes, urban renewal and housing, fire and police, communications, hospitals, health and welfare, ports, parks, libraries, and museums. Metro also was authorized to provide and enforce comprehensive planning, to establish special purpose taxing districts, to set minimum standards of service for all governmental units, and to assume services if the cities failed to meet these standards.

The charter completely revamped the county government organization and established a council-manager type system. The county commission, elected on a non-partisan ballot, was designated as the policymaking and legislative body. It is composed of a chairman-mayor and nine members elected countywide, who must meet district residence requirements. The body has the power to pass local ordinances after public hearings and to appoint and remove the county manager, the county attorney, and the judges and clerk of the metropolitan court. The charter abolished the elective status of the assessor, tax collector, surveyor, purchasing

---

[8] Edward Sofen, *The Miami Metropolitan Experiment* (Bloomington: Indiana University Press, 1963), pp. 14–26.

agent, and supervisor of voter registration, and made these officials and department heads appointees of the county manager.[9]

Metro has produced a number of substantial accomplishments in its organization, processes, and functions. It has simplified countywide government by integrating a formerly complicated administrative organization, and has modernized and coordinated the accounting, budget, information, and personnel systems. A general land use plan has been adopted, along with improved zoning ordinances and a uniform subdivision ordinance to control the development of vacant land. Stringent air and water pollution regulations have been adopted, as well as uniform vehicle inspection and countywide traffic laws. The tax assessment and collection functions for all the cities have been assumed by the county. A department of housing and urban development was created to coordinate the efforts of agencies concerned with urban renewal, prevention of blight, and low-income housing. Generally, the area has benefitted from better fire protection, health, inspection, and sanitation services; more park and recreational facilities; and uniformity in fire, housing, and building codes.

Although the Dade County charter was a breakthrough in metropolitan county government, it has been subjected to continual harassment by various municipal officials and former county officeholders. Hundreds of law suits were filed against it. There were also attempts to secure adoption of anti-Metro charter amendments; one such amendment, providing for the direct election of the sheriff, succeeded.

The conflict concerning the metropolitan government of Dade County has centered largely on the division of powers between the county and the municipalities and on finance and leadership. The charter was ambiguous as to which powers were essentially local and which were areawide. Melvin B. Mogulof, a senior staff member of the Urban Insitute, claims that the authority to enforce comprehensive plans for the development of the county on an areawide basis has been largely unusable.[10] The county lacks adequate control over water supply and sewage disposal, often key factors in shaping area development.

Another source of dissention is Miami-Dade's financial situation. The constitutional amendment creating the new metropolitan government did not provide additional taxing powers. Consequently, the county government has had to utilize its traditional tax structure to finance municipal services to residents of the unincorporated areas. Municipal property owners have not received the same county services as those in unincorporated areas, yet they have been taxed by the county at the same

---

[9] Ibid.

[10] Melvin B. Mogulof, *Five Metropolitan Governments* (Washington, D.C.: The Urban Institute, 1972), p. 59.

rate as residents of unincorporated areas. This is because a state constitutional provision requires ad valorem tax uniformity. In a sense, these residents pay twice for the same services, since they also pay taxes to their municipalities.

While the severe limitations on taxing power, coupled with tax inequalities, are shortcomings of the Miami Metro, the institution of countywide tax assessment and collection of taxes has been regarded as an accomplishment. However, the county has been unable to imple· ment the power granted by the charter to set minimum standards of service for all areas. It has not even had the resources to meet minimum standards in the unincorporated areas that it serves. Consequently, it is not in a position to enforce such standards with first tier governments.

COMPLETE GEOGRAPHIC CONSOLIDATION

Nashville-Davidson County

In the early 1950s, the Nashville metropolitan area was a community with serious, but not unique, governmental problems. The central city, which at that time had a population of 170,000 and covered 22 square miles, provided municipal services with the usual financial limitations. Nashville is located in Davidson County, which had a land area of 532 square miles. By 1960, the county was having difficulty providing services to its rapidly growing population, then totaling 400,000. Consequently, it was widely viewed as a divided and confused local governmental system.[11]

The county was under great pressure to extend sewer systems to the developing suburban areas. The presence of heavy deposits of limestone was undermining the effectiveness of septic tanks. Additional county service problems included expensive water charges and inadequate suburban waterlines. Fire and police protection were provided only on a subscription basis. Certain services, including public health and hospitals, were duplicated, causing a further expense to both city and county taxpayers.

City residents resented the fact that county residents had the use of certain "free services" such as the municipal auditorium, airport facilities, libraries, and a comprehensive park system that located many of the parks in the suburbs. City residents also were paying expensive school taxes, part of which supported the county's school system.

Perhaps the most basic problem was the division of political responsibility within one cohesive economic area, which frustrated administration

---

[11] Herbert S. Duncombe, *County Government in America* (Washington, D.C.: National Association of Counties, 1966), p. 195; and Ed Young, "Three City-County Consolidations: A Case Study," Unpublished Research Paper, American University, July 1969.

and discouraged citizen participation. In addition to Nashville, Davidson County contained six municipalities and six special districts. Though this was a relatively small number of jurisdictions compared to other metropolitan areas, it was enough to fragment public authority at a time when unified action was needed. As the Nashville-Davidson County mayor, C. Beverly Briley, later stated: "I was a county judge in 1950 and saw that the system was wrong. The county had the jurisdiction but did not have the authority: the city had the authority but did not have the jurisdiction."[12]

The Tennessee legislature established the Community Service Commission in 1951 to study the problems of Nashville and Davidson County In 1952, the commission recommended the functional consolidation of health services, hospital, welfare programs, and public schools; the annexation of a 69 square mile area of the County by Nashville; the authorization of county home rule; and the reapportionment of Davidson County to give more representation to the urbanized areas. City-county consolidation was not recommended because it was felt that the state's constitutional obstacles to consolidation were too great.[13] The only tangible outcome of the study was the transfer of the city's public health department and a portion of its welfare functions to the County.

Following the Commission's report, two major changes were made. In 1953, the Tennessee Constitution was amended to permit home rule and the consolidation of city and county functions for counties with more than 200,000 residents. This affected only the cities of Nashville, Chattanooga, Memphis, and Knoxville. The implementation of consolidation was made subject to popular referendum and to concurrent majorities in the central city and the remainder of the county. In 1955, prodded by the Tennessee Municipal League, the legislature enacted a strong annexation law which allowed cities to annex contiguous areas without a popular referendum.[14]

A metropolitan government report, published in 1956 by the City and County Planning Commission, called for replacement of the separate governments with a single metropolitan government. State enabling legislation, passed in 1957, paved the way for the creation of a local charter commission in metropolitan areas with a population of 200,000 or more.[15] According to Alan Campbell, it was sold to the legislators as a "local

---

[12] Patrick Healy and Raymond Bancroft, "Three Mayors Review Their Governments," *Nation's Cities*, November 1969, p. 26.

[13] *A Future for Nashville*, A Report of the Community Services Commission for Davidson County and the City of Nashville, 1952, pp. 3–4, 13–5, 123–34, and 151–78, and Alan K. Campbell, ed., *The States and the Urban Crisis* (Englewood Cliffs, N.J.: Prentice-Hall, 1970), p. 69.

[14] Young, "Three City-County Consolidations," p. 7, and Article XI, Section 9, *Tennessee Constitution.*

[15] *Tennessee Public Acts of 1957*, Ch. 120.

bill," good for the state as a whole, rather than as urban policy. In effect, however, it became state metropolitan policy for Tennessee; each of the four metropolitan counties has tried to adopt the authorized form of government.[16]

In 1958, a charter commission, consisting of five members from Nashville and five from Davidson County, proposed a charter containing the following provisions: (1) consolidation of Nashville and Davidson County; (2) creation of a 21-member metropolitan council; (3) establishment of an expandable urban services district and a general services district; and (4) establishment of a tax rate for each district based upon services rendered. The chief executive would be a metropolitan mayor elected for a four-year term.[17]

The campaign for adoption was conducted by Nashville's two daily newspapers and by most community leaders, including Mayor Ben West of Nashville; County Judge Beverly Briley, later elected as the consolidated government's mayor; and a citizen's committee, which supplied speakers for civic clubs, distributed printed materials, and arranged for radio and television advertising. Emphasizing higher taxes and bigger government, local government officials, suburban small businessmen, and private fire and police companies opposed the charter. They also widely distributed handbills and appeared on radio and television. In June 1958, the proposed charter was approved in Nashville, but was rejected by the remainder of the county.[18]

Shortly after the referendum, Major West moved boldly to employ the strong annexation powers recently provided by the legislature. Nashville annexed 7 square miles of industrial property and 43 square miles of residential areas containing 82,000 persons. As Judge Briley noted: "This upset the people who were annexed, and the people who were not annexed were afraid they were going to be annexed next. . . ."[19] The new residents were being taxed more heavily than before but did not experience a comparable change in the services they received. For example, the city was unable to provide immediately sewers for most of the annexed area. At the same time, the city council passed legislation to make suburbanites pay for using city facilities.

These actions triggered a new consolidation movement. Proponents

---

[16] Campbell, *The States and The Urban Crisis*, p. 69.

[17] Nashville Metropolitan Government Charter Commission, "Proposed Metropolitan Government Charter for Nashville and Davidson County," May 1958.

[18] The 1958 election and the failure of the Metro campaign have been analyzed by David A. Booth, *Metropolitics: The Nashville Consolidation* (East Lansing: Institute for Community Development and Services, Michigan State University, 1963); Daniel R. Grant, "Metropolitics and Professional Political Leadership: The Case of Nashville," *The Annals of the American Academy of Political and Social Science*, May 1964, pp. 72–83; and Young, *Three City-County Consolidations*, p. 8.

[19] Healy and Bancroft, "Three Mayors."

of consolidation campaigned for and elected a state legislative delegation that was committed to the creation of a new charter commission. Such legislation was passed, subject to a favorable referendum, which was obtained in August 1961. In April 1962, the commission filed a charter that was not appreciably different from the one defeated in 1958. Nevertheless, it was approved in June by both city and county voters.[20] The second consolidation attempt was successful partly because of opposition to Nashville's annexation and tax measures. County residents wanted protection from annexation without services.

The Metropolitan Government of Nashville and Davidson County is a strong mayor-council type. The mayor, who serves as the executive head, is elected for a four-year term and is authorized by the charter to appoint the heads of almost all important departments, boards, authorities, and commissions. He directs managerial operations, prepares a legislative program, submits an executive budget to the council, has an item veto over budgets, and is responsible for the functions and conduct of the executive and administrative officials.

The legislative body is a 41-member Metropolitan County Council, consisting of 35 district officials, 5 at-large councilmen, and a vice mayor, all elected for 4-year terms. Exercising broad legislative powers for the total area, the council enacts ordinances, reviews executive budgets, and oversees general administration. An Urban Council, composed of three members selected from among Metropolitan Council members, has the sole function of levying a property tax to finance urban services.

Some independently elected administrative officials were retained to comply with the requirements of the Tennessee Constitution. In addition to judges and officials whose duties are closely related to the court system, the other independently elected officials are the county trustee, the metropolitan tax assessor, and the sheriff. There is also a consolidated metropolitan school system with a nine-member board. The members are appointed for six-year staggered terms by the mayor, and they are subject to confirmation by a two-thirds council vote.

For the administration of services and for tax purposes, the county is divided into two districts. The entire area of Davidson-Nashville County is designated the General Services District (GSD), while the area of the city of Nashville as it existed prior to metropolitan government, including all annexed areas, is known as the Urban Services Districts (USD). Areas requiring urban services may be annexed into the USD only if such services can be provided within a year. All residents receive the same GSD services and are taxed at the same GSD rate. These include services ranging from police and courts, to urban renewal and planning.

---

[20] Brett Hawkins, *Nashville Metro* (Nashville: Vanderbilt University Press, 1966), p. 151.

The residents of the USD pay the GSD tax plus a USD tax for the additional urban services of police and fire protection, water, sanitation, storm sewers, street lighting, street cleaning, and refuse collection. Six small independent municipalities outside the USD continue to zone their own areas and to maintain local streets.

Mayor Briley has claimed numerous substantive accomplishments for the new government, beginning with its very existence as a unified, responsive, and accessible structure, which eliminated intergovernmental conflict. Cooperative efforts on the part of numerous officials have ameliorated many potential problems. For example, the location of new sewer facilities was based on need and engineering feasibility, rather than on artificial political boundaries. Parklands for future recreational needs were purchased under a process whereby school, park, and street officials acted jointly to acquire land needed for coordinated development. Health, hospital, and welfare services have been improving in the old suburban area. The upgrading, integration, and consolidation of the school system have been considered top achievements of Metro. Finally, areas outside the city are served by branch libraries for the first time.[21]

The financial aspects of the new government are among its strongest features. Metropolitan Nashville is the only major Tennessee city that was able to stabilize its property taxes in the 1960s and early 1970s. Also, the consolidated bond structure of the metropolitan government has facilitated the identification and investment of surplus funds. The Tennessee Taxpayers Association estimates that the total savings to the taxpayers under consolidation will total $18 million over a 10 year period.[22]

The government still has a relatively long ballot, too large a council, and too little localized administration. It also has shown some insensitivity in race relations. In short, the new government has overcome most of the structural and service deficiencies of the predecessor governments, but it has been far less successful in providing a high quality social environment. It is not unique in this respect.

Jacksonville-Duval County

The problems that beset the citizens of Jacksonville and Duval county during the 1950s and 1960s comprise a virtual catalogue of all the woes of urban areas across the country. Because of a shrinking population and economic base, the city was stagnating. In 1950, Jacksonville had

---

[21] Healy and Bancroft, "Three Mayors."

[22] T. Scott Fillebrown, "The Nashville Story," *National Civic Review*, May 1969, p. 199.

a population of 204,517 and a budget of $23.9 million. Fifteen years later, the city budget had quadrupled, while the population had dropped to 198,000.[23] Retail establishments were deserting the city and no new major industries were locating there. The area had ominous health and air pollution problems. There were serious water supply problems and city sewage was being dumped into the St. Johns River. Slums were spreading, traffic was clogged on inadequate streets, and the crime rate was spiraling. People in the suburbs were demanding that the county provide traditional water, sewer, street, fire protection, and garbage collection services. The structures of both city and county were so complicated that policy decisions were exceedingly time-consuming, if not impossible to obtain. The archaic governing arrangement included a five-member city commission and a nine-member city council, while Duval County had a five-member commission government. Finally, in 1964, the second annexation attempt by the city was approved by Jacksonville voters but rejected by Duval County residents.

In the face of such problems, the new president of the Jacksonville Chamber of Commerce called a meeting of 23 prominent, but politically inconspicuous businessmen and lawyers who also believed that Jacksonville's government needed rejuvenation. They requested and received state legislative authority to form a Local Government Study Commission to investigate a new form of government for the metropolitan area of Jacksonville and Duval County. As the study commission began its deliberations, the local television station ran a series of highly publicized documentaries that revealed questionable activities of both city and county government officials. A 1966 grand jury investigation culminated in 104 separate indictments, and among those named were two of the five city commissioners, four of the nine city councilmen, the city auditor, the tax assessor, and the former recreation chief.[24] The last group of grand jury indictments coincided with the first public release of the Local Government Study Commission's report. Advocates of reform used these events to justify the need for change and to discredit potential opposition.

Entitled "Blueprint for Improvement," the official report of the Local Government Study Commission was released in 1967. The central recommendation of the report was to consolidate the city and county, abolishing all municipalities. The report was submitted to the state legislature. After more than two months of discussion and debate, during which proponents of the plan made substantial modifications, a charter was

---

[23] Richard Martin, *Consolidation: Jacksonville Duval County* (Jacksonville: Crawford Co., 1968), p. 39.

[24] Thomas A. Henderson and Walter A. Rosenbaum, "The Politics of City-County Consolidation," *New County Times*, August 8, 1972, p. 5.

drafted. A bill was passed calling for a referendum on the proposed consolidation.

The campaign that ensued was complex, involving political officials, citizens, local media, and most civic and professional organizations in the county. Disorganized and shifting opposition was voiced by city and county officials, government employees and some blacks. Aided by civic groups, all of the major daily newspapers and the radio and television stations, the Chamber of Commerce led the battle to secure voter approval. On August 8, 1967, the people of Duval County and Jacksonville voted overwhelmingly (64 percent) in favor of consolidation.[25]

Even voters in four small municipalities containing a total of only 24,500 people voted in favor of consolidation, but chose to retain their municipal government rather than to become part of the consolidated government. The favorable vote created a consolidated government encompassing 841 square miles and a population of 507,200.[26]

The consolidated government is a strong mayor-council form in which the mayor, limited to two four-year terms, is charged with administering the executive organization. He appoints all directors and deputy directors of departments, and all division chiefs, upon approval of the council. He also appoints a chief administrative officer to oversee staff functions. The mayor must submit an annual budget to the council, but has an item veto over appropriations. He also has the power to veto most council ordinances and resolutions, but may be overridden by two-thirds of the councilmen present. Eight executive departments report to him: finance, central services, health and welfare, public safety, recreation and public affairs, public works, agriculture, and child services.

Offices such as sheriff, supervisor of elections, tax assessor and tax collector remained elective. The 19-member council is composed of 14 members elected from districts and 5 elected at-large. Each has a four-year term. The council is responsible for reviewing budgets, making appropriations, and levying taxes on all real and personal property assessments.

As in the Nashville-Davidson County model, the consolidated area is divided into a general services district and an urban services district. The general services district encompasses the entire area of the county and provides services which are paid for by all county residents. The services include airports, child care, courts, fire and police protection, health, hospitals, libraries, recreation and parks, schools, streets and highways, and welfare programs.

Unlike Nashville-Davidson, which has only one urban services district,

---

[25] Martin, *Consolidation*, p. 224.

[26] Young, "Three City-County Consolidations," p. 22 and "Seminar in City-County Consolidation," *The American County*, p. 12.

Jacksonville-Duval has five. The first urban services district is the former city of Jacksonville, and the second, third, fourth, and fifth are defined as the preconsolidation corporate limits of the cities of Jacksonville Beach, Atlantic Beach, Neptune Beach, and Baldwin. Each of these cities retained their local governments to perform urban service district functions, including water supply, sanitary sewers, street lighting, street cleaning, and garbage and refuse collection. The general services district, in which the residents are also taxed, provides the other public services.

The council may expand the territorial limits of the first urban service district (Jacksonville) if particular areas require urban services. These services must be provided within a year after the area's inclusion. Should urban service districts desire consolidation, two-thirds of the council must approve an ordinance and the affected district must pass a referendum.

Although it is too early to evaluate conclusively the new government in Jacksonville, a limited number of tentative judgments can be made. There are already some impressive achievements, including: the initiation of a $90 million water and sewer program to rebuild 133 miles of deteriorating sewers and to remove 72 outfalls that daily pour millions of gallons of raw sewage into the St. Johns River; the extension of full-time professional fire-fighting protection, which has resulted in reduced insurance rates; and the institution and enforcement of a model housing code, a model zoning code based on a county-wide land-use plan, and mechanical, plumbing, and electrical codes. Law enforcement has been extended and improved through the merger of city and county law offices and the establishment of one police communications center. The creation of a department of housing and urban development promoted the adoption of urban renewal enabling legislation. The development of a division of consumer affairs has fostered greater consumer protection.

Consolidation also has resulted in some intangible advantages. Foremost among these is the "rejuvenation" of community interest in local government, and better representation in the new government.[27] Services have been improved and more highly qualified professionals have been hired. For the first time in many years, a large industry has located in Jacksonville, a development that has been attributed to its more positive image.[28] Finally, officials of the new government are proud of its internal budget planning, internal audits, and generally improved fiscal management.

It is not clear yet how the black community will be affected by consolidation. It has been claimed that the creation of at-large seats

---

[27] Healy and Bancroft, "Three Mayors."

[28] Bollens and Schmandt, *The Metropolis,* p. 307.

on the council was an antiblack maneuver. At the same time, it was argued that whites favored district elections because blacks exercise the balance of power in at-large elections.[29]

Melvin Mogulof has raised some questions about the Jacksonville changeover. He suspects that the consolidated government does not exert all its potential power and leverage over areawide and local agencies, which, to varying extents, are independent of the mayor and city council. He has accused Jacksonville of trying to "steer clear of conflict," of trying to conduct bargaining without an overall plan, and of failing to develop a central position in "conflicts over programs and the quality of the area's public life."[30] In spite of these questions, the citizens appear to support the new government. In 1969, a telephone opinion survey administered by a local television station found that about 79 percent of citizens rated the government favorably—an extraordinarily high rating.[31]

Indianapolis-Marion County

Indianapolis differed from Nashville and Jacksonville in that governmental change was not promoted by any serious economic crisis. The city was experiencing a building boom, the amount of taxable property was increasing and the inner city tax rates were decreasing. The citizens were enjoying a period of relative prosperity and low unemployment, although the city was facing the typical large city crime rate, traffic congestion, and service duplication problems.

There was also a need for more efficient and effective services in the metropolitan area. Marion County, once a wealthy agricultural area, was being transformed by new highways, housing subdivisions, small businesses, industries, and shopping centers. Increasing suburbanization required better mechanisms for controlling development. Some 58 separate governments in the area—including 20 towns, nine townships, 11 school districts, 14 special service districts and the county government— claimed a share of the taxpayer's dollars.[32]

Lacking the powers of a responsible executive, the mayor served only as a ceremonial head. The county government had no single executive, but instead was run by two separate groups—a board of commissioners

---

[29] The old city government has a population 43 percent black, with 22 percent of the representation on the council (2 of 9); the consolidated government has 23 percent black within its boundaries and 26 percent representation on the council (5 of 19), according to Young, "Three City-County Consolidations," p. 24.

[30] Mogulof, *Five Metropolitan Governments*, pp. 89–91, 108.

[31] "Seminar in City-County Consolidation," *American County*, p. 16.

[32] R. Steven Hill and William P. Maxam, "UNIGOV: The First Year," *National Civic Review*, June 1971, p. 310.

and a county council. Three county commissioners had quite limited legislative power and general custody of county properties. The county council of five members had some control over the budget, but few other powers.[33] Special districts, over which elected officials had little control, intensified fragmentation of responsibility and undermined citizen control of government.

Mayor Richard G. Lugar, a young Republican businessman and the third Republican mayor of Indianapolis in 40 years, recognized that the local government was a divided and uncoordinated corporation. He wanted to insure public control and political responsiveness. He also wanted to increase Republican chances for election in this suburbanized county.

After his election in 1968, Lugar formed the Greater Indianapolis Progress Committee Task Force on Improved Government Structure. This task force was composed of business and civic leaders, the president of the Marion County Council, the president of the Indianapolis City Council, and other local government executives. They held public hearings, considered various reorganization methods, and finally recommended city-county consolidation. Lugar and the Task Force decided upon a strategy of governmental reform through legislative action. This would avoid the necessity of securing a constitutional amendment, a lengthy and difficult process in Indiana.

Throughout 1968, Lugar and a large group of citizens, businessmen, lawyers, and the League of Women Voters worked on a bill that would provide powers for the proposed consolidated government. At the same time, Lugar used the state elections to gain support and to broaden his power base by vigorously campaigning for state Republican candidates, particularly state senators. After the election, he continued to "court" groups of legislators from outside Marion County, personally explaining the law to 91 of the 127 legislators.[34] With only two exceptions, the local legislative delegation supported the bill. It was passed and signed into law in 1969, and became effective in January 1972.

A strong partisan push appears to have been the most important factor in the consolidation of Indianapolis and Marion County Government, commonly known as UNIGOV. The Republicans simultaneously controlled the governorship, the state legislature, Marion County, and Indianapolis. They conducted a well-organized and unified campaign to push the consolidation bill through the General Assembly. Since many key Republican officeholders considered the bill good for the party, its party apparatus was utilized effectively to help secure the bill's pas-

---

[33] Advisory Commission on Intergovernmental Relations, "Regional Governance: Promise and Performance," *Substrate Regionalism and the Federal System,* vol. II (Washington, D.C.: U.S. Government Printing Office, 1973), p. 51.

[34] Healy and Bancroft, "Three Mayors."

sage.[35] Consolidation was described to the public as a method by which sound business techniques, such as functional consolidation and centralized decision-making, could be applied to make government more efficient and more responsive to its citizen stockholders.

The black community, according to Lugar, was sharply divided on the issue. A portion of those opposing the legislation had charged in federal court that it violated the Civil Rights Act of 1964 and was deliberately contrived to undermine the possibility of securing a black mayor. However, militant blacks supported the plan, because it would enable them to elect black officials in black districts, and thus to obtain leadership with grassroots support.

Certain governmental relationships were not changed by the new plan. The 11 area school systems remained entirely independent. Three incorporated municipalities (Beech Grove, Speedway, and Lawrence) with populations between 10,000 and 15,000, voted not to become part of the new incorporated government. Even the seven county officers provided for in the Indiana State Constitution were retained.

Day to day administration of UNIGOV, with 402 square miles and almost 800,000 inhabitants, became the responsibility of a mayor, elected at-large for 4 years and restricted to serving no more than 2 consecutive terms. The mayor was given the power of line-item veto of budget ordinances, which could be overridden by a two thirds vote of the entire council. His "cabinet" is composed of six departments: Administration, Metropolitan Development, Public Safety, Public Works, Transportation, and Parks and Recreation. The mayor appoints department directors, subject to council approval. A departmental board, composed of the director, two mayoral and two council appointees, govern the four latter departments. Three new departments replaced eight of the formerly independent, single-function, special districts. Five old special districts remained in operation, but the new government gained budgetary control over them.

The UNIGOV Council is comprised of 29 members, 25 elected from single-member districts, each containing about 30,000 residents and four elected at large. As the primary legislative body, the council is empowered to pass ordinances concerning all affairs of the consolidated government. It has the exclusive power to adopt budgets, levy general or special taxes, and make appropriations.[36]

Agencies that operate independently of UNIGOV include the Indianapolis Airport Authority, the Health and Hospital Authority, the County Department of Welfare, the County Home Board, the Building Authority, the Capital Improvements Board, the County Library Board, and

---

[35] George L. Willis, "Indiana's UNIGOV Is a Consolidation Model of Reorganized Urban County Government," *County News*, June 16, 1972, p. 14.

[36] Hill and Maxam, "UNIGOV," p. 312.

the school system. The towns, townships, and existing sewer districts retain legislative powers relative to their territorial jurisdictions. However, they may not issue general obligation bonds or pass ordinances that conflict with or permit lower standards than those of the consolidated council.

Two types of special districts were authorized: a special service district and a special taxing district. The special service district includes only part of UNIGOV. It is a separate corporate body created to provide property owners with special urban services. It is governed by a council composed of City Council members elected from those districts encompassing any part of the special service district. This body may adopt ordinances, approve a budget, make appropriations, and levy taxes for its district.

Property owners in the special taxing district obligate themselves to pay for construction and maintenance of local public improvements. The council must adopt a budget for, and give prior approval to, a bond issue in this district, even if the district boundaries exceed those of the consolidated government.

UNIGOV does not have the power to annex territory beyond its limits, but included towns may annex territory which was unincorporated prior to consolidation. An excluded town and the consolidated government may exchange jurisdiction over territory upon petition of 51 percent of property owners in the affected area and the approval of the governing bodies.

It is much too early to appraise the impact of this new government. Proponents claim that it has enabled the mayor to coordinate and direct operations more effectively, supplied more political leadership for area-wide problems, afforded greater control over short- and long-range development, and provided the city and the suburbs with a common forum for discussing and resolving differences. Opponents point out that, compared with Nashville and Jacksonville, the consolidated government of Indianapolis-Marion County did not drastically alter the governmental structure. They claim that its most decisive effect was to bolster Republican control over what was once a Democratic city. If this assessment is accurate, perhaps enlightened state politics may yet lay the groundwork for more effective government.

MUNICIPAL CONSOLIDATION: TORONTO

The Metropolitan Toronto Federation must be examined in two phases. The first began in 1954 with the formation of an urban federated municipality, unique in North America. This period ended on January 1, 1967, when the Ontario legislature reconstituted the Metropolitan Toronto government.

The legislatively imposed two-tier government, which became operational in 1954, had jurisdiction over 241 square miles and over two million people. The Municipality of Metropolitan Toronto (Metro) was to exercise areawide powers over metropolitan scale functions, while continuing to grant control over purely local functions to Toronto and the other 12 municipalities.[37]

The Metro Council, the areawide governing body, consisted of 24 indirectly elected members—12 from the city and 12 from the suburbs— each serving two-year terms. Council seats were filled by those holding elective office in the municipalities. The suburban delegation included the mayor of each of the 12 municipalities. Toronto's delegation also included the mayor, so that the area's primary decision makers were personally involved.[38]

The council annually elects from within or without its membership a chairman who presides over the council meetings. Frederick Gardiner was appointed to his first term and was reelected annually until 1961. As a presiding officer, the chairman may vote only in the case of a tie.

In apportioning functions between the two levels of government, powers over certain local matters, including police, fire, public health, libraries, and licensing, were left as much as possible to the municipalities. Powers over other functions, such as property assessment, construction and maintenance of expressways, and the development of regional parks, were retained exclusively by metropolitan government. Provision of almost every metropolitan service—including water supply, sewage disposal, parks, roads, and traffic control—was based on shared responsibility between Metro and the municipalities.

Metro became a wholesaler for some functions. For example, it constructed and maintained water mains, pumping stations, and treatment plants. Metro also sold water to municipalities, which maintained their own local distribution system and locally determined prices. In other areas, Metro acted as a financial supervisor in the sharing of areawide programs. For instance, Metro and an independent metropolitan school board issued bonds and determined the amount of funds to be spent, while locally elected school boards operated the schools and levied local taxes for supplemental operating funds. The division of responsibility in some functions was based upon definite areawide need. For example, Metro assumed responsibility for the building and maintenance of arterial highways and for developing and maintaining large metropolitan parks, while the municipalities were responsible for local streets and parks. Metro was empowered to appoint the members of the Toronto

---

[37] Committee for Economic Development, *Reshaping Government in Metropolitan Areas* (New York: Committee for Economic Development, 1970), p. 70.

[38] Ibid., pp. 73–74.

Transit Commission, the exclusive supplier of public transportation in the area. It was also authorized to undertake public housing and redevelopment projects and to adopt an area-wide general plan.

The operation of the metro system is based on the pooling of financial resources through metropolitan assessment and taxation. Metro annually levies its requirements for funds on the basis of each municipality's share of the total area assessment. Since Metro has power to collect taxes directly, the metropolitan and school board taxes are included in the local tax bill collected by each municipality. Since local municipalities were not granted the power to borrow money directly, they must submit their requirements for financing to the Metro Council. Each year, the council determines the total amount of money to be borrowed for local purposes and the proportion to be allocated to each municipality.

In 1957, the metropolitan government widened its jurisdiction to include programs not covered in the original legislation. The 13 area police forces were amalgamated into 1 metropolitan force, which was organized into five districts and which covers the entire metropolitan area without regard for local boundaries. The Metropolitan Licensing Commission was created in the same year to establish areawide standards, regulations and fees for various services and trades that each community previously had licensed separately.[39]

During the first ten years, efforts of the metropolitan government concentrated primarily on expanding the physical services required to sustain a huge growth in population and in industrial and commercial development. Metro considerably improved the area's water and sewer conditions and produced a balanced transportation system. It financed an extensive road and expressway network and an effective public transit facility. A 5,500 acre regional park system was created, and more than 235,000 new pupil spaces were provided in the schools of the city and the suburban municipalities. However, fiscal disparities continued to exist between the municipalities, and a growing concern was expressed regarding representation on the council. Each of the suburban municipalities had only one seat, although they varied greatly in terms of population—from 360,000 persons in North York to 10,000 in Weston.[40]

In 1963, the Prime Minister of Ontario appointed H. Carl Goldenberg as a one-man Royal Commission on Metropolitan Toronto. He was charged with providing an independent evaluation of all aspects of the metropolitan federation. The Royal Commissioner issued the findings of his inquiry in 1965, 12 years after Metro's establishment. He recommended that the two-tiered federated system of metropolitan government

---

[39] Ibid., p. 76.
[40] Ibid., p. 77.

be continued, that the constituent municipalities be consolidated into four cities, that the metropolitan school system be reorganized and that the Metropolitan corporation assume many new responsibilities and powers.

The Metropolitan Toronto Amendment Act of 1966 (Bill 81) became effective in 1967 and incorporated many of the Royal Commission recommendations. The area was reorganized from 13 municipalities to 6, with the following population distribution:

City of Toronto (Toronto, Forest Hill, Swansea)	720,000
Borough of York (York and Weston)	150,000
Borough of East York (East York and Leaside)	105,000
Borough of Etobicoke (Etobicoke, Long Branch, Minimo, New Toronto)	290,000
Borough of North York (North York)	475,000
Borough of Scarborough (Scarborough)	310,000

The Metropolitan Council was enlarged to 33 members including a chairman, elected on a representative basis. East York was given 2 members on the Council; York, 3; Etobicoke, 4; Scarborough, 5; North York, 6; and Toronto, 12. Significantly, the new formula gave the suburbs more votes than the central city. The term of office for these elected officials was extended from two to three years.[41]

The most important functional alterations were in education. The basic function of the Metropolitan School Board was expanded to include providing local boards, through a metropolitanwide levy, with funds necessary for a basic metropolitanwide education program. Thus, the previous disparities in educational financing were eliminated. The school board also was reorganized to give the suburbs greater representation.

The other significant functional transfer was in public welfare, which became the sole responsibility of Metro. This change provided a uniform level of service in all parts of the area. Other new responsibilities assumed by Metro included the administration of waste disposal, the establishment of metropolitanwide public ambulance service, the financing of regional libraries, and the authority to participate in urban renewal in conjunction with the area municipalities.

Since its inception in 1954, Metropolitan Toronto has been subjected to considerable analysis and evaluation. Admirers point to a long list of achievements that have resulted from the reorganized government. The highly critical need for water supply and sewage disposal has been addressed through construction of new treatment plants and pumping stations, and the installation of miles of water and sewer mains. Metro established an advanced transportation system, consisting of expressways, arterial highways, and a showpiece rapid transit facility. Improved

---

[41] Ibid., p. 78.

and unified law enforcement has reduced the crime rate and contributed to a more rapid disposition of cases. The construction of new public housing and homes for the aged, and improved library service and civil defense, are also considered achievements.

In the area of finances, Daniel Grant concludes that the new government did not produce an overall reduction of expenditures, partially because it contributed to a "costly revolution of rising expectations."[42] However, through the pooling of financial resources, it did provide for expansion of services and produced dramatic savings in capital financing. Metro's handling of all capital financing has resulted in tremendous savings in interest costs on bonds, estimated to exceed over $50 million in ten years. Metro Toronto has a "AAA" credit rating in Canada and an "AA" rating in New York City, the highest classification a foreign corporation can receive in the United States.[43] It is commonly agreed that one of Metro's most significant powers is its control over the sale of bonds by municipalities and areawide agencies. However, Melvin Mogulof has charged that the centralized bonding process has allocated approvals to communities on the basis of population rather than on the basis of project merit. This practice may have resulted in the authorization of some marginal projects.[44]

Planning is another functional area that has been subject to criticism. Frank Smallwood and Melvin Mogulof note that there is still no official plan and that it is hard to discern how much decision making is influenced by the "unofficial" plan. They also contend that Metro's planning is "bottom up"; that is, it legitimizes local planning without attempting to apply metropolitan criteria. Mogulof argues that attempts at a "rational" division of functions have resulted in persistent duplication. Further, he sees the system drifting toward an accretion of functions and authority by the central government. Lyle Fitch is critical of the insufficient consolidation of functions and the parochial nature of the bargaining process in the council.[45]

Despite these problems and the continuing issue of tax equity, Metro Toronto has a substantial record of achievement. It generally has accomplished its goals. Clearly, it has demonstrated that it is a more effective government for certain functions than the smaller local governments that make up its first tier.

---

[42] Daniel Grant, "Metros Three Faces," *National Civic Review,* June 1966, p. 318.

[43] Frank Smallwood, *Metro Toronto: A Decade Later* (Toronto: Bureau of Municipal Research, 1963), p. 12.

[44] Mogulof, *Five Metropolitan Governments,* pp. 50–52.

[45] Smallwood, *Metro Toronto;* Mogulof, *Five Metropolitan Governments,* pp. 50–52; and Lyle Fitch, ed., *Partnership for Progress* (New York: Institute for Public Administrators, 1970), pp. 71–74.

THE VIRGINIA APPROACH

Distinct from, but often confused with, city-county consolidation is another form of metropolitan area adjustment, city-county separation. Under city-county separation, a municipality is detached from the county, sometimes with an enlargement of its boundaries. Within its boundaries, the new government usually exercises both municipal and county functions.

During the last half of the 19th century, city-county separation was employed to reorganize local governments in four major metropolitan areas: Baltimore, Denver, St. Louis, and San Francisco. There has been little recent interest in this device, except in the state of Virginia, where city-county separation exists on a state-wide basis. Virginia's approach has evolved through custom rather than by explicit constitutional or statutory provision. When a town's population reaches 5,000, it may become a city and thereafter exercise all city and county functions.[46]

In 1967 the Virginia Metropolitan Areas Study Commission recommended the continuation of this system. Since, with the exception of Roanoke, all of Virginia's metropolitan areas (Washington suburbs, Norfolk, Richmond) contain more than two counties or cities, areawide county government would not be promoted by eliminating the process. Further, the commission stated that any slight advantage gained by abandonment of the present process would be offset by the confusion and the cost of overlapping levels of government, and the duplication of services that characterize local government in other states.

Although Virginia municipalities are not given additional territory when they separate from their counties, they can add territory from the counties that surround them by utilizing another uniquely Virginian procedure. In 1904, the Virginia legislature provided for a judicial panel to accept or reject annexation and consolidation proposals. When a city wishes to extend its boundaries, the case is reviewed by the panel as a civil suit. By this procedure, the issue is removed from purely political settlement.

The Virginia Code states that the statutory standard is "the necessity for and the expediency of annexation."[47] The judicial panels have been guided by the belief that cities should govern urban areas and that counties should govern rural areas. They examine the population and area of a city, the need for additional territory, the need for urban services, the existence of a community of interest, and the benefits to the remainder of the county.

Though the Virginia procedure has been acclaimed widely, some have

---

[46] Virginia Metropolitan Areas Study Commission, *Governing the Virginia Metropolitan Areas: An Assessment,* May 1967, p. 14.

[47] Ibid., p. 29.

argued that circuit court judges are not suitably qualified to decide annexation questions. Further, the review body does not have jurisdiction over proposed incorporations, clearly a related power. On the whole, however, the system has been very successful.

Lately, however, with the increasingly rapid development of Virginia's urban areas, annexation has become less effective in resolving the metropolitan problems. Under current guidelines, financial reimbursements to counties for annexed territory often are too high for the cities to pay, undermining the entire process. Also, the high level of services provided by some of the metropolitan counties weakens a city's argument that it can best provide urban services for the area.

Because of increasing concern with the devices of city-county separation and annexation, more attention currently is being focused on city-county consolidation in Virginia. The statutory procedure for consolidation is basically a simple one and presents no legal barrier to merger. Either the governing bodies or the voters may initiate the process, but it must be approved by majority referendum vote in each affected jurisdiction. The statutes simply outline the procedures and allow the participants substantial leeway in resolving differences.[48] The question of consolidation is largely a political matter, in contrast to the quasi-juridical procedure used for annexation.

Virginia's record of consolidations has been remarkable; six have occurred in this century. The first Virginia consolidations were the merger of the cities of Richmond and Manchester, under a 1910 special act, and the merger of the towns of Waynesboro and Basic City in 1923, under a 1920 general law. Between 1952 and 1963, the greater Norfolk area had four city-county consolidations involving three counties, five cities, and one town. In 1952, the voters of the city of Hampton, the town of Phoebus, and the county of Elizabeth City approved consolidation as the city of Hampton. The county had been faced with the threat of repeated annexation. Evidently, the voters decided to join the city rather than face a succession of annexation suits. In 1958, the cities of Warwick and Newport News became the city of Newport News; in 1962, the city of Virginia Beach and Princess Anne County approved consolidation as the city of Virginia Beach; and in 1963, South Norfolk City and Norfolk County became the city of Chesapeake. As in Hampton's case, the two largest mergers produced completely consolidated cities and the fear of annexation played an important role in influencing voters.

Since all of these consolidations occurred in the Norfolk region, there are now seven contiguous major governments operating there. As of 1970, they had a combined population of a million residents, and were

---

[48] Ibid., pp. 31–32.

beginning to engage in some interesting regional activities. Cooperation between the new consolidated cities of Newport News and Hampton has resulted in areawide approaches to meeting common needs. They are part of area districts to provide sewerage service, water supply, vocational education, and a regional airport. The two cities also operate a stadium and are members of regional housing and port authorities. Such cooperative actions suggest the wide range of untapped possibilities for solutions to common problems.

Further, the old major central cities—Norfolk and Portsmouth—no longer are able to dictate metropolitan policies and decisions. The two city-counties with the largest suburban populations and the greatest potential for future growth—Chesapeake and Virginia Beach—are exerting influence. Hampton and Newport News are now in a stronger position and the new city of Suffolk is likely to grow at a rapid rate and to participate in regional activities.

SUMMARY

City-county consolidations and federated systems, containing local and metropolitan tiers, can provide more flexible mechanisms for delivering services, adapting to growth, and coordinating areawide planning. Such metropolitan governments are alternatives to the kinds of intergovernmental cooperation described in Chapter 9. Decisionmaking becomes more centralized when an elected body is responsible for the entire area. However, there can be no assurance that these reorganizations *will* result in an improved quality of life for the citizens. It depends upon the manner in which government is implemented, the extent to which citizens participate, and the quality of the leadership.

Almost all of the models of these three governmental adaptations, each of which is potentially applicable to urban areas with significant suburban populations, have established special or urban service districts that provide more extensive services to more densely populated areas. In a sense, these systems provide for multipurpose special districts as an intricate part of the metropolitan government. They can be substituted not only for municipalities, which can extend their borders to cover the total urbanized area, but also for special districts already operating in the metropolitan area. Because the extra services are limited to specific areas, it is possible to fund the services by extra property taxes or user charges limited to the areas receiving the benefits.

Since suburbs generally are included in the special service areas, they are treated as urban areas. Thus, from a governmental standpoint, metropolitan governments such as Toronto and Nashville abolish the distinction between central cities and suburbs. However, in the federated systems such as Dade County, and consolidations, such as Jacksonville and Indianapolis, suburbs have been able to retain their identity as suburban jurisdictions. These plans, therefore, can combine some of the best features of *both* the urban and suburban systems, an attractive alternative to the traditional central city-suburban relationships.

Due to their larger size, metropolitan governments can develop and implement metropolitan plans in functional areas such as transportation, air and water pollution control, regional public facilities, solid waste disposal, water supply, and law enforcement. However, as indicated in Chapter 6, there is no guarantee that larger units will be more effective simply because they are larger.

12

National suburban and urban growth policy

As INDICATED in Chapter 1, most future metropolitan growth will be concentrated in the suburbs. In the last decade, political and civic leaders at all levels have become increasingly concerned over problems related to this suburban growth and its impact on the relationship between central cities and their suburbs.

One indication of this concern was the 1968 Advisory Commission on Intergovernmental Relations (ACIR) report entitled *Urban and Rural America: Policies for Future Growth*. This is an extensive statement on the growth problems of the United States and their implications for national policies and developmental planning. The Commission recommended that a policy be developed to deal with urban growth and suggested changes in government structures at the federal, state, and local levels to insure its implementation.[1] At the same time, for widely varying reasons, substantial numbers of individuals and private groups also have put pressure on Congress to adopt some sort of growth policy.

In response to this public interest, Congress enacted the Housing and Urban Development Act of 1968. This was the first time that it applied a comprehensive approach to the solution of urban problems. This action significantly departed from Congress' typical laissez-faire

---

[1] Advisory Commission on Intergovernmental Relations, *Urban and Rural America: Policies for Future Growth* (Washington, D.C.: U.S. Government Printing Office, 1968), p. 123.

orientation in confronting problems associated with the nation's growth, indicating that it must have considered the issue unusually urgent. This chapter will explore the potential effect of urban growth policy on suburban problems.

THE COSTS OF SUBURBAN SPRAWL

Numerous critics of the suburbs have focused upon the issue of suburban sprawl. Little action has resulted, however, because it has generally been conceded that even if some of the consequences of suburban growth are undesirable or costly, the benefits to suburbanites usually exceed the costs and justify the continuation of the pattern. Nevertheless, unplanned and environmentally unsound development projects increasingly have been opposed by suburban newspapers, citizen groups, and, on some occasions, formally resisted by local governments. One striking example of this mounting criticism of growth and its potentially harmful effects is the recent opposition to the construction of urban segments to the interstate highway system.[2] Another example is the expanding "no growth" movement in many suburban areas. Both sewer moratoriums and zoning decisions have been employed by suburbs to retard growth.

A growing body of research documents the social and economic costs of sprawl. Land economist, Marion Clawson, reviewed the existing literature on the subject in his book *Suburban Land Conversion in the United States*. He noted that current patterns in suburban land development involve both quantifiable and nonquantifiable costs. The major source of these costs is the sprawling geographical pattern of modern American suburbs, which distinguishes them from the central cities. This sporadic pattern of development has caused a direct increase in the cost of suburban services.[3]

Many suburban costs are nonquantifiable, including those associated with the sprawling highway system. Since suburbanites must travel greater distances to work, recreation, and shopping areas, their cars emit more pollutants into the atmosphere. This sprawl pattern also has necessitated large expenditures for highway systems. The highway costs are quantifiable, but the societal costs of air pollution, damage to the environment, and the negative effects on health are not easily measured.

A 1974 study by the Real Estate Research Corporation compared the economic, environmental, and social costs of sprawl. The study calcu-

---

[2] Alan Lupo, Frank Colcord, and Edmund P. Fowler, *Rites of Way: The Politics of Transportation in Boston and the U.S. City* (Boston: Little, Brown and Company, 1971); and William J. Murin, *The Politics of Mass Transit* (Cambridge: Ballinger, 1974); and Wilfred Owen, *The Accessible City* (Washington, D.C.: Brookings Institution, 1972).

[3] Marion Clawson, *Suburban Land Conversion in the United States* (Baltimore: The Johns Hopkins Press, 1971), pp. 317–22.

lated the costs of developing 6,000 acres for a new community of 33,000 persons, containing a mix of housing patterns ranging from detached homes with large lots to 6-story apartment buildings. The conclusion was that the single-family detached home pattern is the most expensive in every respect—twice as expensive as the higher density construction. In addition, higher densities, coupled with open spaces, would use only half the road mileage, half the number of sewer and utility pipes, only 44 percent as much energy, and would generate 45 percent less pollution.[4]

In addition to raising the price of public services, sprawl also raises the basic price of land. Due to a number of factors, such as state and federal tax laws, real estate developers find it profitable to withhold land from the market until the demand is great enough to elicit a considerable profit. Normally, this point is reached when undeveloped land is surrounded by already developed property. In this sense, the value of the land results not from its own unique characteristics but from the development that has occurred around it. Inevitably, this also requires public investment in roads, schools, sewers, and other facilities.

These public improvements enable the land developer and the real estate agent to sell the land for a higher price. Both the new home buyer and the existing residents in the community traditionally have paid the full cost of the public services. Meanwhile, the developers gain a bonus because they receive the benefits from the public improvements without paying for them. To reduce this ownership bonus, suburban governments increasingly are holding developers more accountable. Many suburbs now are requiring developers to install roads, parks, and schools, or to contribute a sum to the city to cover some of the costs associated with these benefits.

Whether or not the current patterns of suburban development are inordinately expensive, the total costs of sprawl are clearly substantial and they are unequally distributed. Generally, the suburban home buyer pays an artificially high price for housing to cover the bonus profits and development costs. In addition, the extended public services and highway construction necessitated by suburban sprawl consume local government revenues that could be used to provide other public services. Instead, they are being spent to perpetuate inefficient, costly, and aesthetically unpleasing patterns of land use.

THE RESULTS OF CONTRADICTING POLICIES

Historically, the national government has applied inconsistent policies with respect to sprawl and urban-suburban development. On the one

---

[4] Real Estate Research Corporation, *The Costs of Sprawl—Detailed Cost Analysis* (Washington, D.C.: U.S. Government Printing Office, 1974).

hand, Congress has legislated areawide planning requirements, strong representative regional bodies, and programs promoting the rehabilitation of central cities. On the other hand, the interstate highway program, the activities of the Federal Housing Administration, the absence of effective relocation policies, and various location decisions of the Defense Department and other national agencies often have encouraged population dispersal. In Chapters 9 and 10, we described some of these federal policies which have encouraged sprawl.

One of the best assessments of the impact of nonpolicy was presented by Norman P. Mineta, then mayor of San Jose, California, in his 1972 testimony before the House Subcommittee on National Growth Policy.[5] According to former Mayor Mineta, the federal policies exerting the most powerful influence on growth have not been specific federal and urban programs, but more general expenditures, such as mortgage insurance, tax loopholes, and interstate highway construction. His evidence for this claim was an intensive Rand Corporation study of the rapid population growth of Santa Clara County, California, between 1960 and 1970.

The purpose of this study was to clarify the problems confronting local government officials in metropolitan areas and to formulate recommendations for their resolution. Because Santa Clara County had undergone rapid growth in recent years, it served as an excellent example of the problems encountered in a number of metropolitan areas.

Since 1950, the County had changed radically from a sparsely populated land of orchards and vineyards to one of large suburban populations surrounding an older central city still annexing territory aggressively and based largely on a booming aerospace industry. This change was marked by extraordinary sprawl and acrimonious competition for space between San Jose and its suburbs.

Between 1960 and 1970, the County's population increased from 642,000 to 1,647,000, a 157 percent increase. This trend still was continuing at the time of the study, but the County had begun to restrict development of its remaining open spaces. A clear majority of its residents felt that the beauty and character of the existing open space should be protected from intensive development. However, growth continued despite this opposition.

The Rand researchers traced the sources of the growth in Santa Clara County since 1950 and concluded that the County's boom was precipitated by outside sources. During the "space race" of the 1960s, a number of new aerospace industries subsidized by the federal government located their offices in Santa Clara County, because of its proximity

---

[5] U.S. House of Representatives, Committee on Banking and Currency Subcommittee on Housing, *National Growth Policy*, Hearings (Washington, D.C.: U.S. Government Printing Office, 1972), p. 114.

to other elements of the aerospace industry and its numerous environmental amenities. The new industry provided more employment opportunities in the County, which in turn served as an incentive for additional population immigration. This trend has continued into the 1970s.

The impetus of the federal space program helps explain why the County experienced a rapid rate of growth, but it does not explain why public officials did not attempt to control or retard the growth when they became aware of its negative consequences. In attempting to answer this question, the researchers collected detailed data on population growth, local public finance, and other economic characteristics of the County.

This information was employed in several research models to explain the continued lack of public response. One explanation seemed to explain the absence of growth control in Santa Clara County:

> On the one side, private and public economic well-being in Santa Clara County depend not merely upon a high and stable level of economic activity, but upon a rapid rate of economic *growth* as such; on the other side, such rapid growth degrades the general well-being by lowering the "quality" of living in a number of ways imperfectly subsumed in the phrase "Urban Sprawl."[6]

The earlier population increments moving into Santa Clara County did not require new schools, new highways, or new utilities. Eventually, though, a critical mass of new residents created the demand for large scale public capital investments. The taxable base had to be increased to pay for these investments. To increase the economic base, new industry was encouraged, resulting in an influx of people seeking the new jobs. The sales and real estate taxes generated by this kind of growth were the only means by which the County could meet its new service demands.

Although this might explain why public officials encouraged rapid economic growth in the boom years, it still does not account for their failure to channel it into a more desirable form. Through extensive interviews with the officials of Santa Clara County and case studies of zoning and other public decisions, the Rand investigators came up with two rather interesting findings.[7] The first was that the County officials had very little "policy space." They were unable to respond to the challenges of a rapid growth rate due to outside governmental forces, such as federal income tax laws, which encourage real estate speculation, and state legislation, which limits the powers of local officials in the area of taxation and zoning.

Secondly, in those instances in which public officials have powers

---

[6] Rand Urban Policy Analysis Group, "Alternative Growth Strategies for San Jose: Initial Report of the Rand Policy Analysis Project," in Ibid., p. 164.

[7] Ibid., pp. 226–27.

that might minimize the negative effects of growth, they find themselves in what might be termed the "cat and mouse" game of urban development. This game consists of two kinds of role players, the urban developer who sees profit potential, and the public official who controls the kind of development that will take place. The developer's land represents the desired tax base the public official needs. If the public official does not permit the developer to use his land as planned, the developer can threaten to build in another jurisdiction. The County then would lose the tax base entirely. The fact that developers are able to play off one jurisdiction against another is due largely to political fragmentation in metropolitan areas throughout the United States, and to the failure of states to provide enabling legislation for consolidation or federation of local governments.

In some situations, if a developer is committed to a piece of property, the local governments can induce "underdevelopment" of the land or delay development while the owner must continue paying taxes. In these cases, the governments sometimes play off the developers to secure design changes or contributions for the construction of public facilities. This situation varies from area to area and makes it somewhat difficult to generalize.

The case of Santa Clara County can be considered an accurate example of the growth dynamics operating in a number of metropolitan counties. The findings of the Rand study strongly suggest that many local problems are caused by forces outside the system. The solutions to these problems frequently lie beyond the power of local officials. The study also indicates that federal and state policies designed *without* specific regard to urban and suburban problems have a dramatic effect on growth in metropolitan areas. These policies contrast sharply with formal federal policies, such as intergovernmental aid requirements for regional planning. But even these latter policies, intended to aid urban government, often have failed through lack of federal direction and coordination. Thus, general federal policies, such as tax laws, may have deleterious effects, while federal policies designed to be helpful often may have little beneficial effect on suburban growth. The result is an inadvertent set of federal policies biased toward urban sprawl.

TOWARD A FEDERAL GROWTH POLICY

Many forces are pressuring the federal government to debunk its traditional passive role and to adopt a positive federal growth policy. The 1968 ACIR report first articulated this demand. A wide variety of other groups also feel that some sort of national land use policy is essential. Environmentalists want to preserve open space, to reduce litter and pollution, and to improve the quality of urban life. Groups such as Zero Population Growth also want to control population densities.

In their 1972 platform, the Democratic Party demonstrated concern over housing policies, and the proper distribution of people within metropolitan areas. Other groups are interested in revitalizing communities and encouraging new planned towns. The American Institute of Architects is interested in building and rebuilding on a neighborhood scale.[8] Finally, most Republicans want to make sure that, whatever national growth policy is adopted, the relevant decisions still will be made locally rather than nationally.

There are eight major ways in which the federal government has influenced local growth. Federal influences have included:

1. Making grants and loans to state and local governments;
2. Changing employment levels at national government installations;
3. Establishing new federal offices and installations and closing or relocating existing ones;
4. Expanding the procurement of goods and services;
5. Initiating national public works projects;
6. Developing tax policies that influence growth, such as those permitting most land sales to be taxed as capital gains;
7. Expanding the availability of mortgage money; and
8. Engaging in environmental and other regulatory activities.[9]

These federal activities often have been contradictory in their effects. For example, in one metropolitan area, the U.S. Office of Economic Opportunity (OEO) and the U.S. Department of Housing and Urban Development (HUD) were using the Community Action and Model Cities programs to strengthen neighborhood leadership and organization. At the same time, the U.S. Department of Transportation (DOT) was planning to construct an interstate highway through the area, and HUD's urban renewal office was supporting a project that would supplant the residents with an office building.

In response to the demands for national growth standards and policies, the national government at least could put its own house in order through improved interagency communication and coordination. A more significant response would be to devise a set of policies that would deal directly with urban growth.

National growth legislation

The environmental movement has provided additional new levers for the establishment of urban growth policy with specific impact on subur-

---

[8] For additional information on the various interests involved in a national growth policy, see Congressional Research Service, *Toward a National Growth Policy: Federal and State Developments in 1972* (Washington, D.C.: U.S. Governmental Printing Office, 1973), pp. 1–6.

[9] The Domestic Council, *Report on National Growth and Development*, 1974 (Washington, D.C.: U.S. Government Printing Office, 1974), p. 64.

ban development. In 1969, the U.S. Congress passed the National Environmental Policy Act, which mandated that land use planning be employed in an effort to improve and preserve the environment for the future. The legislation established the Environmental Protection Agency (EPA) as an environmental regulatory agency. The Clean Air Amendments of 1970 required national and state governmental involvement in land use planning as it relates to air quality, and gave EPA the responsibility of enforcing this law. In 1972, the Water Quality Amendments were passed, establishing new federal requirements for local governments to meet.

Congress took a preliminary step toward a national policy on growth in Title VII of the Housing and Urban Development Act of 1970, entitled "Urban Growth and New Community Development." The purpose of this title was to delegate to the executive branch the responsibility for developing a national urban growth policy. The new policy was designed (1) to enhance growth, development, and redevelopment in areas which demonstrate a special potential for accelerating growth; (2) to encourage the prudent use of national resources; and (3) to assure developing communities an adequate economic base, appropriate community services, job opportunities, well balanced neighborhoods, and a socially and physically attractive living environment.[10]

These goals have substantial significance for growth in suburbs, although the congressional hearings preceding enactment of the legislation rarely mentioned suburbs *per se*. This should not be too surprising, since this was the first national statement of comprehensive urban policy, despite the fact that large cities had been a major federal concern for decades. Even the statements presented to the Ad Hoc Subcommittee on Urban Growth in 1969 did not emphasize the fact that most future growth would take place in suburban areas, rather than in metropolitan areas in general.[11]

Discussion about policy recommendations generally focused upon the problems that result from population density rather than on policies to control suburban growth. However, this approach did not result in a consensus of opinion. Some of those who testified believed that it was the conditions that often accompany density, rather than density itself, that generate problems. Others stated that density was a source of problems and that decentralization and a deceleration of population growth would assist in alleviating some of the nation's urban problems. The late Constantinos Doxiadis, a noted urban planner, also testified

---

[10] "The Housing and Urban Development Act of 1970," P.L. 91–609, *U.S. Statutes at Large,* vol. 84, part 2, December 31, 1970, p. 1791.

[11] U.S. House of Representatives, Committee on Banking and Currency, Ad Hoc Subcommittee on Urban Growth, *Population Trends,* part I, *Quality of Urban Life,* part II, *Industrial Location Policy,* Part III, Hearings, 91st Congress, 1st and 2d Sess. (Washington, D.C.: U.S. Government Printing Office, 1969–1970).

about future growth. He stressed the significance of the "daily urban system," the distance people commute each day—"commuting in some way, but not only commuting to the central city, but also between small cities."[12] Current daily urban systems have a commuting distance of 50 miles. According to Doxiadis, by the year 2000, this radius will increase to 80 or 90 miles and, by the end of the century, almost the entire U.S. population will be living within such daily urban systems.[13] According to Doxiadis, the nation's future population will be concentrated in a series of daily urban systems linked together into five basic megalopolises: the eastern seaboard megalopolis from Boston to Washington, D.C.; the Great Lakes megalopolis; the California megalopolis; the Florida system; and the Seattle-Tacoma Vancouver system.

All this testimony implies that most future growth will occur in suburban areas and that metropolitan areas eventually will interpenetrate to form large urban strips. Therefore, if suburban sprawl and population concentration are considered a source of social problems, future growth inevitably will produce a variety of new problems and exacerbate existing problems. The 1970 legislation growing out of these hearings attempted to develop a national growth policy designed to meet these tensions in two ways. The legislation encouraged the development of New Towns and called for preparation of a biannual presidential growth report to focus on policy questions.

New Towns

New Town legislation was examined carefully during the hearings, prior to the 1970 Act. At least one witness, Wilbur Thompson, explained serious weaknesses in the concept. He noted that, in order for cities to be viable, they must be larger than many analysts assume. In general, cities grow stronger as they grow larger. According to Thompson,

> The way that this happens is at least threefold. With greater and greater size a city develops breadth, many different products. In that vast industrial diversification—it develops stability. Not only do big cities have great breadth expressed in terms of the current industry mix that gives them a stability over the near period; not only do they have the great depth that gives them the power to invent and innovate and gain a handhold on the future, but the big city also, of course, offers the great range of choice that is so consistent with our times.[14]

Thompson concluded that a city becomes a viable community once it reaches a population of about 225,000. At this size, cities exhibit a diversity sufficient to withstand changes in the national economy. Conse-

---

[12] Ibid., p. 664.
[13] Ibid., p. 665.
[14] Ibid., Part I, pp. 568–69.

quently, new towns that are not part of larger urban systems might not be economically viable, even though they offer solutions to environmental pollution. Thompson also argued that new towns would not grow rapidly enough or be sufficiently stable to absorb the population increase that would occur in a relatively short period of 30 years. Finally, he noted that the construction of free standing new towns would require a tremendous capital investment in roads, streets, sewers, and schools, which the nation could not afford.[15]

However, other witnesses proposed an alternative strategy of building new towns within the economic area of influence of rapidly growing metropolitan areas. These towns would not be built on completely undeveloped land, but in close proximity to cities with a population of approximately 50,000. This plan would lower the high cost of capital investments because basic facilities already exist and merely require expansion. This strategy also would provide a population nucleus for rapid growth and development.

The approved New Town legislation encouraged and stimulated private enterprise as well as state and local government action, but it did not utilize direct federal action as a mechanism to meet the objectives. Instead, it relied upon loan guarantees for private new community developers and state land development agencies to finance real property acquisition and land development. It also provided for public service grants to state and local bodies to cover part of the costs of central services and public facilities.

New Towns were envisioned as independent, relatively self-contained, planned communities of sufficient size to support a range of housing types and lifestyles. Built on undeveloped land and by staged development over a period of time, they generally specify the amounts of land to be allotted for residential, industrial, and commercial use. Such towns always provide for a greenbelt of open space areas.[16] The mix of housing and the creation of open space and other cultural amenities is to assure that both social and physical planning goals will be met. The key idea is to create an entire urban system.

Four kinds of new towns were to be encouraged: (1) growth centers or additions to existing communities: (2) new towns-in-town; (3) new towns in rural areas with potential for accelerated growth; and (4) free-standing new communities. These four options reflected the variety of views expressed in the congressional hearings.[17]

---

[15] Ibid., p. 571.

[16] Advisory Commission on Intergovernmental Relations, *Urban and Rural America: Policies for Future Growth* (Washington, D.C.: U.S. Governmental Printing Office, 1968), p. 63.

[17] "The Housing and Urban Development Act of 1970," *U.S. Statutes at Large,* pp. 1796–1805.

A growth center is an area near a rapidly growing urban core. It is usually a community that is to be expanded, such as Jonathan, Minnesota, which is within the corporate limits of Chaska, Minnesota. The advantage of this type of community is that many amenities and public facilities are already available. In some cases, the development impetus even comes from residents who want to organize and control growth.

The concept of new-towns-in-town (NTIT) appeals to those who would like to enjoy the benefits of city residence without having to live in a congested or ill-planned neighborhood. The NTIT idea has both strengths and weaknesses. Although the city that surrounds the new community offers advantages such as cultural activities that attract potential residents, it also contains high crime rates and traffic congestion, which repulse them. Roosevelt Island, a project in New York City's East River has been built on previously developed land. However, Cedar-Riverside in Minnesota is an example of a NTIT that has been built on under-developed land. Fort Lincoln in Washington, D.C., with a planned population of 16,000, has been beset with so many community policy and contractor difficulties that it really has not gotten off the ground after eight years.[18]

The concept of a free-standing new city is to convert unused land into a city. Free standing communities must relate to a job base *already* anticipated for the area. Although this may sound exciting and innovative, the risks involved are substantial, and a long term commitment is required by private developers and the government. Soul City, North Carolina, is an example of such a community. It is most difficult to develop these communities in a free market situation. Further, most of them have undertaken substantial social experimentation and community facility development, the costs of which have been badly underestimated.

Most of the successful new towns were really suburban or satellite communities rather than free-standing new towns. The oldest and most successful have been Reston, Virginia, and Columbia, Maryland, both of which are suburbs of Washington, D.C. However, the original developer of Reston suffered a financial collapse before the project was completed, and the developer of Columbia currently is losing substantial amounts of money.

The New Towns programs resulted in 16 proposals but did not have a significant impact on population distribution. Funds for the new communities program were impounded by President Nixon and, in 1975,

---

[18] Muriel Campaglia, "The Sage of Fort Lincoln (cont.): The Citizens Council Rejects its Contract, Planning Proceeds," *City*, April 1969, p. 31. Also see Martha Derthick, *New Towns in Town: Why a Federal Program Failed* (Washington, D.C.: Brookings, 1972).

HUD even stopped accepting applications from developers. Until that time, there had been numerous applicants for new towns throughout the United States.

Most discouraging, however, is the lack of evidence that new communities substantially improve the quality of life. The findings of Raymond Burby, et al., in an extensive market survey and site evaluation comparison of 13 new communities to 13 traditional suburban developments, were rather disappointing. All new communities were ranked in terms of "system characteristics," such as distance from work or school, and in terms of resident satisfaction. Transportation, recreation services, and, to some extent, health care were rated higher in new towns. Schools and shopping centers were rated only slightly better. The number of citizens in new towns who regarded their communities as excellent places to live did not exceed significantly the number of satisfied residents in unplanned communities.[19]

If the New Town experience is typical of the kinds of programs that a national growth policy will develop, one can predict substantial difficulties, both in articulation and implementation. The federal appropriation and expenditure process is never certain. Thus, neither the private market nor other levels of government can depend on federal funding. Furthermore, even if money were readily available, there is no assurance that the social goals of the federal programs would be achieved.

Presidential analysis of national growth

The 1970 Housing Act required the president, with the aid of his Domestic Council, to prepare a biannual report on National Growth Policy. The legislation mandated that this report contain a description of urban growth and identify significant growth trends. The Council also was to evaluate the progress and effectiveness of federal, state, local, and private policies and to make recommendations for national policy. The first report, delivered in 1972, concluded that many of the nation's problems were the result of three demographic trends that occurred on an unprecedented scale during the 20th Century:

1. Population growth—resulting from immigration and longer life spans;
2. Population redistribution—decreasing population growth in the northeast and midwest, and increasing population growth in the west and the south;

---

[19] Raymond Burby III, Shirley Weiss, and Robert Zehner, "National Evaluation of Community Services and the Quality of Life in American New Towns," *Public Administration Review*, May/June 1975, pp. 222–29.

3. Population shifts from rural to urban areas—especially the movement of blacks and other minority groups.[20]

The report concluded that future policy should stress better distribution of growth among both urban and rural areas. The specific policies of the Nixon administration were termed "a new general strategy for national development." This new strategy, based upon a division of responsibility among federal, state, and local governments, was compatible with the developing revenue sharing approach. In 1974, the Community Development Act was enacted to place many of the urban development programs under the revenue sharing bloc grant approach.

This type of strategy was adopted, rather than an overall national growth policy, because the administration concluded that a single comprehensive national growth policy was not feasible. The report cited the following reasons for this position:

1. There is wide-spread disagreement on priorities.
2. Intervention to solve one problem may create new problems.
3. It is debatable that particular consequences of growth actually are problems.
4. It is difficult to specify the link between the growth process and growth problems. Growth is rarely the single cause of a problem: more often a problem or condition both affects the patterns of growth and is affected by them.
5. The decisions that influence growth are made by countless numbers of individuals, families, and businessmen. The factors that influence these decisions may be susceptible to change by altering emerging growth patterns. But, in a nation that values freedom and democratic choice, the decisions themselves cannot be dictated.
6. A single comprehensive growth policy conflicts with the concept of a federal system based upon a sharing of power between states and the national government.
7. The country is much larger than western European countries where national growth policies have been implemented.
8. Patterns of growth reflect many determinations that have primarily local significance, such as local tax levies. These decisions best can be made at the local level. It is not possible for the highest level of government to design policies for development that can operate successfully in all parts of the nation.[21]

The 1972 report concluded that the federal government's involvement in national growth should be limited to fiscal and monetary policy to

---

[20] The Domestic Council, *Report on National Growth and Development, 1972* (Washington, D.C.: U.S. Government Printing Office, 1972), pp. 1–16.

[21] Ibid., pp. 26–28.

keep the nation's economy growing at its full potential, technological advancement, and water and air pollution control. The Nixon growth policy statement asserted that state and local governments have the primary responsibility for shaping growth and dealing with its problems.

This executive growth policy statement was attacked in congressional hearings as a "no growth" policy statement. Those who testified claimed that it is unrealistic to argue that a national growth policy is not feasible; they maintained that such a policy already exists, since many current policies have a negative impact on the nation's metropolitan areas. Most of the federal programs in question had been developed to deal with the specific problems of earlier historical periods and some of them had unintended side effects. For this reason, the congressional report recommended that a national growth policy be developed. Such a policy was deemed necessary at least to minimize the negative secondary effects of existing federal programs.

The second biannual report was prepared in 1974. This report recognized that growth policy is actually an aggregation of policies. It stated that to achieve the Title VII objectives, the government must develop better methods to assess the relative priority of goals and to achieve the interrelationship and coordination of existing and future urban growth programs. It concluded that state legislatures and executive branches must strive for modernization and reform so that comprehensive growth policies can be enacted. But, in order to establish effective growth policies, clear, statewide goals for future growth should be determined and local general purpose governments should be strengthened.

The 1974 report was disappointing in its failure to consider growth in terms of suburban as well as urban and rural areas. It did outline several goals toward which the nation might strive.

These included equal housing opportunity; equality in industrial regulation; safe and livable urban and rural communities; decent and sanitary housing, preferably owner-occupied; preservation of important natural resources, clean air and unpolluted water; and secure and reasonably priced energy sources.

THE FUTURE OF SUBURBIA

Some consensus on a national urban growth policy is essential if any effective action is to be taken at the state or local level. This policy must be developed before an individual growth control program or set of policies can be developed or evaluated. Decisionmakers must address a number of specific questions, including the following:

1. At what rate should economic growth take place?
2. How does a community, state, or country balance individual property rights and community needs?

3. Should the courts compel a suburb to alter its environment to achieve some general social goal?
4. What costs must a community incur to prevent its industries from polluting the environment?
5. What is "fair" in terms of housing opportunity?
6. How can society cope with the social costs of the automobile?
7. What types of economic incentives will encourage local governments to cooperate with neighboring jurisdictions?
8. What price should citizens be willing to pay for a cleaner environment?
9. Should suburban growth be discouraged to focus more attention on central city redevelopment?
10. How will suburbs respond to regional development?
11. What will be suburban responses to regional development?
12. Will discouraging suburban growth increase central city rents, to the detriment of low income residents?
13. How can a metropolitan area distribute the fruits of economic growth in ways that reduce destructive competition among central cities and suburbs?

The future of suburban and urban development depends upon how these questions are answered and how community goals and objectives are established. This future development is likely to occur in one or more of the four broad patterns outlined by Louis Masotti. First, the present pattern of sprawl and uncontrolled land usage could persist if government policymakers take no action. This would be the logical outcome of past and present actions taken by the private market place.

Second, density could intensify in suburban areas and, through a process of reduced expansion, in central cities as well. This pattern would develop from the effective implementation of land use controls. As noted earlier, this outcome would have both negative and positive aspects.

A third scenario suggests that growth and development will be planned according to prudent policies at all governmental levels. New Towns, of course, would be a crucial part of such a program, which involves much more governmental action than merely the decision to support such an approach. The history of the federal program suggests that it is not an easy policy to implement.

Finally, it is possible that the central city will be revitalized by an in-migration of suburbanites and by efforts to discourage the out migration of its present population. This approach can be implemented only by increasing suburban transportation costs and by creating a higher quality urban life. Governmental policies supporting the development of New Towns in Town and eliminating hidden suburban transportation and tax subsidies also could encourage central city revitalization. Perhaps the energy crisis will provide new incentives for the development of such a policy.

As Masotti suggests, these approaches are not mutually exclusive; tendencies in all four directions can be discerned. But it is clear from this review of suburban development that the governmental commitment to the issues posed by growth has fallen considerably short of meeting the challenges. As population concentration and the pressures upon governmental structures increase, the challenges will become even greater.[22]

The most recent effort to construct a federal land use policy was exerted through the "Land Use Policy and Planning Assistance Act" introduced by Senator Henry Jackson in 1973. The bill is designed to provide states with grants for developing land use and power plant construction programs, and for acquiring open space.[23] While the Jackson bill has passed the Senate in the 92d and 93d Congresses, it has not yet been approved by the House of Representatives. In 1975, it was not even reported by the House Committee, despite a lengthy struggle by its supporters. Since a strong core of House members supports it, some bill eventually will be passed, but the necessary compromises may considerably weaken its impact.

The critical question is whether a federated system, with its decentralized decisionmaking process, can mobilize sufficiently to formulate a comprehensive *national* growth policy that will serve the general interest of metropolitan areas. If it cannot, it is extremely unlikely to develop *suburban* growth policies, which necessarily are only a subset of comprehensive metropolitan planning.

Perhaps the impetus for a national growth policy actually is rooted in the actions that states and localities take in attempting to cope with the immediate effects of growth within their boundaries. A number of such measures already have been implemented, including sewer moratoriums, coastline development zones, staged growth zones, and even actual refusals to grant building permits. These actions are not without disadvantages. For example, a sewer moratorium may lead to more use of septic tanks and a freeze on building permits will increase the resale cost of existing housing. Nevertheless, Federal policymakers may adopt these approaches as the foundation of a national growth policy. Such a development would attest to the complexity and vitality of the federal system.

---

[22] These slightly adapted excerpts from chapter 19, "Epilogue: Suburbia in the Seventies . . . and Beyond," by Louis Masotti are reprinted from *The Urbanization of the Suburbs*, UAAR, Vol. 7 (c) 1973, pp. 533–36 by permission of the Publisher, Sage Publications, Inc.

[23] U.S. Senate Committee on Interior and Insular Affairs, *Land Use Policy and Planning Assistance Act,* Report No. 930197, 93d Congress, 1st Sess. (Washington, D.C.: U.S. Government Printing Office, 1973), p. 89.

Index

This book has been set in 10 and 9 point Caledonia, leaded 2 points. Chapter numbers are 30 point Scotch Roman italic and chapter titles are 18 point Scotch Roman italic. The size of the type page is 27 x 45½ picas.